Everyday Taxes

A New Kind of Tax Guide from Th

Kirk Taylor

2016 Edition (2016.1)

Tax rules for use on 2016 tax returns and living life in 2017 (until the IRS changes the rules in December :)

Table of Contents:

1. Read Me First

Welcome to the latest edition of Everyday Taxes. This book is designed to be significantly different from the rest of the tax books out there. For one, it will be written in English, not taxese (made up word of the Day!). I will endeavor to use normal, everyday words to describe the tax rules, and will define any taxese that I use. This does mean that sometimes what I write might not look or sound like what your tax professional or the Internal Revenue Service (IRS) is saying, but that's because I swear they try to make things more complicated than they should be.

I designed the book for the pen and paper crowd, the software crowd, and the pay a professional crowd, but it is not a substitute for the instructions and publications provided by the IRS, your software, or your tax professional. It is designed for everyday usefulness, not just tax time usefulness. It will be organized by life topics, not Form 1040 topics. You can skip right to the sections that apply to you, when they apply to you, and you don't have to read the whole damn thing (that's why I told you to read this first). Getting a divorce? Look up the I'm Getting Divorced (or Already am) section. Having a child? Look up the I'm Having a Child section. I will attempt to cross-link and reference as much as possible so that you can find what you're looking for and not have to wade through a bunch of crap. This also means that the book is deliberately repetitive. I focus on how the tax rules apply to the specific situations addressed in the section title. Relevant information is provided in each section to which it is applicable (as opposed to listing all the tax rules and making you figure out which are applicable).

This book is an ongoing project. I am going to publish whatever sections are done in December of each year. Then I'm going to keep expanding and revising it, publishing a new edition every December. That's why it's so cheap.

Military Members: In 2015 I added a "Military" paragraph at the end of most sections to highlight specific rules that are affected by being in the military. I have also added a very basic state by state breakdown of military rules: State by State Tax Guide for Military.

How to use this book: After reading this section, read sections 3 and 4. After that, the best method is to look up a section based on what's happening in your life. It should link you around until you have everything you need, though I will try to include everything you need in each section. The forms list will tell you a bit about each form, and then reference the appropriate section. So if you get a strange form, just look it up and you're off.

A few notes about my conventions:

1. I tire of saying, "A bigger refund or lower balance due," so for the rest of the book, when I say, "A bigger refund," I mean a bigger refund or lower balance due.

2. As a general rule, your age for tax purposes is determined by your age on January 1st of the tax year. So, for 2016 tax returns, your age is how old you were on January 1, 2016. I won't specify this when referring to age, so you can assume that's the criteria unless I specify otherwise.

3. I will abbreviate Social Security Number as SSN.

4. Despite saying I won't use taxese, there are a few terms I must use:

      a. Adjusted Gross Income (AGI): This is so frequently used that I need to define it. AGI is your total income, minus a few specific deductions listed on the front page of your tax form. For Form 1040 and 1040A filers, it's the bottom number on the front page, and the top number on the second page. Most of the times you use it, you're using it to determine some limitation or maximum income above which you don't get a deduction. When this happens, they almost always use a "modified" AGI, where you add or subtract some other tax number from the AGI. These numbers almost never apply, so your AGI and modified AGI are almost always the same. For the most part I'm going to use AGI and modified AGI interchangeably. If you have Puerto Rico income, excluded savings bond interest, or have a Foreign Earned Income Exclusion, you'll want to pay more attention to modified AGI. I'll try to identify things that commonly affect modified AGI when talking about them, as opposed to defining modified AGI every time it comes up.

      b. Deduction: This is something that reduces your income subject to tax.

      c. Credit: This is something that reduces the amount of tax you owe (which is obviously better than a deduction.)

      d. Refundable Credit: This is a credit that you get even after you've reduced your total taxes to zero. (Allowing you to get more money back than you paid in.)

5. I'm going to try to avoid using lists of tests for claiming something. Generally, I will list only the things you need to pay attention to in a given situation. For example, under "I'm Having a Child," I list the assumption that it is your own child and that you live in and are residents of the U.S. I won't then list those requirements during the discussion. This means that my list of requirements will differ from what an IRS publication or tax professional will say, but that's because there are a lot of stupid tests that are obvious. A good example is when you are married but don't live with your spouse and are trying to file Head of Household (HH), one of the tests is that you don't file Married Filing Jointly (MFJ)—duh!

6. I'm not using any specific layout for all the sections, though you will notice patterns in many of the sections:

- an introduction with assumptions I'm making,
- a discussion of the most common scenarios,
- a discussion of more complicated situations, and
- lists of the nit-picky details.

Some sections will be different. I want the sections to be as easy to use as possible, so I'm going to lay them out in whatever way I think meets that goal.

7. The unextended deadline for filing taxes is April 15th, or the next business day, if April 15th is a holiday. This includes weird Washington, DC holidays, such as Emancipation Day (for example the deadline for 2015 was 4/18/16 because of

Emancipation Day). That said, I will use April 15th as the deadline throughout this book, and will only talk about extensions in sections where they are likely to apply.

8. Unless otherwise specified, I'm going to assume that your tax year is a calendar year: January 1st through December 31st. There are very few situations where the average taxpayer will have any other tax year. So, if I say tax year, I mean calendar year.

9. Many times in the book I'm going to suggest to get professional help. This doesn't mean you have to use a professional to file your taxes (though many times it will); it means to get advice or assistance from a professional with expertise in the area we're talking about. Some tax issues are difficult to explain on paper in a way that assures there won't be confusion. You can research it yourself; just be aware that an experienced professional will be familiar with the rules and able to explain them as they apply to you. Be careful when doing your own research!

Which brings me to the disclaimer. I have attempted, to the best of my ability, to ensure that the information contained is as accurate as possible. However, the IRS is constantly changing the rules, and I am, in fact, a human being. So, do your due diligence and don't rely solely on this book for your tax information. It is designed to get you doing the right things, but I take no responsibility or liability for any issues that arise based on you relying on this information. Sorry. I also must say that this book is my interpretation of the tax code only, and does not necessarily represent the opinion of the IRS or my employer.

All client anecdotes are semi-fictional. In order to protect client confidentiality, it's necessary for me to modify, aggregate and twist the stories sufficiently to prevent identification or embarrassment. While the underlying point of the anecdote will be based in fact, the actual story will be mostly made up. If you are my client, and you think you recognize your story...it's not you.

2. Do I Have to File a Tax Return?

For most people, the determination of whether or not you have to file is fairly straightforward. The basic answer is determined with the following calculation:
- Take your standard deduction
- Add the exemption for you and your spouse
- Add any increases for being 65 or over.
- If your income is equal to or more than the number calculated above, then you have to file.

Of course, you have to know your filing status first, which is covered in another section: Filing Status. Once you know that, you're home free.

Here are the details:

1. You need to know your Gross Income. Your gross income is everything you made, anywhere in the world, that is not exempt from tax. It includes gains on sales of investments or properties, but not losses. It includes income from a business, before you take expenses into account. It includes only the taxable portion of Social Security, which is a complicated situation and you pretty much need to prepare a tax return to figure it out. If you are filing MFJ, you include both you and your spouse's income.
2. You are considered 65 or older if you were 65 on December 31st of the tax year.
3. For Single filing status, you have to file if your Gross Income is at least $10,350 ($11,900 if you are 65 or older).
4. For MFJ status, you have to file if your Gross Income is at least $20,700 ($21,950 if you or your spouse are 65 or older, $23,200 if both of you are 65 or older).
5. For Married Filing Separately (MFS) status, you have to file if your Gross Income is at least $4,050.
6. For HH status, you have to file if your Gross Income is at least $13,350 ($14,900 if you are 65 or older.)
7. For Qualifying Widower (QW) status, you have to file if your Gross Income is at least $16,650 ($17,900 if you are 65 or older.)
8. You must also file if any of the following apply to you, regardless of income:

 a. You owe Alternative Minimum Tax (there's a whole section on this later).

 b. You owe a penalty on early retirement plan withdrawals. (You'll get a Form 1099-R with a Code 1 for the distribution code.)

 c. You owe taxes on household employees, such as a maid or house cleaner.

 d. You owe taxes on tips you didn't report to your employer. I have a section on this, too.

 e. You have to pay back a First-Time Homebuyer Credit.

 f. You owe other recaptured taxes or penalties.

g. You receive distributions from a Health Savings Account, Archer MSA, or Medicare Advantage MSA.

h. Your NET profit from self employment (your business) was at least $400, regardless of your gross income.

i. You made at least $108.28 from a church that was exempt from Social Security and Medicare taxes.

j. You received an Affordable Care Act Premium Tax Credit (you should get form 1095A if this happened.

9. If you are claimed as a dependent by someone else, you have a more interesting problem. To determine if you need to file, you need to know your earned income, unearned income (investment income, unemployment, annuities, etc.) and the total. You have to file if one of the following applies:

- Your unearned income was over $1,050
- Your earned income was over $6,300
- Your total income was larger than your earned income plus $350, or $1,050, whichever is larger (basically if you have earned income and more than $350 of unearned income, you have to file)

10. Even if not required to file, you should file if you have withholding or other credits that you can get back.

11. Generally, if you are not required to file a federal return, you don't have to file a state return, but you should check the website for your state.

Bottom line is that unless you have a very simple tax life, you practically need to finish your tax return to know if you have to file, or if you should file to get money back.

Military: Combat zone time can reduce your income below your filing threshold causing you to not have to file, but you should generally check to see if you qualify for a refund.

3. How Should I Be Preparing my Taxes?

The tax preparer in me says use a professional, preferably me. I know, we're expensive, inconvenient and can be a bit arrogant and prickly. Still, unless you have a very simple return, you should at least have it reviewed by a professional every couple of years. You can find many willing to check it for free, in the hopes that they can find a mistake and charge you for fixing it. If you do this, make sure you know up front that the review is free, and that there is no obligation to allow them to be the one to fix it if they find an error. That said, one of the biggest mistakes I see is people thinking their tax return is simple when it could be more complicated and result in a bigger refund. That's why you need to get it checked. You can fix a return for a bigger refund for 3 years after it's filed or due (April 15th)—no extensions for the oldest tax return! If you have a tax return reviewed every 4 years and they find a mistake, you can have them check the prior three that weren't reviewed.

So what are your options for filing? You have a few: you can do it pen and paper, online, with store-bought software, or you can use a professional. The IRS is not a fan of pen and paper, and it is the slowest method of getting a refund, so keep that in mind. Anyway, let's go over the ins and outs of each option.

So you want to do it yourself...

Pen and Paper. For pen and paper, make sure you download the current year's forms (the internet is the best way to get them—the post office and libraries don't carry them anymore.) They are available at www.irs.gov, and there is a prominent link to forms and publications. Download the form you need and the instructions. I would also recommend downloading a copy of the Publication 17. It's the basic tax publication that covers the majority of individuals' tax situations. So how do you know which form to use? That's the first problem with paper filing. It's the only method that doesn't answer this automatically. The short answer is that the instructions will tell you if you qualify for a given form. Anyone can file the Form 1040 (the long form), but there are restrictions for using the 1040A (short form) or the 1040EZ (the easy form). To be honest, I would use the 1040, because it ensures you don't miss any potential deductions, and it's not that much more difficult than the A or EZ, even if you qualify for using them.

When ready to start writing, read the general instructions, and then follow the line-by-line instructions. Don't assume that you know what goes where! Write legibly and carefully—start in pencil! When you are done, check all your calculations TWICE, and then copy the numbers in pen. Then check it again. Sign the return, and mail it to the appropriate address. The instructions will tell you where to send it based on where you live, and if you are getting a refund or owe money. Make sure to put the right postage on it, and mail it by the due date (generally the 15th, unless that falls on a holiday, then it's the following Monday.) If it is in a mailbox, before the postman picks up at that box on the 15th of April, you're good.

Online Software. For online software, you need to do a few more things before you start. First, pick a good provider. Most of you already have one you're satisfied with, but, if you are just starting, or think you might want to change, I would suggest using one of the big boys—you know who they are. Check reviews to decide which one you like, then stick with them. Switching providers can result in loss of carryover information from the prior year. This not only creates more work for you, it could cause you to screw up your tax return. While you're at it, check www.irs.gov to see if you qualify for Free File. Depending on your income, you might be able to file your federal taxes for free! Income limitations and other restrictions are set by the IRS, so you can be comfortable that if the service charges you, it's because you didn't qualify, not because they are trying to rip you off. You will most likely have to pay for your state taxes, even if the federal is free. Which reminds me, many providers will lure you in with a free federal, and then stick you with a state fee. This is common practice, but make sure you know the state fees before you buy. Military personnel can check with Military One Source to see if you can have your taxes prepared online for free.

Once you've decided who to use, you're ready to start. First, don't use public Wi-Fi! Are you insane? This is identity theft gold for those evil bastards! Do it at home, and make sure your internet connection is secure. This is the only real difference between online and at-home software. With this method, everything you do goes over the internet. With home software, just the actual filing goes over the internet. You should be able to trust the connection between you and the provider. They have enough incentive to make sure it's secure. You just need to make sure it's secure at your end. Second, I would have IRS Publication 17 downloaded and ready to review just in case you have questions.

Now you just follow the software prompts, making sure you enter your information accurately. The key here is to not just answer the questions off the top of your head. Use your documents, and think! This is the biggest problem with software. It says, "How much did you pay for uniforms?" and you enter how much you paid for those logo shirts your company makes you wear. But they're not deductible! Even military uniforms are mostly non-deductible. Generally, the software will have somewhere you can click for more information. ALWAYS click it! At least for your first time through. In subsequent years, you can be a little more casual when your situation stays the same. A note of caution: most programs will provide values for Goodwill type contributions, but they are awful! Check the charitable deductions section for more information—that's probably where this book will make people the most money with their refunds.

Once you finish your federal return, the software will do some sort of review, and prompt you to check some things (maybe). Then it's time for state. For the most part, state will be dragged directly from your federal, without a lot of input from you. That said, state is where software starts to show its weaknesses. Federal gets all the attention by the software developers, and the states get the leftovers. Even the amazingly expensive professional software I use to prepare taxes has its shortcomings regarding states, so you can imagine what you get for $14.99. Some states are more complicated than others. You need to be even more cautious navigating the state screens. If you have a complicated situation (more than one state, moves between states, military spouses) I would urge you to either have it prepared or checked by a professional.

Now we come to another major problem with software tax preparation: you don't get to review the return until you pay for it. Sure, it tells you your refund and you can look at what you put in, but you can't look at the forms! Most people who use software never even look at the forms. They just electronically file and save a copy to their hard drive (or just rely on the online company to retain a copy). This is a MISTAKE! Go ahead and pay for your return, and, if possible, print a copy before filing. If you have to file before printing, go ahead and file and then print. Review your return line-by-line, or have a professional do it. Then electronically file it (you can mail in a paper copy, but this will delay your refund). If you had to e-file and then you find a mistake, the software should have a method for correcting it. Now take the copy you printed and put it somewhere safe with all the documents you used to prepare it. I would also suggest making notes of anything you might want to remember about how you prepared it in case you are audited.

A note on guarantees: You'll see many a proclamation about the Maximum Refund Guarantee and Accuracy Guaranteed! Read the fine print. First, they generally only guarantee the software's programming, not the entire return. They will assume (correctly for the most part) that any error on your return was a result of you not following the instructions (or even reading them), mis-entering information, or misinterpreting the rules—they won't pay anything for this. If their software is wrong, you will probably hear about it on the news—it happens, but rarely. Even if their software is wrong, they generally only pay interest and penalties, with maybe a refund of what you paid for the software. They don't pay any extra taxes you owe, unless you pay for some magical extended guarantee with a fancy name.

Store-bought Software. For software you buy in a store, the process and problems are pretty much the same as with online preparation. You do all the preparation at home, and the only thing that goes over the Internet is the actual electronic filing. Follow the same suggestions I made for online software, and you'll end up in the same place. Most of the at-home versions of a company's software are very similar to the online version. One good difference is that your work and final tax return are automatically saved on your home computer, vice the company's servers.

Using a Professional:

Using a professional brings on a whole new set of concerns. The first step is deciding who to use. The IRS gives great advice on this subject, and I'll mirror some of it here. To select a preparer, I recommend going online and searching for someone in your local area.

Experience. You don't want someone with little or no experience providing the final look at your tax return. However, if nobody uses new preparers, how do they get to be experienced preparers? The mercenary in me says that's the problem of the people who don't know how to pick a good preparer. The tax preparer in me who works with and relies on new preparers to help staff an office is a little more understanding. The way my office handles new preparers is that we initially have them observe experienced preparers, then prepare under the direct supervision of an experienced preparer (sitting right there as they work), and then have them prepare tax returns that are thoroughly checked by an experienced preparer. How does this matter to you? If you find yourself in front of an inexperienced preparer, make sure that an experienced and qualified supervisor will thoroughly check your return. Always feel free to refuse an inexperienced preparer if you don't feel comfortable. As for volunteer services, such as Voluntary Income Tax Assistance for the Military and AARP, use the same criteria for evaluating them as you would a paid preparer. Be prepared to not find any volunteers with extensive experience. You do get what you pay for.

Qualifications. I highly recommend a licensed preparer. Shockingly, there is no requirement to be licensed to prepare taxes. You could hang a sign on your door tomorrow and start preparing returns for money. That said, the IRS and other agencies do issue licenses and certifications that help you identify knowledgeable preparers.

- Registered Tax Return Preparer is the lowest level license issued by the IRS. This certification came about as a result of the IRS trying to require licenses for return preparers. However, the courts ruled that the IRS did not have the authority to do so, so the program is voluntary. I feel the exam for this license is rudimentary, but better than nothing.
- Enrolled Agent is another license issued by the IRS. This isn't actually a license to prepare taxes, it's a license to represent people in front of the IRS, such as at audits. The testing and continuing education are serious. You can be pretty sure that Enrolled Agents know their stuff about taxes.
- Certified Public Accountants (CPAs) are licensed within their state. CPAs must meet education and experience requirements established in their state of license. If you are running a complex business, you want a CPA to prepare your taxes. The catch is to make sure that they specialize in and are experienced in the areas you need. You don't want a CPA specializing in Trusts doing your Rental Property tax return.

Check online for reviews of their performance, check their Linked In profile, and figure out how long they've been preparing taxes. Five years is a minimum for me for an unsupervised preparer. I thought I was pretty awesome at five years—I was wrong.

Fees. My next piece of advice is to make sure that they won't charge you unless you are satisfied, at least for the first year. What I mean is that if you are trying out a new preparer, you should be able to see the results, and the fees, before deciding if you want to use them. Most preparers can't quote you a fee until they see what they are getting into. Many charge by the hour. Don't be surprised if you ask how much, and they give you a ballpark, but tell you that there's no guarantee that's what the price will be. You just never know what's in a tax return until you're done. My policy has always been to do the whole tax return, tell the client the results, and tell them the price. If they don't want to pay, I give them their paperwork back and send them on their way. No hard feelings. I would expect that policy from any preparer for at least the first year. Point is, ask up front to make sure.

Transparency and Communication. The next thing you want to check is to make sure the preparer you researched is the one preparing your taxes. If you sit through the whole preparation process, this is obvious. However, if you drop off your paperwork and leave, you need to ask who will prepare your taxes. I have people assist with my preparation, but I always disclose that to the clients affected, and I always go over EVERYTHING. That's what you want your preparer to do. If you drop off your paperwork and leave, make sure you establish how you will communicate and a basic time frame when it should be done. Don't expect a guarantee of when your taxes will be done—sometimes a client's tax issues are more complicated than they originally appeared. Many preparers will have you fill out a questionnaire for dropping off, and have you sign an engagement letter or client service agreement. Make sure to read these carefully.

Guarantees and Representation Practices. The last things to consider before deciding who to use are their guarantees and representation practices. At a minimum, and this is the industry standard, they should pay interest and penalties that result from a mistake they made. If you fail to disclose something or bring in a form, that's on you. You have to pay extra for an extended guarantee if you want your preparer to be financially accountable for any tax shortfall due to their error. Whether to get it or not is a tough question. Most of these guarantees are backed by insurance companies, who don't want to pay. If your preparer is making a lot of judgment calls, paying for the guarantees might be a good idea. As for representation, we're talking about what happens when you get a letter from the IRS, or have to be audited. Most preparers will charge you hourly for this kind of work, and it's not included in the price of preparation. Some will review letters and provide limited assistance as part of the price (think interpreting the letter and suggesting how to respond). Going to an audit with you or for you is almost always extra (a lot extra) but sometimes that's included free if you pay for the extended guarantees. Keep in mind, face-to-face audits are very rare, and letters are certainly not common, but they can be a NIGHTMARE when they happen. Make sure you know what you get, preferably in writing, before you agree to use a preparer.

Once you've chosen a preparer, make sure to give them EVERYTHING. They should provide a checklist or discuss it verbally with you. Include a copy of last year's tax return if it wasn't prepared by them. When in doubt, include it. Try to be organized. Many preparers charge extra for sorting through a grocery bag of receipts (I don't, unless it's ridiculous). Whether dropping off or sitting face-to-face, the preparer should communicate with you as necessary to ensure they have complete information, and they should review the tax return with you before filing it. I would suggest electronically, for speed of refund, and because the IRS requires professionals to do it unless you give them written authorization not to. Plus, e-filing avoids humans, which can be a good thing with taxes.

I'll close with a brief discussion of time to get refunds (see the How Fast Can I Get my Refund section for more). If a preparer promises to get you your refund faster than someone else, they are full of crap, and possibly breaking the law. No preparer can get you your refund faster than any other preparer, assuming you e-file. When a tax return is sent to the IRS and accepted, the timing is in the IRS' control, and no one else's. Some places will give you a loan as an advance on your refund, but this is not your refund, and they're not allowed to say it is. Most of the places that offer this nowadays are fly by night and should be avoided. It takes 6 to 21 days to get an e-filed refund, just wait for it.

Military: Look for free military editions of popular software, though the warning about paying for state tax returns still applies. Be careful of VITA free tax preparation; some are awesome, others not so much. I would strongly consider having a professional check your tax returns, especially the state.

4. 10 Simple Pieces of Tax Advice

Here are a few of my best pieces of advice when it comes to taxes, in no particular order:

1. If you are doing something just for the tax benefit, you're probably making a mistake. Buy a house because it's the right time, not for the tax break. Buy equipment that makes your business more profitable or efficient, not to get the deduction. By all means, take the deduction, but don't make it a critical part of the decision.

2. When in doubt, donate it. If you have stuff you don't want, and you're not sure if it's worth the trouble of selling, give it to charity. Make sure to deduct its REAL fair market value, not what Goodwill is selling it for. Clothes and other used items should be valued based on what a for-profit thrift store would sell it for. If you have a garage sale, don't give in to the temptation to mark everything down to nothing at the end. Ask a fair price, dicker a little, but don't just give it away. After the sale, while everything left is still on the tables, take pictures of it all, load it in the car, and take it to a charity.

3. Depreciate your rental property. This isn't advice—it's a NO BRAINER! You can't avoid depreciation recapture by not taking it.

4. Have your taxes checked by a professional, or a different professional once in a while. Especially have it checked after some big changes have happened. You can usually find someone to check them for free. You would be stunned at the errors I've seen made, and the money left on the table. You have three years after the due date to fix it, so don't wait too long.

5. Don't cheat or lie. Claim all income, don't make up deductions. Stretch the rules as far as you can, but don't break them.

6. Along those lines: Don't be afraid of the IRS. If you're not cheating, you have very little to worry about beyond money and hassle. Professionals like to scare you with the IRS, and, if you're cheating, you should be scared. I prefer to scare people with the prospect of not getting all they deserve. Let's put it this way: Say you've got a nice desk to donate to charity. You check some stores and eBay, and the values are between $500 and $1,000 dollars. Assuming the $1,000 isn't a huge outlier (5 sites between $500 and $550 and one at $1,000), take the $1,000. It's reasonable, defensible, and not frivolous. If you're in the 25% tax bracket, that's $125 on your tax return (25% of the difference between $500 and $1,000). Now let's say the mean old IRS does its worst, and audits you face-to-face. The auditor looks at your documents and tells you the desk is only worth $500. You argue a bit, but they insist and you have to pay back the $125, plus a bit of interest. No handcuffs, no jail-time, no yelling or beatings. You shake hands, sign some paperwork and write a check. Now let's pretend we're in Vegas. You find a table

that gives you $125, then you spin a wheel to see if you have to give them the $125 back, plus $15. The chance of losing is 1 out of 100 times! Who wouldn't make that bet? That's the same thing we're talking about with the desk. JUST DON'T CHEAT!

7. Don't count on getting your refund when promised. You probably will, but don't have things depending on getting the money. The IRS gives estimates of 10 to 21 days from e-filing. However, this gets screwed up enough to make it worth being aware of, and nothing stops them from reviewing your return and adding delays. That's also 10 to 21 days from acceptance, and there are a number of reasons a return might not be accepted the first time it's submitted.

8. Don't over-complicate your records, and don't obsess about organizing every receipt. Keep a good notebook, or series of notebooks that document income and expenses and deductions. Keep them up to date and save your receipts where you can find them. They don't have to be in perfect order—the odds that you ever need them are pretty slim. If you get audited, you can match up your receipts with your books. Odds are good you'll only have to do this once in a lifetime (literally).

9. Don't claim kids that aren't yours, even if the parent gives you permission. Your tax professional can tell you what the rules are to claim kids, and, if you don't meet them, don't do it.

10. Pay your child support and your student loans. The number one reason I see for people not getting refunds is delinquent student loans and unpaid child support. If you're marrying someone with kids from a previous marriage, make sure they're up to date on their child support because their problem is about to become your problem, and it's not that easy to get around it.

BONUS: Don't believe everything you hear about taxes. The myths out there are LEGION. Talk to a professional or look them up on the IRS website.

Military: The advice about not doing something for the tax benefits does not apply if you have the opportunity to tie a big bonus to time in a combat zone. The bigger the bonus, the more benefit you can get from receiving it in a combat zone.

5. How Fast Can I Get my Refund?

That's the most common question, and the answer is, despite anything anyone tells you: "I don't know." Anyone who promises to get you your refund faster than someone else is, as I said before, full of crap. There are things you can do to make sure it doesn't go slower: file electronically, make sure it's accurate, don't owe any government agencies money, and use direct deposit. Owing the government agencies money means delinquent student loans, child support, government benefit agencies, and of course, back taxes. If you do, the government can, and will, take the money out of your tax return, and it often delays the return as well. If you ever get less money from the Feds than you expected, this is a likely culprit. Check out the Where's my Refund section for more info if this happens.

I'm sure the answer above isn't very satisfactory, so I'll expound on it. The IRS says you can expect an electronically filed, direct deposited refund in 10-21 days assuming there are no issues. In fact, last year the IRS wouldn't even talk to you about your refund status unless it had been at least 21 days. This pissed a lot of people off, but I agree with the IRS (this time). People start calling the IRS after 14 days and tie up the lines that should be getting used to answer real questions and deal with real problems. Do yourself and everyone else a favor, don't worry for 21 days. You can check the status of your refund at www.irs.gov using a prominently marked, "Where's my Refund" button. You need your SSN, filing status, and your refund amount. If you use a professional that takes your fees out of your refund, make sure you use the original refund amount, not the amount you will be getting after fees. The honest truth is that the most people will get their money in 6 to 14 days, and the vast majority within 28 days. If it takes longer, either you (or your preparer) did something wrong, the IRS is taking a longer look (nothing you can do about this) or the IRS is messing up (not too likely, but it happens). The Where's my Refund system at www.irs.gov should give you an update as to the cause of the delay, and sometimes tell you what to do. You will also generally get a letter if the IRS decides to take an extended look.

Tax Identity Theft has become a big deal, and the IRS keeps trying to stop it while still getting the majority of people their refunds within 21 days. Even so, more and more people are facing delays as a result of these scumbags. States are taking it far more seriously. Dozens of states delayed refunds last year and I expect more to follow suit this year. Some of these delays are weeks and months. Check out your states tax website to see how this might affect you.

Having said all of the above, those dates are from the time the return is accepted, and are the timeframes for your money to get to the bank (your bank can legally hold a direct deposit for 4 days after receiving it, but if they do, I'd find a new bank). When you send your return to the IRS electronically, they do a number of checks immediately, and, if they fail, it is rejected. The following are common causes for returns to be rejected:
- Names, SSNs, or birthdays on the return do not match IRS records

- A person on the return has already been claimed or already filed
- Last year's Adjusted Gross Income that you provided to software isn't correct
- The First-Time Homebuyer Credit payback was not included on the return when required

There are literally hundreds of other reject causes, but suffice it to say, the clock in the paragraph above doesn't start until you correct the problem and resubmit. Most rejection problems are easy to solve, and if you use a professional, they should walk you through solving them. I would say that 80% of my client's rejected returns are resolved over the phone in 24 hours. Another 10% require modifications to the return that affect the refund. About 5% require the return to be mailed in, and 5% don't get resolved because the client disappears, or is unable or unwilling to make the changes required to the return. If your return is rejected, don't panic. Your software support or tax professional should be able to help.

Now let's mention a few wrinkles that some tax companies will introduce. The first one is a system for withholding your tax preparation fees from your refund. The way this works is that you agree to have your refund deposited with the tax company's bank, who immediately forwards the money (minus fees) to your bank account. The main thing to understand about this is that they have no control over the speed of your refund. They don't send you your money until the IRS sends it to them. If the IRS sends you less, you get less. If the IRS doesn't send enough to cover the fees, the company will expect you to make up the difference. They will also take any back fees that you owe them from prior tax returns. Also, if you are a careful tax return reviewer, you might panic that the direct deposit information on the back of the Form 1040 is wrong. That's because it's the bank's information, and that's okay. There is almost always a fee for this service, but it's usually not too much. My mantra is that the fastest and cheapest way to get your tax return from a professional is pay the fee up front, electronically file, and use direct deposit.

The last thing is getting your money faster than the IRS sends it. No matter what your tax professional calls it, this is a LOAN. They are required to disclose this fact, but not all are as conscientious about it. There are a couple of things to know about these. First, they are EXPENSIVE. Since the loan is for only a couple weeks, the interest has to be outrageous to make the company loaning you the money any profit. Plus, your fees have to cover them for the people who don't end up getting a refund. The second thing is that you are not guaranteed to get a loan. Once you e-file, the bank can approve or disapprove the loan. Generally, if they say no, you only get charged for the conventional product of having your fees withheld and the timing is just like any other product. The big thing to know is, if they loan you money, and the IRS doesn't issue you a refund to pay it off, the bank will want their money back. This can be a lot of money. My advice is to avoid these like the plague.

Military: No real changes here for you.

6. Where's my Refund?

I'll answer that with a question: Has it been at least 21 days since you electronically filed your return and the IRS accepted it (28 days if they are mailing you a check)? If not, wait. This is the normal processing time and you should not call the IRS or your tax preparer until this much time has passed. You will probably know people who filed after you and got their refunds faster, but that's because the timing can vary, between 6 and 21 days, and there's no way of knowing who gets it when. For the first 21 days, the best way to track it is at www.irs.gov using a prominently marked, "Where's my Refund" button. You need your SSN, filing status, and your refund amount. If you use a professional that takes your fees out of your refund, make sure you use the original refund amount, not the amount you will be getting after fees. You will be given the status of your return and contact information if they need you to do something. If there's a problem, they'll let you know, though they may not tell you anything useful besides that. If they indicate there's a problem, now is the time to call your tax preparer or contact the IRS at the number they give you when you check the status. Be prepared to wait, and wait. The IRS phones are VERY busy during tax season.

Starting with 2016 tax returns, the IRS will be holding refunds that include Earned Income Credit, Additional Child Tax Credit and (rumor has it) American Opportunity Credit until February 15th. Practically, this means you might not get your money until February 27th if you claim these on your taxes.

Now let's talk about a few of the more common reasons you might not get your refund on time:

The IRS is taking a harder look at it: The timing guidelines from the IRS are not obligations. They sometimes pull a return for additional review. Sometimes this is quick, sometimes it can take a long time. If it takes more than a few days, they will usually send you a letter telling you they are doing it, but not always. Feel free to harass the IRS for answers if you have the patience.

You owe the IRS or other government agency money: This is called an offset. If you have delinquent student loans, Veterans (VA) overpayments, military credit card delinquencies, back child support, back taxes and/or many other things, they can deduct the payment from your refund. "Where's my Refund?" will tell you if an offset was deducted, and give you a number to call to find out the organization they took it for and their phone number. Make sure to check with your spouse to make sure it wasn't their offset. If it was taken for your spouse's debts, you may be able to file as an Injured Spouse to get some of the money back—contact a professional for help. If you think this has happened, or may have happened to you, you can call 1 (800) 304-3107 and this automated system will tell you if you have offsets, and who to contact about them.

You owe your tax preparer (or their bank) money: When you use a preparer and have them pull your fees out of the refund, you generally give them permission to collect any debts you owe them or their bank. Check the paperwork, it's in there.

You gave them bad Direct Deposit information: Make sure you get those numbers right. Check your actual checks and match them to your tax return. If you had your fees pulled from your refund by your preparer, the numbers won't match the return, since your money goes to the preparer's bank first. Check the paperwork for pulling the fees out, your direct deposit information should be in there somewhere. If you made a mistake, chances are that you will simply get a check mailed from the IRS, or, if you had fees withheld, your preparer's company will process a check for you using their own processes. It shouldn't be more than a couple weeks of delay. Worst case is if your direct deposit error matches an actual account for someone else. In that case, you have a long road of pain ahead—though you will get your money. Contact the IRS or your preparer for help.

The IRS corrected your return and you don't get a refund: Sometimes the IRS finds errors and corrects them on the spot, sending you the proper amount of money. If this results in a balance due, you won't get any money—you'll get a letter asking you to pay.

Military: No real changes here for you.

7. I Owe Taxes and Can't Pay

This sucks. I see it all the time and it can be nerve racking. You don't want to owe money to the IRS. They have some of the most effective methods of getting money from you and can do a lot more than other creditors can. That said, don't freak out completely. The IRS can be understanding and does have a number of programs available to you, especially if this is the first time. Also, you need to immediately take the steps in the next section to ensure you don't owe again next year. This can be a double whammy, because anything you do to lower your tax bill next year will generally lower your take-home pay just as you're trying to pay the IRS for this year!

Here are some general considerations. First, pay them what you can, as soon as you can. Send every penny you can afford in with your tax return (or the voucher you'll get printed if you're e-filing) by April 15th. Second, don't try filing an extension to avoid this. It's an extension of time to file, not time to pay. Third, don't ignore the IRS. If they send you a letter or a bill, you need to reply, preferably with some money and an explanation.

A word on those tax resolution companies you see advertised on television. While I'm sure that some of them are honest and helpful, I think most of them are one step above con artists. Some are one-trick ponies who will try to file an Offer in Compromise for you, the vast majority of which are not approved. They are telling you the truth when they say they can stop garnishments and levies, but what they don't tell you is that this is only while the IRS considers your Offer in Compromise. Be very careful and do your due diligence if you try to use one of these firms.

Keep in mind that it is highly unlikely that you can avoid paying the taxes you owe, and that the IRS will charge interest, and often penalties, on the amount that you don't pay by April 15th. You should consider all sources of money that are available to you in order to make the payment (though talk to a tax professional before pulling money out of a retirement account). By the way, even if you file before April 15th, you don't have to pay until April 15th.

Here are some details on what the IRS has available when you can't pay:

1. The most common method used is the installment agreement. There is a fee to apply, but the IRS has to accept an installment agreement that will get the taxes paid within 3 years, as long as you have filed and paid your taxes on time in the past, and owe less than $10,000. Interest and possibly a late payment penalty will still be assessed. Go to www.irs.gov and on their front page there is a section titled "Paying your Taxes." You will find the installment agreements there.
2. You can pay your taxes with a credit card, though the IRS uses third-party vendors who will charge you a fee. Information on them is available at www.irs.gov/e-pay.

3. You can file for a payment extension. You can ask for up to 6 months, and, if approved, you will not pay a penalty if paid by the extended date. You will still owe interest the entire time. DO NOT apply for one of these if you aren't sure you can pay by the extended date. Make sure to apply for the extension before April 15th. You file for the extension using Form 1127.

4. You could try for an Offer in Compromise (OIC). These are difficult and not approved very often. The IRS will accept an Offer in Compromise in two situations. One is a situation in which it is unlikely that you will ever be able to pay the amount due. You will need to PROVE this with tons of financial documentation, as well as substantiation as to why your financial situation will never improve. The other reason is if there is doubt as to whether you owe the money. This normally comes up when you are fighting the IRS over something on your tax return. The IRS may accept less than what's owed if there is a possibility that they might lose a fight in court on the issue in question. You should seek some professional advice before filing an OIC, even if you are going to file it yourself. You will save yourself a lot of trouble talking to an EA or CPA to ensure you at least stand a chance.

I want to reiterate two points here: pay as soon as possible, and fix your tax situation so you don't owe again.

Military: If you are on active duty, or National Guard called up for more than 30 days for an emergency, you can request a deferral for the time you are on duty and have interest capped at 6%. You'll need to talk to an expert about this. There are also payment deferral programs for active duty military, but they are complex and confusing, so you will want to seek expert advice.

8. I Owe Taxes and Want to Get a Refund Next Year

This is a tough situation to fix with accuracy and certainty. You usually ensure that they withhold enough from your paycheck by filling out a W-4 and providing it to your employer. The problem is that the W-4 form is a complete piece of crap. If you are anything other than a single income family, it won't get you the right answer. If you are a single income family, follow the instructions on the W-4 and file it with your employer. This should get you the right amount of withholding, though you should make sure your paycheck changes to reflect your updates (I'm assuming your original W-4 was not filed correctly). Some payroll people aren't so good at getting this done.

I'm going to just list things to do and considerations to take into account. Unfortunately, there is no magic bullet other than having a professional analyze every detail of your situation, or delving into a bunch of tax tables yourself. I don't recommend that, and, my experience says you won't do it anyway.

1. Tax withholding is a zero sum game. Any change you make to get a bigger refund is going to reduce your paychecks by EXACTLY the amount your refund goes up. Make sure your budget can sustain the changes you make, and if it can't, work on your budget.
2. Don't try making less money. Making less money very rarely improves your tax situation more than it hurts your paycheck. In fact, one of the best ways to fix this is to make MORE money, and have the extra income (or a lot of it) withheld and sent to the IRS.
3. Don't try to be perfect. People will tell you that a refund is an interest free loan to the government, but I can tell you based on thousands of tax returns that getting a $5,000 refund is infinitely preferable to owing even $500.
4. You are already behind on this. Every paycheck you received during the year before filing your taxes and seeing that you're screwed had the wrong withholding. The changes you make now, if you make them exactly right for a full year, will still be short for the part of the year you were not paying enough. The later you filed your taxes, the worse this is (that's why you should at least prepare your taxes as soon as possible.)
5. If the problem is that you have multiple incomes, such as a working spouse or a second job, my advice is to fill out a W-4 for the highest income using the instructions, and enter Single and 0 on all other W-4s. This is usually overkill, but you can adjust later if you get too big a refund.
6. No matter what you do, you should be able to see if it's working by noting how much your paycheck changes once you adjust your withholding. Take the change in Federal Tax Withheld on your paystub and multiply it by the remaining pay periods in the year. This should be at least as much as your balance due was.
7. The more things that change your income, the more difficult it's going to be to get this right. Make bigger adjustments if a lot of stuff is changing.
8. If you only owed a few hundred dollars, consider figuring out your withholding allowances as they are, and adjusting DOWN, by a single number. You can find

your withholding on your pay stub, on your payroll online account, or by talking to your payroll office. If you are at Married and 4, change it to Married and 3. If you owed much more, make a change by two or even three numbers. If you get to zero, change from Married to Single. After making the change, calculate number 6 above, and adjust further if necessary. Don't worry about putting Single when you're Married, it doesn't matter. There is a box for Married, but withhold at higher Single rate; checking that box does the same thing as checking Single.
9. If you want to be more exact, you can make estimated payments. Estimated payments are made on April 15th, June 15th, September 15th, and January 15th of the next year. You can make them more often. I used to hate this idea, because you had to send a check, but now you can make estimated payments online at www.irs.gov. To do this simply take your balance due and divide it by 4. Make those payments on the above dates.
10. Keep in mind that using your prior years balance due as the basis for changing withholding or making estimated payments won't be perfect unless your income and tax rates (and tax laws) stay the same. The more your income changes, the more error will occur. You can account for some of this by being more aggressive and having them withhold extra.
11. Some payroll managers will automatically match your state withholding to your federal withholding allowances, so make sure you see what's happening on the state side as well on your paycheck.

Military: You can see your withholding allowances on MyPay and can make changes there. Be careful making changes in years when you get promoted or transferred. That said, when your pay goes up due to advancement or moving to an area with COLA or higher BAH, this is an opportunity to increase withholding without taking a big hit in take-home pay.

9. I Get a Big Refund and Want a Bigger Paycheck

If you are willing to do a lot of math and your tax situation is fairly static, you can do a pretty good job at adjusting your deduction for a smaller refund and bigger paycheck. On the other hand, there are a lot of ways to screw this up, so be very careful. If you want a smaller refund and you don't want to do a lot of work, the easiest way is to increase the allowances you claim on your W-4 by exactly one number. If you have multiple jobs, do this with the highest paying job. Nowadays, you typically do this through your online payroll program, but you might have to submit a paper W-4 to your payroll department. You can also talk to your payroll people to have them make the change manually, if you work for that kind of company. Then make sure to check your next couple of paychecks to ensure the change is made: typically your take home pay will go up.

If you want to be more accurate, I still recommend the following:
- Increase the number of allowances on your W-4 one number at a time (2 to 3, 3 to 4, etc).
- Take the amount your federal withholding goes down on your next paycheck, and multiply it by the number of pay periods in the year. This is roughly how much your refund will go down.
- If you still want less money in your refund, make another adjustment to your W-4 (increasing the number of withholding allowances) and repeat the calculation. Don't try to cut it too close.

Note that since the year already began at this time (assuming you are doing this after filing your return and seeing the result), you won't get the full benefit (because you've already received some paychecks). I would adjust the W-4 based on a full year anyway, otherwise your next year you might go too far. If you get a lot of refundable credits, like Earned Income Credit or Education Credits, you may not be able to get the refund down, even if they take out nothing. This is because you might already be paying zero taxes, and the IRS is kicking in some bonus money. You should be careful if you get some of these credits, because if they disappear due to policy changes, program expiration, or life changes, you could end up owing money.

Before jumping on this too fast, I recommend you read the next two sections, which are taken from posts I wrote on my blog about why it's not awful to get a big refund, and things you can do with a big refund.

One more thing: be careful of financial advisors who encourage you to go exempt or claim nine withholdings so you'll have more money to invest. They are generally not looking out for you. It is appropriate to talk about your refund and suggest small and careful changes to lower your refund and increase the monthly amount available to invest. Your financial advisor should either refer you to your tax professional, or, if they are smart, help you run through the numbers to make an accurate change to your withholding.

Military: You can see your withholding allowances on MyPay and can make changes there. Be careful of making changes during years in which you are advanced, get bonuses, or have served in combat zones. All those things make it difficult to predict your tax situation accurately.

10. In Defense of a Big Refund

I know what everyone says, "A refund means you made an interest free loan to the government!" And they're right, but really, have you seen interest rates lately?

I'm not here to argue that their opinion or facts are completely wrong. To be honest, they're pretty much spot on. But that doesn't mean it's the whole story. I'm here to reassure you that you shouldn't feel guilty about the big refund, and I'll tell you why. First, however, let me tell you when a big refund really would be bad:

If you're really struggling to make your monthly bills, barely getting by paycheck to paycheck, but get a big refund, you really should adjust your withholding to cut down the struggles. Aside from that, here are a few reasons it's okay:

1. Interest rates suck. If saving the money for a big purchase is your plan, you really aren't losing much letting the government keep it and getting it on your refund. If you're saving for long-term things, such as retirement, then you should get it in your paycheck rather than the refund. If it's for short-term goals, there's not much of a difference. Combined with a few more of the following reasons, you can make a compelling case for a big refund.
2. Most Americans (myself included) suck at saving. We tell ourselves that we'll save the money, and maybe we even set up an account to do it. Then the money is there: mocking us, tempting us. So we spend it! Or even more likely, we never get around to setting that account up, or we end up "needing" it for "just this one time." Next thing you know, we've saved bupkis!
3. Getting a big refund is a good way of ensuring you can catch up if you have a bad year with bills. You get a little behind because, as most Americans, we're not really great at budgeting. The credit cards build up a little more than we wanted, and maybe even get a little hard to pay, then BAM! It's refund time and we can do a reset. Now I'm not recommending this as a planning method, but, I see a lot of reality in the tax office, and this is a big helper for a lot of people.
4. It's really difficult getting a small refund without ending up going too far. I can say with absolute certainty that virtually every person I do taxes for would consider a $500 balance due as nearly end-of-the-world bad. It SUCKS owing the government money. Even the ones who want to get a small refund would rather get too big a refund than owe one thin dime! Trying too hard for a small refund risks the evil balance due.

So relax. Tell the naysayers to mind their own business. If you want a big refund, that's fine with me.

Military: The variability of military pay can make the act of getting a small refund even more difficult.

11. I Get a Big Refund and Don't Know What to Do With It

These are some ideas for making your big refund work for you. They're a little preachy, but I think it's good advice:

1. If you're behind on any bills, please, for the love of God, catch them up and keep the bill collectors at bay. After that...
2. If something important, like your car or your HVAC system is broken, get it fixed. After that...
3. If you don't have $1,000 dollars saved for an emergency, open a savings account and put $1,000 dollars in it. Please, for the love of God, Don't Touch It, unless you have an emergency. After that...
4. Spend some of it, no more than 20%, on you or your family for something that makes you, and them, happy. You should enjoy the fact that you've accomplished steps 1 through 3. That's more than many families will accomplish in their lives. A $1,000 emergency fund is a BIG DEAL, and you should be proud of it. After that...
5. Pay off credit card or other high interest debt. All of it, and shred those credit cards, and get a debit card only. After that...
6. Pay off student loan or car debt. After that...
7. Put away 3 to 6 months of expenses in that savings account we talked about in Step 3. Leave It Alone! It's for emergencies. After that...
8. Feel free to spend the rest on something you want, or a vacation you desire. If you've accomplished Steps 1 through 7, you probably have a good budget, and a good plan for your future. Everything that follows is optional, and you can do any of the steps in any order. If you want...
9. Fully fund your Roth Individual Retirement Account (IRA) for the year (or traditional if appropriate for you—talk to your tax professional and your financial advisor). You have until April 15th. Or...
10. Sock some money away for the kid's college fund...maybe an Education Savings Account or a 529 plan. Or...
11. Put a big chunk towards the house. Big payments now increase the power of the normal payments you make. Don't listen to the morons who say you should always have a mortgage. They don't know what the hell they're talking about. The Super Tax Genius rules say NEVER do anything just for the tax benefit, and owing money to the bank qualifies as one of the dumber things you can do. Or...
12. Upgrade the house. Maybe new counters, new bathroom. Whatever. You've demonstrated that you're smart enough to spend your money the way you want. I would probably jump on Step 11, but if you've got 1 through 7 done, you don't need me to nag you.

If some of these ideas seem familiar, that's because many of them were inspired by listening to Dave Ramsey. I don't think his advice is absolutely necessary for everyone, but if you've tried to get your financial life in order and failed, you should follow his plan, TO THE LETTER. If you're out of debt and your retirement plan is on track, you probably don't need all of his advice, though we can always learn something.

Military: No real changes for you on this subject, except that all of the above advice applies to any bonuses you get.

12. I Want to Lower my Taxes

Don't we all! There are a lot of guru's out there claiming they can lower your taxes. They range from frauds, kooks, and one trick ponies all the way to legitimate tax experts. Avoid the scam artists like the plague. You can always tell who they are because they over promise and make it sound easy. The fact of the matter is that it's hard to lower your taxes without causing problems with your life. As I said in my advice chapter, you should rarely be doing anything just to lower your taxes. Sure, buying a house can lower your taxes, but you should buy a house when it makes sense for your life - not just to lower your taxes. So I won't be talking about things that might lower your taxes, but that should be done based on other factors.

I'm going to cover two types of things here. Things that directly lower your taxes and things that defer your taxes. Deferring taxes is usually good, unless you'll pay taxes at a higher rate later. Even then, deferring taxes is often the right plan, especially over a long timeline.

I'm going to try to put things in the order of best to worst, based on my opinion, and the extent to which they are likely to apply to more people. Some of them I will advise based on things other than just taxes, though I might not specify why - it's kind of like my personal preference. There are probably more ways than these, but these are the ones that apply most often, or that don't require 7 CPA'S to make happen.

Last thing before the meat - some of these require you to itemize. If you don't normally itemize, some of these things won't help you unless big numbers are involved. I'll identify these with a "Requires Itemizing" closing sentence.

1. The first thing you should do if you want to save on taxes is talk to a tax professional and have them review your last three years tax returns. Many will do this for free and only charge you if they find some more money for you. A good tax pro will not only use the review to find you money in the previous years, but also use what they learn about your tax situation to give you advice for the future.
2. Funding tax deferred accounts such as 401k's and Individual Retirement Accounts is almost always a good idea. Talk to BOTH a tax pro and a financial advisor to figure out what types of accounts are best for your situation. If your employer matches contributions to your 401k, investing up to the match is a no brainer. For accounts with your employer, you might not see the reduced taxes reflected in your paycheck, since the withholding will drop with the reduced taxable income. Health Savings Accounts are another good option for deferring taxes on current income.
3. Giving stuff to charity is a great way to save on taxes. One of the things I like to tell people is that anything you pay that reduces your taxable income (mortgage interest, job expenses, etc.) is money out of your pocket. The return on your deduction is whatever your state and federal tax rate is; so it's a net loser. Cash

contributions to charity work exactly like that. Non cash donations however, are like the proverbial free lunch. You give away crap you don't want to someplace that will do good with it, and you pay less in taxes. I have a whole chapter on this: I'm Donating to Charity. Requires Itemizing.

4. Selling investments (in non tax deferred accounts) for a loss during the year. You can do this both to offset taxable capital gains, or you can deduct up to $3,000 of net capital losses right off of your other income ($1,500 if MFS). Do this only if it makes good investing sense. Also, don't try to sell for a loss and buy it right back - that's called a wash sale. You have to wait more than 30 days after selling in order to deduct the loss.

5. There's a weird trick on Capital Gains, but you might need your tax pro's help with it. If you have long term capital gains (generally on investments held at least a year) and are in the 15% or lower tax bracket (including the gains) you pay ZERO taxes on the gains. You won't see a direct reduction on your current taxes, but you will NEVER pay taxes on those gains, even if you buy the investment back the next day (wash sale rules only apply to losses.) This is the most under-utilized tax strategy out there. I don't recommend doing this without the help of a tax pro, because there's a lot more to it than I can discuss here.

6. Some deductions come with a threshold you have to be above before you can deduct them. Job expenses and medical expenses are two of them. If you don't normally get above the threshold, but have an unexpected expense in one year that puts you above it, this strategy can help. Once you know you will be above the threshold, move any planned expenses for early in the next year into the current year. For medical this might mean moving physicals or procedures up, or buying new glasses or contacts. For job expenses you might move a business trip or big purchase up into the current year. This also applies to itemizing itself. If you are below the standard deduction, but close, donate to charity every few years, instead of every year. This will allow you to get some use out of the donations. Requires Itemizing.

7. Keep better records. You can't deduct something you forgot about. I like notebooks that are always at hand. In the car, on the desk, in your purse, in your shirt pocket. Write things down right away!

8. Don't miss mileage deductions. Keep a mileage log in the car, and write down the mileage after every trip. Mileage mostly applies to home businesses, people who deduct job expenses, medical trips and charity trips. Requires Itemizing (except businesses).

9. I almost didn't want to write this one down, because I wouldn't personally do it, but the math for taxes works out. You can make purchases that wouldn't ordinarily be deductible, with home equity debt, that might make the interest deductible. For example, you might buy a car with a home equity loan, making the interest deductible. Two BIG things to consider first: First, there are limitations on home equity debt not used to buy or improve your home - so talk to a tax pro first. Second, if you can't answer yes to this question: "Are you willing to lose your home if you can't make the payments on that other thing you bought?" then don't borrow money on your home to make the purchase. This strategy puts your HOME on the line if you don't make the payments.

Military: If you can reenlist in a combat zone for a bonus, do it. If this involves taking a smaller bonus, talk to a tax pro to see if the taxes saved is more than the bonus given up. The Thrift Savings Plan qualifies as a tax deferred account as discussed in suggestion #2.

13. I Can't File by April 15th

First things first, relax. This is not as big a deal as most people make it out to be. In fact, for most people, this is an absolute non-event. I'm going to start by clearing up some myths and explaining some important things everyone should know about the filing deadline:

1. If you are getting a refund, for all intents and purposes, the IRS doesn't give a crap when you file, and, there's very little they can do to you if you don't. Almost worst case, you get a letter telling you to file, you file, and they send you your refund. No penalties, no jail, no yelling. So if you are SURE you are getting a refund, you really don't need to do anything. You can file an extension to avoid letters and hassle for six months, but you probably don't need to. Now, to be 100% accurate, there are some possible issues for not filing - so you should file as soon as you can. These are the issues: they can hold up another refund until you file, they might calculate a tax return for you that says you owe money and send you a bill (but your tax return for a refund as a response will fix it), you might need the return filed to get a loan, job or security clearance, and, if you wait more than three years from the deadline to file for the refund, the IRS won't give it to you.
2. You can get an extension of time to file for an extra six months, and it's approval is (almost) automatic, but...BIG BUT, it is an extension of time to FILE, not time to PAY. When you file the extension, you are expected to estimate your balance due, and send the money with the extension. Failing to send the amount you owe will result in interest and failure to pay penalties. The extension avoids failure to FILE penalties. So, if the reason you can't FILE by April 15th is really that you can't PAY by April 15th, then you're in the wrong section. You want: I Owe Taxes and Can't Pay Them.
3. As a corollary to the above, even if you can't pay your taxes, you don't need to wait to file. Your money is not due until April 15th, even if you file in January or February.

All that covered, what to do if you can't file by April 15th depends on why you can't file, and when you can file. Here are a few reasons, with suggestions for what to do:

Waiting on paperwork: This is the most common one, and, the one that ticks me off. I'm not mad at you, I'm mad at companies that make people wait for paperwork. Assuming you keep places up to date with your address, there's no excuse for this. Keep calling and harassing them to get the paperwork. I really can't provide much better advice than that. If the paperwork won't be received by April 15th, complete your tax return as much as you can, including a best guess for the numbers from the missing paperwork. Then file an extension using the estimated balance due, and send the extension with payment by April 15th. Make sure when you file that you include the payment amount as part of the tax return, so you get credit for it in the final results. Make sure to file the tax return by

October 15th. Your tax pro or tax software should handle this smoothly, and you can probably e-file the extension. If you are getting a refund, don't send any money with the extension. One other little thing: if you can get 100% accurate numbers for the document, and it's not a W-2 or 1099-R, you might be able to file without getting the actual document - check with a tax pro.

Waiting on Spouse availability to sign: If your spouse is unavailable temporarily, you can try to file on time by getting a Power of Attorney, getting his or her signature on the documents via fax, email or something else, or your tax pro may have ways of helping. Otherwise, complete your tax return then file an extension using the tax return data, and send the extension with payment by April 15th. Make sure when you file that you include the payment amount as part of the tax return, so you get credit for it in the final results. Make sure to file the tax return by October 15th. Your tax pro or tax software should handle this smoothly, and you can probably e-file the extension. If you are getting a refund, don't send any money with the extension.

Waiting on Spouse availability to provide needed information: In this case, you can obviously attempt to get the information, but I'm assuming that you already tried that. Depending on the amount of missing information, the extension might be just a little off, or wildly inaccurate. You need to work with your spouse to get the tax return done as much as possible, before filing the extension. If you KNOW you are due a refund, you can wait for them to get home and file without bothering with an extension, or send an extension in with 0 as the balance due. If your spouse is more permanently unavailable, you'll need to work with a tax pro on what options you have. If they are deceased, I'm sorry for your loss, but I have a section on that: My Spouse Died.

Divorce or Separation Issues: This can be tough. You can always file Married Filing Separately or Head of Household (if qualified). Read the sections I'm Getting Divorced and I have to File Married Filing Separately first. Otherwise, you should talk to your divorce lawyer AND a tax pro to cover your options. You really need to do both since there's no way I can cover this well enough to help you with all possible scenarios in this book.

Don't have time: This one really doesn't work. In order to file an extension, you practically have to do the whole tax return in order to know how much to send them, so you might as well do the whole thing and be done with it. Seriously, no one has time, but the IRS couldn't care less. Make time for this and get the damn thing done. There's no reason to have the IRS hanging over your head for any longer than necessary.

Military: The IRS and all states will accept a military POA as long as it authorizes the filing of taxes. When stationed outside the U.S. at the time the tax return is due you get an automatic 2 month extension of time to file (not time to pay) and this applies even if only one spouse is overseas. If you are in a combat zone, you get an automatic extension that lasts until 180 days after you exit the combat zone. If your spouse is deployed to a combat zone when the return is due, you can sign the return for them and attach a statement to the return explaining that they were in a combat zone.

14. Filing Status

This is the first decision you need to make about filing your taxes, though for most people they don't have a lot of choice. This is sometimes the easiest question to answer, and sometimes the most complicated. I'm going to try to put the facts you need down, in an order that will help you make the decision as easily as possible.

Just to make things easy, here are some situations that are pretty cut and dried:
If you are unmarried and live alone, you're probably going to file SINGLE.
- If you're married and live with your spouse, you're going to file MARRIED FILING JOINTLY (MFJ) or MARRIED FILING SEPARATELY (MFS).
- If you are a single parent of your own minor child and it's just you and your children in your home all year, you're probably going to file HEAD OF HOUSEHOLD (HH).

Here are the details:

1. There are five filing statuses available. They are SINGLE, MARRIED FILING JOINTLY (MFJ), MARRIED FILING SEPARATELY (MFS), HEAD OF HOUSEHOLD (HH) and QUALIFYING WIDOWER (QW).
2. If you are married and not legally separated on December 31st of the tax year, you are MARRIED. This means you have to file MFJ or MFS, unless you meet very unique requirements to file HH by being considered unmarried for tax purposes (covered next). Legal separation requires the involvement of the courts and is governed by the laws of your state.
3. If you aren't divorced or legally separated, you can be considered unmarried if ALL the following apply:
    a. You did not live with your spouse after June 30th of the tax year. This doesn't count if it's a temporary absence, such as school or military orders. The idea is that they left and aren't coming back.
    b. You paid over half the costs of maintaining a home, which was the main home for your child, stepchild or foster child (foster child must be placed with you by an authorized placement agency or court) for at least 6 months and a day of the tax year. Note that the relations are VERY specific. One way to think of it is that you as a parent have been forced to take care of a child for whom you are responsible due to being the birth parent, step-parent or foster parent. I should also note that step-relationships established by marriage do not end by divorce or death.
    c. You claim that child on your tax return as a dependent, unless you could claim the child, but are allowing the child's other parent to claim them under special rules for divorced or separated parents (which I will discuss in the I'm Getting a Divorce section).
4. The requirement of paying more than half the cost of maintaining a home discussed in this section are different from most times we will talk about paying more than half the costs for kids. In this case, it is just for the home. You include

taxes, interest and rent paid (later situations will talk about Fair Rental Value—here it is rent PAID). You also include utilities, repairs and insurance for the home. Other than that, it's food consumed in the home, and not much else. You need to have paid more than half of that total during the period of time the child lived with you (at least 6 months and a day).

5. If you meet all the requirements in 3 above, you can choose to file HH. You can also file MFJ if the other spouse agrees. If you file HH, the other spouse must file MFS, unless they meet the requirements of 3 above with a different child.

6. If you are married as discussed in 2 and don't meet the requirements of 3 (or are simply happily married), you can file MFJ or MFS. Generally MFJ is better, but you can figure out your taxes both ways and choose the one that gets better results. I have a whole section on MFS, but I'll list a few reasons to consider that might make you want or have to file MFS:

    a. You don't want to be responsible for your spouse's taxes. If you file MFJ, you have to sign the return saying that everything is true under penalty of perjury, and the IRS will hold you accountable for what's on the tax return, even if all you did was sign it. It is very difficult to get the IRS to accept that you are not responsible for a joint return you signed (though there are ways). By filing a MFS return, you are taking responsibility only for the information on YOUR tax return.

    b. You might have to go MFS if you can't get your spouse to file jointly with you. You can't make them. This happens sometimes because your spouse doesn't want to be responsible for YOUR tax return, or during divorces or separations.

    c. Your spouse owes debts that will be collected out of their refund, such as back child support or taxes. If you file separately they won't take it out of your refund if you weren't responsible. There are ways to avoid this without filing MFS, but you should get professional help in these cases.

    d. There are certain tax situations that do work out better MFS. Mainly they involve big differences in income, and either medical expenses or job expenses. You'll have to run the numbers both ways to be sure.

7. If your spouse or child died during the year, you may consider them to have lived with you and/or been married to you through the end of the year. If your spouse died during the year, you will still file MFJ or MFS with them. However, if you get remarried during the same year, you have to file MFJ or MFS with your NEW spouse, and you will file your deceased spouse's tax return as MFS.

8. If you have never had any children, and aren't married, your filing status is SINGLE.

9. If you aren't married, you may be able to claim HH if you pay half the costs of maintaining a home for someone who lived with you for more than half of the year. I discussed paying half the costs of maintaining a home in 4 above. The person has to meet very specific requirements:

    a. If they are your parent, they don't have to live with you, but you have to pay the costs discussed in 4 above for the home they live in (can be a nursing home). You also have to meet the requirements for claiming them as a dependent on your tax return, and you have to claim them to qualify for HH.

b. If they are your son, daughter, stepchild, foster child (foster child must be placed with you by an authorized placement agency or court), brother, sister, stepbrother or stepsister, or a direct descendent of one of them (meaning nieces, nephews, grandchild, etc.) they must meet the following requirements:

- They must have lived with you more than 6 months and a day,
- You must claim them as a dependent,
- They must be under 19, or between 19 and 23 if a full-time student for at least five months, or if older, permanently and totally disabled, and
- They must not have provided more than half of their own support.

(You'll learn more about this when you read the sections that apply to you with regard to claiming people as dependents.)

c. If you don't claim the relative just above only because they are married, someone else can claim them and does, or you allow the other parent to claim them under rules for divorced or separated parents (covered in I'm Getting a Divorce section) they still count for HH.

d. For people who live with you who don't meet the relationship or age requirements above, they may still qualify if they are the following relationships: son, daughter, stepchild, foster child (foster child must be placed with you by an authorized placement agency or court), brother, sister, or a direct descendant of any of those, father, mother and any sibling or descendent of them, a stepbrother, stepsister, stepparent, son-in-law, daughter-in-law, brother-in-law, sister-in-law, or parent-in-law. You must also provide more than half of their support (discussed in chapters you will read about trying to claim them as dependents), and be able to claim them as a dependent on your tax return.

10. If none of the requirements for MFJ, MFS and HH apply, you are Single, with one major exception, covered next under 11.

11. If you were married and your spouse died during the year, we've already discussed what to do for the tax year they died in. However, there are special rules that might apply for the next two years AFTER the year their death, if you have dependent children. You must not have remarried, the dependent must be your child or stepchild (not foster child), they must have lived with you ALL year, you must claim them as a dependent, you must have paid over half the cost of maintaining the home (discussed in 4 above) and you must have filed a MFJ return with the spouse in the year they died. If all those requirements are met, you file as QW, which basically gives you a lot of the benefits of being married, even though you technically aren't.

12. When discussing living with you in the above discussions, temporary absences for school, work, military, etc. still count as living with you.

Military: Being separated from your spouse due to being deployed does not count for not living with your spouse for purposes of claiming unmarried for tax purposes (though geographical bachelor probably does). If a dependent lives with you at the time you are deployed they continue to count as living with you during the deployment, even if you send them to another household (such as your parents) for the time you are deployed. Some people might debate this, but a good rule of thumb is that a non-permanent deployment or assignment does not change the living situation for taxes so long as the intention is for the dependent to return to the pre-deployment living situation when the deployment or temporary assignment ends (sending the child to your ex-spouse who is the child's parent might be trouble). Geographical bachelor or Permanent Change of Station orders would not count for as "temporary".

15. Itemized Deductions

This section is just generic information about itemized deductions. I'm going to cover more details of the various deductions during sections on specific life events or situations. For example, I'll cover charitable deduction requirements and details in the I Give to Charity section. Here I'm going to go over the broad strokes and the overall way that itemizing works.

The first thing you need to understand is that for every filing status, the IRS gives you a deduction that you can take, without having to prove anything or save any receipts. This is called the standard deduction, and it's pretty generous. If you don't have enough qualifying itemized deductions, you generally take the standard deduction. However, there are situations where itemizing is done even though you are below the standard deduction (mainly it saves you more money on the state return). The standard deductions are (2016 values): $6,300 for Single, $12,600 for MFJ and QW, $9,300 for HH, and $6,300 for MFS (there are caveats to this so make sure to check the MFS section if this applies). You also get an additional $1,550 for being over 65 or blind if you aren't married, and $1,250 for each if you are married. There are special rules for children and people being claimed on other persons tax returns, but I'll cover those in the relevant sections.

As you can see by the numbers, you need quite a few deductions before it's worthwhile not to take the standard deduction. I often have people bring me $200 worth of deductions, not realizing it won't make a difference. I tell them about it, but don't make a big deal of it. I'd rather have them keep track and not need them, than not keep track and then need them. Here's why: Say you don't keep track for the first ten months, and then an opportunity comes along, or you end up with a huge deductible expense that gets you over the limit. Now all those deductions you didn't keep track of are either gone, or a big pain in the butt to reconstruct. That's why you keep all your potentially deductible receipts, even if you're pretty sure you won't itemize. It's also why you bring things you think are deductible to your tax pro, and let them tell you they're not deductible. Better to ask and be told no, than not to ask when it would have been deductible.

There is also an income at which the IRS starts limiting how much you can deduct, and some of the individual deductions have limits of their own. I'll cover the individual limits both here when I give the broad strokes, and in the sections where I get specific. The overall limit kicks in at an AGI $311,300 if MFJ or QW, $285,350 if HH, $259,400 if S and $155,650 if MFS. The limit applies only to certain itemized deductions, essentially all of them except investment expense, casualty losses, gambling losses, and medical expenses. The limit is a bit weirdly calculated, but here goes: Take the amount your AGI exceeds the threshold just discussed, and take 80% of your deductions subject to the limit (the ones I didn't just list). The smaller of those two numbers is subtracted from your total itemized deductions.

Here are some general categories of itemized deductions:

Medical expenses: Medical deductions are available, though there are also many caveats. These are limited to the amount that exceeds 10% of your AGI. This number is 7.5% if you and/or your spouse were born before January 2nd, 1951. Check out the I Have Medical Expenses section for more.

Taxes: You can deduct real estate taxes, state income tax withheld from your check or paid with your return, personal property tax that you pay to register your car (not the fees, just the taxes) and sales tax. If you deduct state taxes withheld, your refund will generally be included as income next year (this is very confusing but it does make mathematical sense).

Mortgage Interest: You can deduct the mortgage interest you pay on a first and second home. You can also deduct points paid with some restrictions (these restrictions mostly apply to refinancing or home equity lines). You can also deduct mortgage insurance premiums, including VA and FHA funding fees. There are limits on the amount of debt you can deduct interest on, but I'll cover those in the I'm Buying (or Already Own) a Home section.

Charitable Contributions: You can deduct contributions made to properly established charities. You can deduct cash and non-cash donations, but not the value of your time. There is a maximum contribution that you can deduct in a single year that varies between 20 and 50% of your AGI, but any not allowed can be carried over to the next year. See the I Donate to Charity section.

Casualty and Theft Losses: This is when tragedy strikes and insurance doesn't fully cover it. There are lots of restrictions, you don't get the first $100 per event, and you don't get a deduction until the loss exceeds 10% of your AGI.

Job Expenses: This can be a tricky one. They have to be unreimbursed, required or for the convenience of your employer, and there are a myriad of rules on what can and cannot be deducted. See the I have to Pay Things for my Job section for more details. They also don't count until they exceed 2% of your AGI.

Gambling Losses: You have to keep good records and can only deduct them up to how much you won (which you should have claimed as income).

Claim of Right Repayment: This one can seem a little weird, but, if in the past, you received money that you honestly believed was yours (VA benefits, military pay, sick pay, Social Security, etc.) that was reported on your tax return when you got it but then was taken back in a later year, you have a claim of right repayment. If the amount you paid back during the tax year was $3,000 or less, you must deduct it on Schedule A. If it was more than $3,000, you can either deduct it, or figure out the amount you paid in taxes on it originally and then claim that amount as a credit on your tax return. If it is more than $3,000 you should figure it both ways and do the one that gets you the best result. If you have control of the repayment, you should try to repay at least $3000 in a given year to maximize your options.

Tax Preparation Fees: What you pay to prepare your taxes, including software purchase, is deductible. So are research items like books, including this one.

Investment Income Expense: If you pay interest or other fees to generate investment income, you can deduct them up to the amount of investment income you have.

Military: Generally you won't have medical expenses since it should be mostly covered, but fertility treatments will sometimes get you there. Make sure to include non-taxable allowances and combat pay when calculating your sales tax deduction. Don't miss the VA funding fee as mortgage insurance. Your December LES will have a year to date charity amount for your CFC and other payroll deduction charity. Uniforms are generally not deductible. If you have to repay a bonus, the Claim of Right repayment discussed above might apply.

16. I'm Getting Married

Congratulations! We have a lot to talk about. For this section I'm going to assume that you're marrying a U.S. citizen and that you plan on living with your new spouse. If the marriage falls apart quickly (let's hope not) you'll want to read this section and the section on divorce. That's because for this section I'm going to assume that your marriage actually lasts through 12/31 of the year with you both still living together. The nice thing about this section is that most things are going to apply to most people, so there won't be a lot of hopping around for you. The not so nice thing is that marriage has a lot of tax surprises if you're not prepared. That's one of the things that separates this book from others. If you're doing it right, you're reading this section well before tax time, so you'll be ready.

Filing Status:

You only have two choices now: MFJ and MFS. I'm going to tell you now to plan on filing MFJ. You can run the numbers both ways just in case, but MFJ is usually best. The only reason to file MFS if it doesn't get you a bigger refund is if there is some reason you need to keep your finances separate from your spouses, or they owe money that will be taken from their tax return. If you are considering filing MFS for a reason other than a bigger refund, read the section: I Have to File Married Filing Separately.

Tax Effects:

As a general rule, two basic Single tax returns combined into a MFJ tax return will be unchanged AS A COMBINED RETURN. If one person gets a big refund, and the other a balance due on a Single return, the combined return will be a disappointment to one, and an improvement for the other. I'm about to list a lot of reasons why your combined tax return might change, but, if none of them apply, you should be okay with your current withholding. One of the biggest mistakes newlyweds without kids make on taxes is changing their withholdings to Married. This lowers withholding and causes the combined refund to be lower than the combined refunds were when they were single. The following factors should be considered, as they may cause refunds to change:

Head of Household: If one of you is filing HH before you get married, at the very least, the combined standard deduction and tax tables will not be as good MFJ. I'll talk about kids next, but you obviously have at least one if someone filed HH. The MFJ standard deduction and tax tables are exactly double the Single tax tables: you would see no difference going Single/Single to MFJ if nothing else applied. HH has a higher standard deduction and better tax tables than Single, so going HH/Single or worse, HH/HH to MFJ, is going to impact the tax return. For middle income couples, HH has higher limits at which various benefits start phasing out, though most are the same as Single. Retirement Savings Credit is an example of one where you might get hurt.

Children: The big thing with children is Earned Income Credit. I'm not going to run the numbers on every scenario, but suffice it to say that a combined income is going to hurt when compared to an individual income. I cover the exact numbers for EIC in the I'm Having a Child section. EIC involves BIG numbers that can be dramatically affected by marriage, and you can't avoid them by filing MFS. A person with a child making $13,000 who marries a person making $50,000 is going to see a refund drop in the THOUSANDS! I often say to emphasize that there's no support test for EIC: "You can live with Donald Trump and still get EIC. However, you can't MARRY him and get EIC." The point being that you can live with someone and they don't affect your EIC, but you can't MARRY them without having it affect your EIC.

AGI Limited Items: Itemized deductions are the best example of this, where medical expenses and job expense deductions are limited based on a percentage of your AGI (10% for medical and 2% for job expenses). If one person has the deductions, the combined income will make less deductible. The limit for charitable deductions (in most cases) is no MORE than 50% of your income, so if you give a ton to charity, the combined income might let you deduct more.

Federal Debt: If one of you owes back taxes, student loans, child support, excess VA payments, or a number of other things, they can be taken directly out of your federal refund. Talk to your future spouse to find out about these things BEFORE you get married. You can file an Injured Spouse claim to prevent the entire refund from being taken, but it's a bit of a pain. I would get professional help.

Others: Most of the rest of the tax provisions are affected by filing MFJ, but the numbers are usually exactly doubled, so they rarely make a big difference. It's possible that if one of the newlyweds has something that's affected but the other doesn't that the increased limit might be helpful. A good example is that a Single person can exclude up to $250,000 of gain on the sale of a main home, while a couple can exclude $500,000 (there are a lot of other rules so be aware that this is just an example).

There might be a few things I'm missing, but those are the big things. If none of the reasons that cause refunds to change applies to you, and you're happy with the total that your previous year's Single tax returns would get you (assuming no other big changes), leave your withholding alone.

Withholding:

So the question is: Do you adjust your withholding? The answer is: maybe?

If none of the discussions above apply to you, I would leave things alone and see what happens. Sometimes you can be too proactive.

If any do apply and you feel a need to adjust your withholding, I usually suggest taking the highest income source, and following the W-4 instructions to the letter to come up with good numbers for that income source. For all other jobs and sources of income, have them withhold at the maximum rate (usually Single and 0). If the refund that year is too high, start adjusting them.

A good trick is to run a fake return for you as a couple using the information from your previous year's returns. If you use software, you can probably just add your new spouse to your last year's return. Make sure to save a copy of the original!

Sorry this is so nebulous, but withholding is not an exact science.

Military: If you are going to be deployed, make sure to get a Power of Attorney that covers taxes. A POA prepared by the military must be accepted even if it doesn't fully match state requirements. You can adjust your withholding on MyPay.

Military Spouses Residency Relief Act: The spouse of an active duty military member has two choices for state of residency. The state they live/work in, or the military member's state. In order to choose the military member's state they must have at some time established a domicile/residency in that state (this is the hard rule), and they must be in their current state only to be with the service member (this one is the easy rule).

The choice is not as easy as it sounds. Obviously, if the military member is from a tax free state like Florida or Texas, it's a no brainer. Be careful if they are from a state that is tax free FOR MILITARY. Also, be aware that some states (like California or South Carolina) treat military spouses very well. Consider seeking professional help to make the decision.

17. I'm Having (or Already Have) a Child

Congratulations! Kids are just about the best tax deduction out there; unfortunately, they're going to cost you a lot more in life than they save you in taxes! First big piece of advice—get them a SSN (should be automatic unless you are living abroad), keep it safe and secret, make sure you know how to spell their name exactly as it appears on the Social Security Card and make sure you remember their birthday. The name, SSN and birthday on the tax return must match the Social Security Card and IRS records EXACTLY. This is one of the most common causes of problems on tax returns. Also, as I said, protect the SSN. If someone else has their name, SSN and birthday, there's nothing stopping them from claiming your child before you do, and that will create big problems for you. I'm going to spend a lot of time talking about weird situations involving children later in the book, but for this section, I'm going to assume a traditional parent/child/family situation, and go over what's available from start to finish. I'm also going to assume that you and the child are U.S. citizens living in the U.S., and that at least one of the following applies:

- You are either married to the other parent,
- The other parent is not in the picture, or
- The other parent does not have custody and has no rights to claim the child.

NOTE: Support is discussed periodically below, and is usually obvious and straightforward. I have included a Support Worksheet in Appendix A if you need more details.

I'm going to cover things chronologically, starting with the things that disappear first. Before that, some fine print:

1. If the child is born before midnight on 12/31 of the tax year, they count as living with you all year.
2. This one's a little depressing, but if the child dies before 12/31 at midnight, they still count as living with you all year. Be careful on this though—file early if your child dies. For some stupid reason, it's really easy for identity thieves to get a deceased child's information and fraudulently claim them. You can recover, but it's painful.
3. Even more depressing, if your child is born and dies in the same year, you still get to claim them. This applies for any amount of time. If the child is born alive, even if it immediately dies, you may claim the child. You have to make sure to get a SSN and birth certificate, which will unfortunately be the last thing you will be concerned with if this happens to you. If the child is stillborn, you may not claim the child.

Claiming the child as a dependent: Generally speaking, the assumptions we talked about for this section will make claiming the child a slam dunk, at least for the first 16 years or so. Claiming a child is actually one of the more complex things, but, when you are the parent and the child lives with you, most of the requirements are covered right there. There are a few things to be aware of:

1. The child must live with you for at least 6 months and a day. They can be absent for vacations, school, medical care and even detention in a juvenile facility—those still count as days living in your household.
2. The child cannot have provided more than half of their own support (Appendix A Test 1). Note that this does not mean that YOU have to support them, they just can't provide more than half of their own support. This test changes if they are too old based on item 3 below. If they are too old, then YOU (together with your spouse if MFJ) must provide over half of the child's support (Appendix A Test 2). More details below under 5 - 7.
3. They must be under age 19, or under age 24 if a full-time student for at least 5 months, or any age if disabled. If not, additional tests must be met:
    a. Support test listed under bullet 2 above changes as noted in the bullet.
    b. The child's taxable income cannot exceed $4,050. Sometimes a child receives Social Security benefits due to a deceased parent. Social Security benefits won't affect this test because even though it could be taxable, the income levels that make it taxable would be higher than $4,050, so you would have already failed the test.
4. Note that when a child starts making their own income, turns 18, or goes to college, things start to change. A child can simply move out once they're 18, and no divorce decree, custody document or anything else can get you back to claiming them (assuming they move out before July 1st). They also start messing with who provides over half their support.
5. Support **from** the child includes: wages, investment income, scholarships, student loans that the child is obligated to pay back, unemployment income and savings withdrawals. Any of the above that are not spent for support (generally this means added to savings) don't count as support from the child.
6. Support **for** the child includes: cost of the home (fair rental value of the home plus utilities, repairs, taxes, insurance and other household costs divided by number of occupants), education, entertainment, clothing, medical, travel and other necessary expenses.
7. If the child is young enough that 3 above doesn't apply, you simply determine if the support **from** the child (total from 5) is less than half of the support **for** the child (total from 6). If the child is old enough that 3 does apply, then you determine if YOU (together with your spouse if MFJ) provide over half of support **for** the child (total from 6).

Daycare: Up until your child turns 13 (to the day—not the age on January 1st), you can get a credit of between 20 and 35 percent of any daycare expenses that you pay while you work or look for work (though you must ultimately earn income). If you are married and filing jointly, both you and your spouse must be working or looking for work, though one of you may be a student or disabled. Being self-employed counts as work, as long as you make a profit. What they do is take either your income (and your spouse's if MFJ), how much you pay for daycare, and the limit for how much the IRS allows, whichever is smaller. You then subtract any money you get from your job for daycare (will be reported on your W-2 in Box 10), and then multiply it by a percentage between 20 and 35, depending on your income. This amount comes right off of your taxes due, but cannot reduce them below zero. If you are a student or disabled, you obviously don't have income, so the IRS allows you to use $250 per month ($500 for 2 or more qualifying children) for every month you are disabled or a student as your income (one spouse must be working and have earned income, the other may be a student or disabled). Now for the fine print:

1. The 13-year age limit is waived if your child can't take care of them self due to a disability. You will need to back this up with a doctor's statement.
2. The limit for how much you can get a credit for is $3,000 if you have one child under 13, and $6,000 if you have two or more. They don't both have to be going to daycare, they just have to qualify based on age. This is a common source of lost refund money.
3. You can't get this credit if you are filing MFS.
4. It has to be daycare, not school. You don't get squat for private school or home school. You can get credit if you pay for after school care, even if it is to their regular school. It just has to be separately stated from other payments.
5. Speaking of statements, you should get a receipt from the provider. You will need the amount paid, the name and address, and their Employer Identification Number (for a professional) or their SSN (for an individual).
6. That said, make sure that the person taking care of your children gives you this information up front. It is a very awkward conversation at tax time when you find out your provider won't give it to you because they don't plan on claiming the income on their taxes! This would be illegal, of course. You generally don't need to worry about this if they are a professional daycare provider, such as a Child Development Center.
7. You generally cannot claim the credit for money paid to your children, your spouse or the child's parent, even if they aren't your spouse.
8. Day camps can count, but not overnight camps. The day camp can be activity related, like band camp, and still qualify.
9. If you get daycare money from your job in excess of what you spend on qualified daycare, it's taxable income and is reported on the same line as your wages. If your job reimburses more than $5,000 of daycare expenses, the excess is taxable income. (Most software handles this smoothly if you enter everything from your W-2 right.)
10. If you have a live-in nanny or housekeeper, you can claim payments that are specifically for child care. If the primary purpose is child care, and they do some minor household tasks, you can take the entire amount paid.
11. If the daycare provider provides transport, you can include that expense. You cannot include cost of transport you provide.
12. Unemployment compensation is not earned income for determining eligibility for this credit.
13. You generally must claim the child as your dependent (see above)

14. The child must live with you for at least 6 months and a day (they can be away at school, on vacation and other temporary absences and still count as living with you, they basically just can't be living with someone else).

Child Tax Credit (CTC): Up until the year your child turns 17, you get a $1,000 credit off your taxes. This credit can't reduce your taxes below zero, but once you hit zero, another credit immediately appears. This additional credit has a confusing name that makes no real sense—the name is a carryover from when the credit was different. Anyway, I prefer to treat it as an extension of the CTC. Basically, you can get $1,000 for every child you have under 17, no limit on the number of children (there is an income limit, discussed later). You calculate your taxes, and then reduce them by all your credits, in a certain order (most are taken before the CTC, leaving a lot of it behind to potentially reduce your taxes below zero). You take whatever wasn't needed to get you to zero, and do a calculation based on your income to figure out how much you get back from the government even when you are already at zero taxes owed! Here's the fine print:

1. The credit phases out by $50 for every $1,000 your AGI exceeds $110,000 if MFJ, $75,000 if Single, HH, or QW and $55,000 if MFS.
2. Don't look for a loophole around age 17, there isn't one. This is one of the few times when there is no exception to the age rules. You get 16 years of Child Tax Credit per child, no more.
3. The child must live with you for at least 6 months and a day (they can be away at school, on vacation and other temporary absences and still count as living with you, they basically just can't be living with someone else).
4. You must claim the child as a dependent (see above).
5. The credit can exceed your total taxes if your earned income (generally wages or business profit) exceeds $3,000. After reducing your taxes to zero, you take your earned income minus $3,000, multiply it by 0.15, and take the smaller of that number, and the amount of credit that was left after you reduced your taxes to zero.
6. Refunds with refundable Child Tax Credits may not arrive until after February 27th.

Earned Income Tax Credit (EITC or EIC): If you have kids under age 19 (24 if in school at least 5 months out of the year, or disabled), and don't make a lot of money, EIC is a HUGE benefit. Because of this, there is a ton of fraud, including those people trying to steal your kid's identities. The IRS is focusing a lot of attention on the credit, and there are a lot of hoops to jump through. The idea of EIC is to encourage people with children and limited income to work more, and earn more money. In return for this, the IRS gives them a tax credit against their tax due. (It gets better, the EIC can reduce your taxes below zero, resulting in free money from the government). In order to do this, the Credit works weirdly with income. If you have no Earned Income, you get no EIC. As you make small amounts of money, the EIC goes up until it reaches a point where the government thinks you're doing okay, so it levels off for a while as your income goes up, then, when you reach even more income, it starts to go down until finally it fades away. You get more money for every child up until three, then you get the same for more than three as you get for three. I'll cover the specific ranges in the details so you can get an idea how much we're talking about.

1. If you are self-employed you cannot manipulate your business expenses to qualify for more EIC.
2. Your child cannot file a joint return with their spouse unless they are not required to file, and are only filing to get back their withholding. Your child can be married, but they must still live with you.
3. There is no support test for EIC. I state this because many people will fail to claim EIC because they don't support the child. You can live with Donald Trump and still get EIC!
4. The child must live with you for at least 6 months and a day (they can be away at school, on vacation and other temporary absences and still count as living with you, they basically just can't be living with someone else).
5. You cannot get EIC no matter how little you earn if you have investment income of over $3,450 for the year. Investment income includes taxable and non-taxable interest, dividends, royalties, capital gains (profits from selling investments) and other income reported on Schedule E (rents and royalties). You also include your children's investment income if you are subject to Kiddie Tax (discussed later).
6. Your earned income is generally your wages and business income (self-employment income) from your tax return. If you had taxable scholarships you subtract them off. If you had non-taxable combat pay, you can include all or none of it, whichever is better for you. If you have non-earned income, such as unemployment compensation, you get the lower EIC amount calculated when including it and not including it (in other words, most unearned income can hurt, but not help EIC).
7. Speaking of unemployment, the following are NOT earned income: unemployment compensation, pensions, annuities, Social Security, alimony, child support, welfare benefits, workman's comp, VA benefits, non-taxable military allowances, investment income and tax-free foster care payments. Disability payments may or may not be. You'll want to ask for help with this if you are receiving taxable disability payments.
8. The IRS is serious about EIC fraud. Don't claim it if you don't qualify. They do want you to get it if you deserve it. Don't be surprised if your paid preparer asks a lot of questions about your life situation when discussing EIC. The IRS puts extra due diligence requirements on us for EIC, and we can be fined if we ignore things that make an EIC claim questionable. Also, if you claim EIC when not entitled to it, the IRS can require you to file additional forms for subsequent years. They may even bar you from claiming EIC for a child for 2 to 10 years, depending on how flagrant you were.
9. You cannot get EIC if you file MFS.
10. Everyone needs a valid Social Security Card.

11. You cannot be filing Form 2555 for the Foreign Earned Income Exclusion and also get EIC.

12. Refunds with EIC may not arrive until after February 27th.

13. EIC amounts vary depending on how many children you have (one, two, and three or more), your income, and your filing status (one amount for MFJ, another for all the rest. Here's a rundown.

a. If you have one child and are MFJ, the credit goes up from 0 to a maximum of $3,373 when your earned income reaches $9,900. It stays at $3,373 until your earned income exceeds $23,750, then it drops down as your earned income increases until it hits 0 again at $44,846.

b. If you have two children and are MFJ, the credit goes up from 0 to a maximum of $5,572 when your earned income reaches $13,900. It stays at $5,572 until your earned income exceeds $23,750, then it drops down as your earned income increases, until it hits 0 again at $50,198.

c. If you have three or more children and are MFJ, the credit goes up from 0 to a maximum of $6,269 when your earned income reaches $13,900. It stays at $6,269 until your earned income exceeds $23,750, then it drops down as your earned income increases, until it hits 0 again at $53,505.

d. If you have one child and are not MFJ, the credit goes up from 0 to a maximum of $3,373 when your earned income reaches $9,900. It stays at $3,373 until your earned income exceeds $18,200, then it drops down as your earned income increases, until it hits 0 again at $39,296.

e. If you have two children and are not MFJ, the credit goes up from 0 to a maximum of $5,572 when your earned income reaches $13,900. It stays at $5,572 until your earned income exceeds $18,200, then it drops down as your earned income increases, until it hits 0 again at $44,648.

f. If you have three or more children and are not MFJ, the credit goes up from 0 to a maximum of $6,269 when your earned income reaches $13,900. It stays at $6,269 until your earned income exceeds $18,200, then it drops down as your earned income increases, until it hits 0 again at $47,955.

College Savings Plans: You can contribute to a college savings plan for your child. There are two kinds: Qualified Tuition Programs (QTP) and Coverdell Education Savings Accounts (ESA). QTPs are set up by individual states and are sometimes called 529 plans or college savings plans. ESAs are set up by an individual for the benefit of their child. I'm not going to go into a ton of detail because you should discuss these with your financial advisor, but I will hit some high points:

1. Contributions are not deductible (though your state may allow you a deduction on your state taxes for contributions to your state's QTP).

2. There is a $2,000 per year limit for contributions to an ESA. There is no limit for QTPs.

3. Contributions grow tax deferred (earnings are not taxed).

4. You do not need to be related to set up and contribute to a QTP for someone. An ESA is limited to parents and children.

5. Withdrawals are subject to taxes and penalties if not properly used for education. ESA contributions must be withdrawn when the beneficiary turns 30.
6. Talk to your financial planner AND your tax professional before setting up one of these, or withdrawing from one.

Education Credits and Deductions: If you can still claim your child while they attend college, you can get an education credit or deduction for them. I'll cover them in more detail in the I (or my Spouse or Child) is Going to College section.

Student Loan Interest Deduction: You can deduct student loan interest you pay of up to $2,500 per tax return for student loans that you are obligated to repay. This means that if you pay your child's student loan for them, you cannot deduct the interest. I'll cover them in more detail in the I am Paying on Student Loans section.

Kiddie Tax: Having kids isn't all roses and sunshine for tax purposes. The dreaded Kiddie Tax is designed to prevent you from shifting your investments to your child's name so that you can pay taxes at a lower rate (since your kid probably doesn't have a high tax bracket). This sucker is COMPLICATED, but I'll do my best to put it in plain English. Kiddie Tax kicks in when your child has unearned income of more than $2,100. Some people call this investment income, but that's really not true. For Kiddie Tax, unearned income is ALL taxable income that's not wages, salaries, tips, or payments for services (like running a lawn mowing business). That means it includes unemployment, Social Security payments (if taxable—which happens if the child has a lot of other income), and investment income (also Alaska Permanent Fund Dividends, which means 2015 is going to be an interesting year for Alaska residents). Kiddie Tax applies until the child turns 18, but if the child doesn't provide more than half of their own support at age 18, the Kiddie Tax applies in that year as well. Also, if the child is a full-time student, Kiddie Tax applies until they turn 24, unless they provide over half of their own support. There's more, but I'll hit it in bullets now:

1. The Kiddie Tax applies even if you're not claiming the child.
2. The Kiddie Tax works by taxing your child's income above $2,100 at YOUR tax rate. If they have no earned income, the first $1,050 of their income is tax free, the next $1,050 is taxed in the 10% tax bracket, and the rest is taxed at YOUR highest tax rate.
3. You calculate their tax using Form 8615, which will take their income, and calculate taxes based on your tax rate.
4. You can elect to include the child's income on your tax return instead of filing Form 8615. You do this by filing Form 8814 with your tax return.
5. There's more about who has to claim the income in weird parental situations, but this section isn't about that—Thank God.
6. I'm going to add this just to be clear: If your child has a small amount of investment income in their name, as long as the earnings don't exceed $1,050, you

don't have to do anything with it (unless the child has a job that requires them to file, of course).

Itemized Deductions: You can claim itemized deductions paid on behalf of your children.

1. You can claim medical expenses you paid for your child while you are still claiming them as a dependent.
2. Even if you aren't able to claim them as a dependent, you can still take medical expenses you pay for them if the reason you can't claim them is they filed a joint return or their gross income was over $4,050 (see above on claiming your child as a dependent if you don't understand why these matter.) There are other exceptions but they'll be covered in the I'm Getting a Divorce and various I'm Living with... sections.
3. You can generally take a charitable deduction when you give away your child's stuff while they are under 18. After that, it's a bit shaky. However, if you paid for it while they were a child and they left it behind, I'd deduct it.
4. Other itemized deductions that you pay on behalf of your child will depend on a case-by-case basis. If you buy your child a car, titled and registered in their name, and pay the personal property taxes on it for them, they are probably not deductible. If the car was titled and registered to you, even though you considered it their car, you probably can deduct them.

The next section dovetails directly from this one, and it's about your child getting a job!

Military: If a child lives with you at the time you are deployed they continue to count as living with you during the deployment, even if you send them to another household (such as your parent's) for the time you are deployed. Some people might debate this, but a good rule of thumb is that a non-permanent deployment or assignment does not change the living situation for taxes so long as the intention is for the dependent to return to the pre-deployment living situation when the deployment or temporary assignment ends (sending the child to your ex-spouse who is the child's parent might be trouble). Geographical bachelor or Permanent Change of Station orders would not count as "temporary".

Combat pay can be all included, or all excluded for EIC and most AGI limitations.

If you are stationed outside of the U.S. that still counts as living in the U.S. including for your family.

Not discussed: Unusual parental situations.

18. My Kid's Getting a Job

I'm going to start with the first and most important thing, even though it's not technically a tax law: As long as your child lives at home (even if they go away to college for a while) make them get their W-2 come tax time and IMMEDIATELY give it to you. Under no circumstances are they to file their taxes without going through you! Way too many tax returns are screwed up by a child filing their taxes without consulting their parents. Now it may turn out that you can't claim them, but that doesn't mean they don't affect your tax return (see medical expenses in the previous section). The only way to be sure the returns are both done correctly and the most advantageously is to compare the documents side by side. This applies even if your child has children of their own (especially if they have children of their own!) As long as they live at home, taxes go through you.

NOTE: Support is discussed periodically below, and is usually obvious and straightforward. I have included a Support Worksheet in Appendix A if you need more details.

Now that we've covered that, let's talk about you and your kid's taxes. The first thing to consider is whether you can still claim them as a dependent. Let's revisit the requirements, and talk about where their getting a job might impact.

1. The child must live with you for at least 6 months and a day. They can be absent for vacations, school, medical care and even detention in a juvenile facility—those still count as days living in your household. This shouldn't be a concern unless they move out permanently before July 1st.
2. The child cannot have provided more than half of their own support (Appendix A Test 1). Note that this does not mean that YOU have to support them, they just can't provide more than half of their own support. This test changes if they are too old based on item 3 below. If they are too old, then YOU (together with your spouse if MFJ) must provide over half of the child's support (Appendix A Test 2). More details are below under 5 - 7. Now you have to take their income into account and compare how it applies to the support test.
3. They must be under age 19, or under age 24 if a full-time student for at least 5 months, or any age if disabled. If not, additional tests must be met:
    a. Support test listed under bullet 2 above with changes as noted in the bullet.
    b. The child's taxable income cannot exceed $4,050. Sometimes a child receives Social Security benefits due to a deceased parent. Social Security benefits won't affect this test because even though it could be taxable, the income levels that make it taxable would be higher than $4,050. If your child is 19 or older, and not in college for 5 months out of the year, or 24 or older, regardless of school, they can't make more than $4,050 and you still claim them as a dependent. This does not apply if they are permanently and totally disabled, but you'll need a doctor's statement to that effect.

4. Note that when a child starts making their own income, turns 18, or goes to college, things start to change. A child can simply move out once they're 18, and no divorce decree, custody document or anything else can get you back to claiming them (assuming they move out before June 30th). They also start messing with who provides over half their support.

5. Support **from** the child includes: wages (this is what we're talking about!), investment income, scholarships, student loans that the child is obligated to pay back, unemployment income and savings withdrawals. Any of the above that are not spent for support (generally this means added to savings) don't count as support from the child.

6. Support **for** the child includes: cost of the home (fair rental value of the home plus utilities, repairs, taxes, insurance and other household costs divided by number of occupants), education, entertainment, clothing, medical, travel and other necessary expenses.

7. If the child is young enough that 3 above doesn't apply, you simply determine if the total support **from** the child (5 above) is less than half of the total support **for** the child (6 above). If the child is old enough that 3 above does apply, then you determine if YOU (together with your spouse, if MFJ) provide over half of support **for** the child (6 above).

Their income won't affect EIC, assuming they qualify based on age.

Kiddie Tax isn't significantly affected by getting a job. The Kiddie Tax is based on unearned income.

The other major item to consider is them filing their tax return. You could just review all the sections of this book to do their taxes, but that would be cruel. I'll cover the gist here. If you can't claim them as a dependent, all the usual rules for filing taxes apply. I'm assuming in the bullets below that you are still claiming them and that they are not married, and have no children of their own:

1. Generally if they make less than $6,300 of total income, they won't owe any income tax (assuming no Kiddie Tax). They might have to file anyway, and should, if there was any state or federal withholding on their W-2, so they can try to get some of it back.

2. They will probably file Form 1040EZ, which is really easy, as long as you follow the instructions. Make sure that they check the box indicating that they are being claimed by someone else. If for some reason they are filing Forms 1040A or 1040, they need to make sure NOT to check the box for claiming themselves as an exemption (they should have 0 exemptions).

3. Their filing status will be Single.

4. If they have education expenses, you get the credit or deduction, even if they pay them. This is because the education credits go with the exemption, and we assumed you are claiming them.

5. To determine if they need to file, you need to know their earned income, unearned income (investment income, unemployment, annuities, etc.) and the

total. They have to file if their unearned income was over $1,050, their earned income was over $6,300 or their total income was larger than their earned income plus $350, or $1,050, whichever is larger (basically if they have earned income and more than $350 of unearned income, they have to file.)

6. Just to be safe, in case you mess up, electronically file your tax return before you e-file your kids. That way, if you accidently have the kid claim themselves, their tax return will be rejected, and yours will go through. Don't sweat a rejection in this case, there's nothing you can be held accountable for since a rejected return isn't considered to be a filed return. The IRS can't hassle you for incorrectly filing it. Just correct it and e-file it again.

Military: If your child joins the military, for active duty, and leaves for boot camp before July 1st, you probably can't claim them. If they leave on or after July 1st, their age and income will determine if you can claim them. Talk with them about this before they leave!

19. My Child had (or is having) a Child

Congratulations Grandparent (feel old yet?). If your child is off on their own, and don't live with you or receive significant support from you, then relax, nothing has changed about your taxes. If they live with you or you support them, read on...

Hopefully you've read the previous sections on children and have some pretty good ideas about how you're claiming your child. The questions to be asked now are, does this affect me claiming my child? Can I claim my Grandchild? Any other effects?

I'm not going to rehash all the requirements for claiming a child since you should have been through them for your kid before they had your grandchild. If not, please reread the sections on having a child. I'm going to highlight the things that change or are weird about your child having a child:

1. If your child and/or grandchild both move out permanently such that they don't live with you for more than 6 months during the tax year, you're pretty much done and need not worry about the rest of this. You can't claim much of anything for either of them, even if you're sending a bunch of money their way.
2. If your child moves out, leaving their child with you, such that your grandchild spends more than 6 months with you, but NOT more than 6 months with either parent (even if some or all of the 6 months is in your home), then you treat the grandchild just like it was your child in the discussions previous to this about having a child. You'll still list the child as your grandchild, but all the rules for dependency, education and daycare apply to a grandchild, just like your child. Again, this assumes that you (and your spouse if married) are the ONLY ones that the child lived with for more than 6 months out of the year.
3. In contradiction to what I just said, the one time that a grandchild isn't exactly like a child in the scenario above is if you are married, and trying to be considered unmarried in order to claim HH filing status. A grandchild does not qualify for that exception.
4. If you live together with your child and grandchild in your home, that complicates things. The fact that your child had a child does not change any of the requirements for you claiming him or her, and, generally if you still qualify to claim your child, your grandchild will fall right in line to be claimed by you.
5. That said, it's possible that you might not end up claiming the child. The parent of a child has a higher claim than a grandparent, so, if there's a dispute about who gets to claim the child, you have to run through some scenarios and tests. It is generally a good idea for people to be agreeable about determining who claims a child, and, in a lot of cases, you can decide who gets to claim the child based upon what are the best financial results overall.
6. For the dependency exemption, if there is a dispute, the parent gets to claim the child over the grandparent. If you and your child agree, either can claim the child for tax purposes.

7. For EIC, if there is a dispute, the parent gets to claim the child, unless they meet the requirements for you to claim them (your child) for EIC. You can't get EIC if you are the qualifying child for EIC of another person, so, since we've already discussed that your child lives with you, and they are your child, the only question is age. If your child is under age 19, or under age 24 and a full-time student for 5 or more months during the year, or your child is any age but permanently and totally disabled, they are a qualifying child for EIC, and they CAN'T claim their child for EIC, and you should. If you want to be agreeable, and put the child on the tax return that gets the best EIC, you first need to check the age thing we just talked about, and then, if the child qualifies for both of you, you can only put the child on your tax return if your AGI is higher than your child's.

8. For HH, only the person who pays more than half the cost of maintaining the home can be HH, and they must claim the dependent on their tax return to get it. So, if you agree that your child will claim the dependency exemption, but you pay more than half the cost of maintaining the home, neither you nor your child gets HH (unless there are other children).

9. For all of the above discussions, if the other parent of your grandchild lives with you, you need to include them in the determinations (keeping in mind that they won't be your qualifying child for EIC since they aren't your child). If they are married, see the next section...

Military: If a child lives with you at the time you are deployed they continue to count as living with you during the deployment, even if you send them to another household (such as your parents) for the time you are deployed. Some people might debate this, but a good rule of thumb is that a non-permanent deployment or assignment does not change the living situation for taxes so long as the intention is for the dependent to return to the pre-deployment living situation when the deployment or temporary assignment ends (sending the child to your ex-spouse who is the child's parent might be trouble). Geographical bachelor or Permanent Change of Station orders would not count for as "temporary".

20. My Child is Getting Married

I hope this is a happy situation! If your child is off on their own, and don't live with you or receive significant support from you, then relax, nothing has changed about your taxes. If they live with you or you support them, read on...

NOTE: Support is discussed periodically below, and is usually obvious and straightforward. I have included a Support Worksheet in Appendix A if you need more details.

The real question that comes up here is can you still claim your child once they get married. The answer is yes, but a few more potential roadblocks come up. The biggest one is that you generally can't claim your child if they file MFJ (though there are a couple of exceptions). You should definitely go over the filing requirements section of this book with your child and their spouse, and while you're at it, you should be preparing your taxes at the same time as them, so you can evaluate the positives and negatives to both tax returns. There is also the question of your child's spouse. If they are living with you, can you claim them? The answer is not as easy as it is to claim your own child, though it's actually easier to figure out. You also have to take into account your child's spouse's income sources and how they affect you supporting your child.

Let's revisit claiming your child, and add how their marriage affects it:

1. They must live with you for at least 6 months and a day. They can be absent for vacations, school, medical care and even detention in a juvenile facility—those still count as days living in your household. This shouldn't be a concern unless they move out permanently before July 1st.
2. They cannot have provided more than half of their own support (Appendix A Test 1). Note that this does not mean that YOU have to support them, they just can't provide more than half of their own support. This test changes if they are too old based on item 3 below. If they are too old, then YOU (together with your spouse if MFJ) must provide over half of the child's support (Appendix A Test 2 and their spouse's income now comes into play as a source of support not from you). More details below under 5 through 7.
3. They must be under age 19, or under age 24 if a full-time student for at least 5 months, or any age if disabled. If not, additional tests must be met:
	a. Support test listed under bullet 2 above with changes as noted (again, their spouse's income can count against this calculation).
	b. Their gross income cannot exceed $4,050. Sometimes a child receives Social Security benefits due to a deceased parent. Social Security benefits won't affect this test because even though it could be taxable, the income levels that make it taxable would be higher than $4,050. If your child is 19 or older, and not in college for 5 months out of the year, or 24 or older, regardless of school, they can't make more than $4,050 and you still claim them as a dependent. This does

not apply if they are permanently and totally disabled, but you'll need a doctor's statement to that effect.

4. Note that when a child starts making their own income, turns 18, or goes to college, things start to change. A child can simply move out once they're 18, and no divorce decree, custody document or anything else can get you back to claiming them (assuming they move out before June 30th). They also start messing with who provides over half their support.

5. Support **from** the child includes: wages, investment income, scholarships, student loans that the child is obligated to pay back, unemployment income and savings withdrawals. Any of the above that are not spent for support (generally this means added to savings) don't count as support from the child.

6. Support **for** the child includes: Cost of the home (fair rental value of the home plus utilities, repairs, taxes, insurance and other household costs divided by number of occupants), education, entertainment, clothing, medical, travel and other necessary expenses.

7. If they are young enough that 3 above doesn't apply, you simply determine if the total support **from** the child (5 above) is less than half of the total support **for** the child (6 above). If they are old enough that 3 does apply, then you determine if YOU (together with your spouse if MFJ) provide over half of the support **for** the child (6 above).

8. The biggest one is that they can't file a joint return with their new spouse. This means they must file as MFS (or not file a return) in order for you to claim them. The only exception to this is if they are only filing MFJ in order to get back ALL of their withholding. In essence, this means that they are not required to file due to low enough income, and are only filing to get back money that was withheld from their paychecks.

Now let's see about claiming their spouse:

1. Since they are not your biological child, they do not meet a relationship test to be a qualifying child so YOU must provide more than half of their support (as discussed above).

2. They have to live with you ALL year (January 1 through December 31), though the temporary absence rule for school, temporary jobs, etc., still applies.

3. They cannot be the qualifying child of another taxpayer. This means that if they lived with you all year in order to meet the above test, then a relative of theirs must also have lived with you in order for them to fail to meet this test for you. This would be someone like their parent, sibling, aunt or uncle.

4. Their gross income cannot exceed $4,050. Sometimes a child receives Social Security benefits due to a deceased parent. Social Security benefits won't affect this test because even though it could be taxable, the income levels that make it taxable would be higher than $4,050. This test applies to the spouse regardless of their age, due to not being YOUR child.

5. They can't file a joint return with your child that they married. This means they must file as MFS (or not file a return) in order for you to claim them. The only exception to this is if they are only filing MFJ in order to get back ALL of their

withholding. In essence, this means that they are not required to file due to low enough income, and are only filing to get back money that was withheld from their paychecks.

Military: If a child lives with you at the time you are deployed they continue to count as living with you during the deployment, even if you send them to another household (such as your parents) for the time you are deployed. Some people might debate this, but a good rule of thumb is that a non-permanent deployment or assignment does not change the living situation for taxes so long as the intention is for the dependent to return to the pre-deployment living situation when the deployment or temporary assignment ends (sending the child to your ex-spouse who is the child's parent might be trouble). Geographical bachelor or Permanent Change of Station orders would not count for as "temporary".

21. I'm Getting Divorced (or already am)

Tax issues for divorcing couples have become more complex every year, and recent tax law changes have made it even more imperative that good preparation and advice be given during and after a divorce is final. Tax planning begins at the moment of separation. Many individuals are unprepared for the effect that separation has on their tax situation. Most only discover the difficulty when they go to file their taxes and discover that they can't file as Single. Keep in mind that marital status is determined on 12/31 of the tax year in accordance with the laws for marriage established by your state. If you are still married and living together on this date, all the stuff about custodial vs. non custodial parent doesn't apply. Children are claimed via standard tie-breaker rules (# nights, then AGI, which we will discuss later).

Couples who are still married generally can only file MFJ or MFS. This is why it's critical to get a legally binding separation agreement that is accepted in accordance with the rules of your state. Your divorce lawyer can help you with this. MFS has significant disadvantages due to disallowed deductions and lower income thresholds. It is rarely a good way to file (I have a full section on MFS). In order to avoid this quandary, you have limited options (listed in general order of preference):

I. The custodial parent (the one the child spent more nights with—forget what the divorce court says—more later on custody) may be able to file HH if they meet all the following requirements:
(The non-custodial parent would be MFS, unless they had another child)
    A. You are unmarried or "considered unmarried" on the last day of the year.
        1. You are considered unmarried on the last day of the tax year if you meet all the following tests:
            a. You file a separate return (not necessarily MFS, just not MFJ).
            b. You paid more than half the cost of keeping up your home for the tax year.
            c. Your spouse did not live in your home during the last 6 months of the tax year.
            d. Your home was the main home of your child, stepchild, or foster child for more than half the year. (Once you are the step-parent of a child that status does not change, even due to death or divorce from the child's "natural" parent.)
        2. You paid more than half the cost of keeping up a home for the year.
        3. A "qualifying person" lived with you in the home for more than half the year (except for temporary absences, such as school). However, if the "qualifying person" is your dependent parent, he or she does not have to live with you. (Keep in mind that if your parents live in their own home, the Fair Rental Value of the home counts as support provided by them, even if they pay no mortgage or rent.)

4. You must be able to claim an exemption for the child. However, you meet this test if you cannot claim the exemption only because the noncustodial parent can claim the child using the rule for divorced or separated parents (or parents who live apart). We will discuss the rule for divorced or separated parents later.

II. They may file Single if they obtain a divorce or separation agreement prior to 12/31 of the tax year (this must meet the requirements of your state's laws.)

III. They may file MFJ with their spouse and divide the refund.

Once divorced or separated there are a number of issues to consider. I'll start with the biggie: Children.

Who can Claim the Child:

The IRS uses many of the same terms that lawyers and laymen use, but they don't mean the same thing. Many people believe that custody as granted in a divorce decree is custody for taxes. It is not. The IRS defines custodial parent as the parent the child spent the most nights with during the tax year. In the event of a tie, the parent with the higher Adjusted Gross Income is the custodial parent. Nights are counted based on spending them with the parent or in the parent's home. If the child is not with either, the night counts for the parent who would normally have the child in their home. This could happen for sleepovers or when the parent is deployed while in the military, resulting in the deployed individual's family taking care of the child.

Again, the IRS does not care what the divorce decree says. A divorce decree cannot force a parent to grant the exemption to the non-custodial parent (except decrees before 1985). After 1984 and before 2009, a divorce decree may be used for the non-custodial parent to claim the exemption if it provides the following:
- Gives the claim to the non-custodial parent WITHOUT ANY ADDITIONAL REQUIREMENTS (such as up-to-date on child support).
- States that the non-custodial parent can claim the child and that the custodial parent will not for specified years.
- Signature by the custodial parent is on the decree (judge's signature not required).

After 1985, only the custodial parent can release an exemption—the divorce decree was simply the method by which it was done. The exemption can be revoked by providing (or in good faith attempting to provide) written notification to the non-custodial parent that the custodial parent is revoking permission for the non-custodial parent to claim the exemption. This notice and proof of attempted delivery must be enclosed with the tax return. After 2008, only a signed IRS Form 8332 or similar statement may release the exemption. There is some argument as to whether a judge can compel a parent to provide an IRS Form

8332; prevailing opinion is leading to the idea that a judge cannot. However, a judge can hold YOU accountable for failing to provide this form if you are ordered to do so.

My recommendation to the non-custodial parent is that they get a Form 8332 signed at the signing of divorce papers. The form should specify all years that the non-custodial parent may claim the child. Form 8332 is still revocable, but this is still the best way. If I was representing the custodial parent, I would recommend they not provide the form upfront, rather that they provide it each year. Obviously the tenor of the divorce will affect this decision.

The non-custodial parent will have to attach this form to their return (or mail in with IRS Form 8453 if electronically filing) each year they claim the child.

Who can Claim What for the Child:

This is vitally important and regularly done wrong. When the non-custodial parent is claiming the child, it is vital that BOTH parents file the child correctly. They are "splitting" benefits. As a general rule, the non-custodial parent only gets the exemption and the Child Tax Credit. The custodial parent is the ONLY one who can get Earned Income Credit (EIC) and the Daycare Credit, as well as file as HH. Even when the non-custodial parent makes too much money to get EIC, they must still file as the non-custodial parent. No divorce decree, judge or lawyer can change this. Other items are less obvious...

- Medical Expenses go to who paid them.

- Education Credits go with the exemption (custodial, unless Form 8332 signed).

Child Support and Alimony:

Child Support is never taxed or deducted. Alimony is generally deducted by the payer, and taxed for the recipient. If alimony and/or child support are not up to date, payments are presumed to be child support first, and then alimony. Alimony has special tax requirements and recapture rules, so don't assume that just because the divorce decree calls it alimony that it qualifies to be deducted. You must talk to a tax professional before deducting alimony or claiming it as income—it is too complex to read in a book.

Three (I keep changing this number!) Final Points:

First, make sure you have your children's and ex (or soon to be ex) spouse's SSN and birthday—you will need them for taxes! Second, do not assume your divorce lawyer understands taxes—they probably don't. Third, get copies of your joint tax returns—you are entitled to them and might need them.

Military: If a child lives with you at the time you are deployed they continue to count as living with you during the deployment, even if you send them to another household (such as your parents) for the time you are deployed. Some people might debate this, but a good rule of thumb is that a non-permanent deployment or assignment does not change the living situation for taxes so long as the intention is for the dependent to return to the pre-deployment living situation when the deployment or temporary assignment ends (sending the child to your ex-spouse who is the child's parent might be trouble). Geographical bachelor or Permanent Change of Station orders would not count for as "temporary".

If you send military retirement benefits to your ex-spouse, they might be alimony, but this is complicated. Normally, DFAS should be sending the payments to your ex-spouse. In this case, your 1099-R will reflect only what you receive, and your ex-spouse will get their own 1099-R. This avoids all the alimony questions.

22. My Spouse Abandoned Me and/or Our Children

I'm sorry about that. The main concern here is the effect on your filing status and claiming of the children. Also, if there was domestic violence, either physical or otherwise, that actually has tax effects. For the purposes of this chapter, I'm assuming you were legally married and that they're GONE, as in no or limited contact and things like filing taxes will not involve the spouse. I'm going to cover things very simply based on the date of abandonment, and then go over the details. You should read the details anyway to make sure these apply to you, but the initial scenarios will help you understand what you should be thinking.

Abandoned between January 1st and June 30th of the tax year: Assuming the children remained with you and qualify to be dependents, you will most likely file as HH and claim the children.

Abandoned between July 1st and December 31st of the tax year: Assuming the children remained with you and qualify to be dependents, you will most likely file as MFS and claim the children.

Abandonment after December 31st of the tax year: For the tax year before the abandonment, you will most likely file MFS, and the parent with the higher income (AGI) will claim the children. This applies even if your spouse was not the biological parent of the children. The next year you will most likely file HH and claim the children. To be clear, if you are abandoned January 15th of 2017, you will likely file MFS for 2016 and HH for 2017.

Here are the details you should understand:

1. If domestic violence was involved in any way, go to the police and file a police report. I'm not saying this to be preachy and to tell you what to do in your personal life, but because domestic violence victims have some special tax protections (though not a ton) and the police report is good evidence if needed with the IRS. I'm also pretty sure there are a lot of non-tax things that make this a good idea. One of the biggest non-tax issues has some big effects on taxes anyway. If you've been abandoned, you need a divorce or legal separation in order to remove the specter of MFS from over your head. More about that later.
2. As for the children, assuming you were abandoned before the end of the calendar year (December 31st), and the children lived with you all year, you have a slam dunk, higher right to claim them than the spouse who abandoned you. That said, this does not mean he/she won't try to claim them anyway. Document the date he/she left, making sure to notify people, such as schools and doctors and (I would suggest) a good divorce lawyer. File your taxes early and if the other spouse claims them—fight. See the chapter titled Someone Claimed my Child if that happens.
3. If your spouse left after December 31st, you have a bit of a problem. In this case, standard tie-breaker rules apply. This means that if you lived together all

year, the person with the higher income (technically AGI) gets to claim them. If that's not you, don't try to claim them, even if morally you feel you have the right. Wait until next year.

4. The biggest issue you have to face is Filing Status. Marital status is determined as of December 31st of the tax year, so you will probably still be legally married for tax purposes in the year they abandoned you. If they left on July 1st or later, you have to file MFS. If you have no children, you pretty much have to file MFS. Married Filing Separately sucks. I have a whole chapter on it, so make sure to read the I have to File Married Filing Separately section. If you have children, you can be considered unmarried if ALL the following apply:

a. You did not live with your spouse after June 30th of the tax year.

b. You paid over half the costs of maintaining a home, which was the main home for your child, stepchild, or foster child (foster child must be placed with you by an authorized placement agency or court) for at least 6 months and a day of the tax year. Note that the relations are VERY specific. One way to think of it is that you as a parent have been forced to take care of a child for whom you are responsible due to being the birth parent, step-parent, or foster parent. I should also note that step-relationships established by marriage do not end by divorce or death.

c. You claim that child on your tax return as a dependent.

Note that the requirement of paying more than half the cost of maintaining a home discussed in this section are different from most times we will talk about paying more than half the costs for kids. In this case, it is just for the home. You include taxes, interest, and rent paid (later situations will talk about Fair Rental Value—here it is rent PAID). You also include utilities, repairs, and insurance for the home. Other than that, it's food consumed in the home, and not much else. You need to have paid more than half of that total during the period of time the child lived with you (at least 6 months and a day). If you meet all the requirements, you can choose to file HH.

5. Some of the MFS problems can be avoided if you were a victim of domestic violence. The one that is likely to come up is if you get an Affordable Care Act (Obamacare) subsidy. MFS really messes up this subsidy, and can cause you to pay back all or most of it. There is an exception for victims of domestic violence, but you should seek a tax professional's help to get it right.

Military: A military spouse deploying would not normally be considered abandonment. If a child lives with you at the time you are deployed they continue to count as living with you during the deployment, even if you send them to another household (such as your parents) for the time you are deployed. Some people might debate this, but a good rule of thumb is that a non-permanent deployment or assignment does not change the living situation for taxes so long as the intention is for the dependent to return to the pre-deployment living situation when the deployment or temporary assignment ends (sending the child to your ex-spouse who is the child's parent might be trouble). Geographical bachelor or Permanent Change of Station orders would not count for as "temporary."

23. My Spouse Died

I'm very sorry to hear that. Take a few weeks and don't worry about taxes, or much of anything other than taking care of yourself. Come back when you're ready (but don't take forever).

Okay. Let's first remind ourselves that this is a tax book, so this isn't about estate resolution, finances, or other complexities—talk to the experts. Also, there are situations where you should talk to an expert rather than relying on this book. Here are a few:

1. Your (or your deceased spouse's) net worth is in the millions
2. Trusts are involved
3. Other heirs beside you will get more than a few personal items or some money (especially Real Estate and/or retirement accounts)
4. There are disputes about the estate
5. You were estranged from your spouse or there were other unique factors, such as separate finances or businesses

Also, read the next section I Inherited Money or Property.

For the most part, the tax implications for a surviving spouse should not be too complex. Most of their assets should automatically transfer to you or be specifically laid out in their will. Bank accounts and investment accounts are probably joint tenant accounts or have a designated beneficiary, which means they automatically become yours. This may require paperwork, but the transfer is tax-free. I'll cover specifics of things that don't quite work that way.

If you are the beneficiary for your spouse's retirement plan accounts (i.e., IRAs) and/or pension plans (i.e., 401ks), the good news is that you can treat your deceased spouse's accounts as your own. You just contact the plan administrator and they will tell you what you need to do. If you are not the beneficiary, the beneficiary should talk to BOTH an investment advisor you can trust, and a tax expert before pulling the money out of these accounts. There are a lot of rules that apply to withdrawal, depending on the relationship to the original owner. You generally must take the money out within a certain period of time, which can have big tax implications.

For a house (or houses) in both your names, you may increase your BASIS (your "investment" in the home—usually what you paid for it—that is used to determine gain or loss when sold). If you live in a community property state, your BASIS becomes the value of the house on the date of death—get an appraisal! In non-community-property states, YOUR half of the house keeps its original BASIS, and your spouse's half goes up to the value on the date of death. Again, get an appraisal. The math on this is to take half your original BASIS and add it to half the appraised value. This is the new BASIS. If you didn't own the house 50/50, get expert help.

Also, if you plan on selling the house you both lived in at the time of death, you get the MFJ Principal Residence exclusion for two years after the date of death. See the I Sold my Home section.

For other items that pass on to you, such as investments that were in their name only, you get the stepped-up basis discussed in the next section: I Inherited Money or Property.

The last thing to worry about is actually filing your tax returns. If you don't remarry before the end of the year, you can file a joint return with them, and get all their deductions as if still living. You'll sign the return as surviving spouse. For years after that your filing status will be based on your new situation, without considering your deceased spouse, UNLESS you have dependent children. For the next two years, if you meet the following requirements, you can file as a Qualifying Widower: you have not remarried, the dependent is your child or stepchild (not foster child), they lived with you ALL year, you claim them as a dependent, you paid over half the cost of maintaining the home and you filed a MFJ return with the spouse in the year they died. This gives you almost all the tax benefits of being married.

Military: The Thrift Savings Plan is a retirement plan that you can treat as your own as discussed above.

24. I Inherited Money or Property

First things first. if any of the following occurred, you should seek the advice of a competent tax expert, financial advisor, and/or an attorney:

1. You are the executor of the estate
2. You inherit more than a couple million dollars
3. You inherit property that will not be immediately liquidated or occupied by the person inheriting it
4. You inherit retirement accounts
5. You inherit an on-going business
6. You inherit from a trust account
7. You inherit anything significantly different than the things I discuss below

Second thing—a misconception—if you inherit money, you are not responsible for estate taxes. The estate should pay the taxes BEFORE it sends you money or property. This is why I say if you are handling the estate (as executor) you should get help from an estate attorney. This means that, generally, when you get money or property from an estate, you won't have any tax issues, except in a couple cases discussed later (selling property and tax sheltered accounts).

So let's talk about what you should do or know if you inherit the following:

Cash: This includes bank and money market accounts, and life insurance proceeds. In general you simply receive a check from the estate or assets are transferred to your name. You can be almost certain that this cash is yours, free and clear with no tax implications. The only thing to be sure of is that the estate didn't liquidate tax-sheltered accounts and send you the money (they should absolutely NEVER do this, but you want to make sure.)

Stocks or Bonds: You don't pay any taxes on these when you get them, and you don't pay taxes on increases in value until you sell them. Any money they earn for you (dividends and interest) is taxable in the year you receive it (even if it's reinvested). If you inherit a lot of stocks or bonds, this can be a big addition to your taxable income that will affect your taxes for the year, so make sure you understand how much they earn, and how it will impact the tax return. Adjust your withholding if necessary. The biggest thing you need to do when you receive these is to know their value on the date of death (of the person you inherit them from). The brokerage house that holds them for you can tell you this, and you should get the information and save it. When you sell them, you only pay taxes on the increase in value (or take a loss if they go down in value). This is why you need to know the value on the date of death (this is your BASIS).*

Real Estate (Personal Residence): We're talking about the house the person who died lived in when they died (or just before). Make sure the estate had the property appraised, and get a copy of the appraisal. If they didn't, get it appraised immediately. If you plan to live in it, this appraisal will tell you what your BASIS is in the property, which will be important when you sell it or convert it to business use. Essentially, this value acts the same as the price you pay for a home, had you bought it. It's your "investment" in the property. Similarly, if you plan to sell it, this BASIS determines if you have a gain or loss on the property. Generally, if you sell the property immediately, you shouldn't have any appreciable gain on the property, and any loss wouldn't be deductible. If you hold it for a while, or make improvements to it, the gain is taxable and the loss deductible. Read the chapter on I Sold a Home that wasn't my Principal Residence and it will tell you everything you need to know, just remember that the BASIS discussed there is the appraised value we just talked about.*

Real Estate (Investment Property): This is mostly the same as we just talked about for Personal Residence, so go ahead and read that, then come back here...Okay. The main difference is that if there is a loss, it's deductible. The idea is that you don't get to deduct a loss on "personal" stuff, just investment and business stuff. When you inherit someone's "residence" it's "personal", at least for a while. Here it never was personal. Now if you move into it, it becomes personal for you, and you treat it just as if you bought it. The appraised value is like your purchase price, becoming your BASIS for the future. If you don't sell the property right away, and don't move into it, talk to a tax expert.*

Collectibles: In a lot of ways, these are just like stocks. They have a value, which you need to know at the time of death. The problem is that there's no broker to tell you what that value is. If the estate appraised them, get a copy of the appraisal. If you sell them right away for as much as you can get for them (not to a relative), you can pretty much assume they were worth what you got and you have no gain. If it's not much stuff, not worth much money, and you're hanging onto it, you can probably not worry much about it. You can deal with it when/if you eventually sell it. If there's a lot of value, get it appraised. Just be aware that when you sell it, you pay taxes on the increase in price, but you can't deduct a loss if it goes down in value (if you are in the business of buying and selling collectibles this does not apply to you and you need expert help).*

Personal Items: If you're keeping them, then treat them just like all your other stuff. You will probably never face any tax implications. If you're selling them and sell them right away, you can pretty much assume you sold them for what they were worth, and thus have no taxable gain.*

*Okay. For all those things with an asterisk I've said a lot of complicated things, so here's the simple explanation: you basically treat all those items as if you had bought them, on the date of death, for what they were worth on that date. If you think about it that way, it gets pretty simple.

Tax Sheltered Accounts: These include IRAs, Pension Plan Accounts (401k, 403b, pension, etc.), Tax Sheltered Annuities, and any other accounts that had contributions or earnings sheltered from taxation. The reason these matter is that the previous owner avoided taxes on some or all of the money in these accounts. Now the government wants those taxes. You should talk to BOTH an investment advisor you can trust and a tax expert before pulling the money out of these accounts. The applicable tax rules depend on your relationship to the original owner. You generally must take the money out within a certain period of time (except when it was your spouse that died). I will give you my best, generic advice on what I think should be done:

1. Talk to the experts discussed above to determine if and/or when you have to take the money out.

2. Make a plan for the money before you get it.

3. Unless you have a pressing need for the money, leave it in the accounts as long as possible without breaking the rules.

4. When you take the money out have your tax pro estimate the tax liability and either have that amount (plus a little extra) withheld, make an estimated tax payment for that amount, or save that amount until tax time. This is "found" money, so there's no need to spend it until you are sure how much you get to keep. My favorite plan is to put the money in an account until after you file your tax return for the year.

5. You'll get a tax form (probably a 1099-R) that you'll use when filing your taxes.

Military: The Thrift Savings Plan is an example of a Tax Sheltered Account.

25. I'm Buying (or already own) a Home

Buying a home is normally the final hurdle that gets someone from claiming the standard deduction to itemizing. In the course of this discussion I'm going to spend some time talking about how owning a home affects itemizing. You need to read the Itemized Deductions section to make sure that you get all the deductions that you're entitled to.

I first want to talk a little bit of taxese. I know I promised to try not to, but there's some information about owning a home that you need to calculate and track: BASIS. Basis comes up all over the tax world, and applies in this instance to the house you just bought. Simply put, Basis is the amount of money (or value of property) that you put into something, minus what you take out of it. You need to know the basis of your house. You won't use it for a while, but it will come up when you sell it, or if you convert it to business or rental use. (This is a good time to say that if you bought this house for a reason other than personal use, such as a first or second home, then you are in the wrong section.) The good news here is that the basis of your house is usually easy to figure out. All the information will be in your closing packet, so put the closing packet in your files, label it as "house" and have it available for your tax professional if you sell the house, or convert it to rental or business use. Assuming that you purchased the home with a standard mortgage (or cash) and that there weren't any really weird things involved (like the loan for the house was also used to buy a car, or you paid expenses for the seller) your basis is the cash you paid for the house plus the mortgage you took out on the house, including amounts for settlement costs that weren't a part of getting the loan or placed in escrow for future insurance or tax costs. It's more complicated than that in taxese, but all the details of basis are pretty much encapsulated within the cash, plus mortgage calculation. If you traded properties or did anything weird with the purchase contract, you'll want to talk to a tax expert, but this cash plus mortgage gets you a good basis to start with. If possible, you'll want to know how much of that basis represents the value of the land, which you can usually find in the appraisal paperwork. Going forward, you want to track things that change your basis (putting money in, or taking money out). Generally, the only things that will change the basis are home improvements; assessments the government makes you pay to improve sidewalks, sewers or streets; or money the government pays you to use your land (such as an easement to widen the road). If you pay it, it is added to basis; if they pay you, it's subtracted from basis. Also if there is a big fire or other accident, the event will likely affect your basis. If anything like that happens, put the receipts in your "house" file. An improvement is something that increases the value, like redoing the kitchen or floors. Repairs and upkeep are not improvements, unless you upgrade the item repaired to a more expensive type that increases the value. Put receipts for this in your "house" file. If keeping track of the basis seems like too much trouble, just keep the file up-to-date and let your tax professional do the math if the house is sold, or converted to rental or business use.

Sorry about that paragraph, but it could save you a lot of trouble later. Now just to be clear, you don't get any current benefits for home improvements (unless they meet a very narrow list of energy efficient home improvements, discussed later in this section), but you need to track them.

The next thing to talk about if you just bought a home is the HUD-1 settlement statement (I'll just use HUD from now on). This form is usually one of the first forms in the stack of crap that they made you sign when you closed on your home. Go through the big folder they give you, and look for this form. It's the one with two columns about paid by buyer and paid by seller. You want to set aside a copy of this form for when you do your taxes. Sometimes you'll get multiple copies, other times just the one. Make a separate copy for this year's taxes and leave one with the big package of crap. This form is going to detail where every dollar of your down payment and what you financed went toward. It will also document everything that the money the seller provided went toward. We're going to need this as we try to figure out what you can deduct from your home.

The main deductions you get from your home are mortgage interest, real estate taxes and mortgage insurance premiums. Most years, it's easy to get these numbers since your lender is going to send you a Form 1098 that will generally have all of these numbers. Some banks, like Bank of America, make you search for the real estate taxes on a second page, but they'll be there. The problem you face in the year of purchase (and sometimes later years) is that the mortgage company or bank that you get your initial loan from will usually immediately sell the loan to another mortgage company. You generally get informed of this so you can make your payments to the right company. Most people don't really pay too much attention to this, BUT YOU SHOULD! At the end of the year, you're going to get a Form 1098 from EVERY company that received money from you. Generally speaking, in the year of purchase you will get at least two, and sometimes three. If you don't realize that you should be getting more than one, you can miss out on some serious deductions! Sometimes, you never get one of them, and you have to call the mortgage company to get another copy and/or get the numbers. I highly recommend getting online access to all of your mortgage accounts so you can get copies online if needed. The other wrinkle in the year of purchase is that sometimes the Form 1098 doesn't report everything that you paid. In that case you need to go through the HUD and your 1098s to make sure you take every penny your entitled to. Be careful not to duplicate deductions reported on multiple forms.

As a general rule, the 1098 will have everything that's on the HUD, but you need to double-check. Commonly missed items are mortgage insurance premiums, which on the HUD may have other names such as FHA funding fee, VA funding fee or USDA funding fee. Make sure these are reported on the 1098, and, if not, you can use the number from the HUD. Also make sure all points, discount points, and other prepaid interest items are included on the 1098. Again, you can use the HUD if they aren't on the 1098. Also you sometimes won't even make a payment to the original lender, so make sure that you get a 1098 from the lender listed on the HUD, or use the numbers directly from the HUD. If you use any numbers that differ from the 1098s you receive, or your name (or spouse's if MFJ) or SSN are not on the 1098, you must attach a statement to your return explaining why. Most tax software has a system for doing this. It can be a good idea to have a professional assist you if your 1098 numbers don't match what the HUD says.

Having said all of the above, here are the details on deducting mortgage interest and taxes:

Mortgage Interest:

1. You can deduct mortgage interest on a first or second home, but no more. If you have more than two homes, or buy a third or replace one during the year, you have special rules to follow on selecting which home to deduct. The main rule is that you cannot change which home you count as your second home unless you change your primary home, or buy or sell your second home.
2. On the original loan, you get to deduct points immediately—if you paid them. If you had a no money down loan, you probably have to spread the points out over the life of the loan (divide by loan term in months and multiply by months you paid the loan in the tax year). Generally you will either get all or none of the points right away, but it is possible to get a portion if you put some small amount of money towards closing costs. You get points even if the seller pays them, though they would have to be spread out since you didn't pay them. The 1098 from the original lender (the 1098 is from the same lender that appears on the HUD) can generally be relied upon to accurately reflect the points you can take right away. Just make sure to compare the HUD to the 1098 and spread any points not on the 1098 across the life of the loan as we just discussed.
3. You can elect to spread the points out over the life even if you qualify to deduct them immediately. This is a good idea if you buy the house late in the year and don't end up with enough deductions to itemize.
4. Points might be called discount points, loan origination fees, maximum loan charges, or loan discount (they are the same thing).
5. Points cannot be fully deducted on a mortgage that is 15 years or fewer if the points are more than 4%. On a mortgage that is 15 years or longer, points cannot be fully deducted if they are more than 6%, unless the loan amount is less than $250,000.
6. You cannot fully deduct points on a loan of more than 30 years. If the loan is 10 years or more, the terms must be similar to other loans in your area (you can't be getting some special magic loan from your brother's bank, or a desperate seller).
7. To deduct points or interest the loan must be secured by your home (you don't pay, you lose the home).
8. You can deduct interest on a construction loan for up to 24 months before you move in, but you have to move in by that 24-month point. You don't have to start deducting the day you take the loan out; you can choose any day as long as it's

within 24 months of you moving in (this might apply if it's going to take 2 years or more to build your home).

9. You can deduct late payment fees and prepayment penalties.

10. The loans must be to buy, build or improve your home.

11. If the total loans on both homes exceed $1 million ($500,000 if MFS) you only get to deduct the interest on the first million.

12. Home equity debt not used to buy, build or improve your home can be deducted on equity debt up to $100,000.

13. Your mortgage must comply with the laws of your state or locality.

14. If your home is destroyed you can continue to deduct the interest on your home as long as you rebuild it or sell the land within a reasonable time (reasonable time is nebulous, but as long as the delay is not primarily procrastinating, you can usually meet reasonable time. Reasonable can be 10 years or more if you're fighting to rebuild the home against opposition from neighbors or government). If you just let it sit there and make no effort to rebuild or sell, you're running into problems.

15. Your first or second home can be a boat, mobile home, condo or RV/fifth wheel as long as it has sleeping, toilet and cooking facilities.

16. You must own or co-own the home, or be legally liable for making the interest payments.

17. For low-income taxpayers, there is a Mortgage Interest Credit you can get if you set it up during the purchase. You get it by following the rules for your state that involve location and income requirements set by them. It is set up BEFORE closing so you need to work with your real estate agent and bank to see if you qualify. If you get the credit, you can't use the same interest paid for the credit and the deduction (but any excess interest above what is used for the credit can be deducted).

18. You generally have to be the one who pays the payment, but there are situations where that might not be true. If you are divorced, see the I'm Getting Divorced section. If you get government assistance paying it, seek professional help with your taxes.

19. When you refinance your home, you generally have to spread any points you pay on the refinancing out based on the life of the refinance. Any unused points from before the refinance are spread out over that same period. If you do a cash-out refinance and use the proceeds to substantially improve your home, you can take the points immediately. If you use some for improvement and some for other things, you can pro rate the points based on the use of the money and deduct the portion related to the improvements.

20. Any untaken points can be taken in the year you sell the home.

21. If you receive a refund of mortgage interest in the same year you paid them, only include the amount that was actually kept by the bank. If you receive a refund in a later year, you must include the refund as income in the year you get it, but only to extent that it benefitted you. If your itemized deductions were only $100 above the standard deduction the year you deducted them, and you receive a rebate of $500, you only include $100 as income since you would have gotten the full standard deduction anyway.

22. Military and clergy housing allowances do not affect the deductibility of mortgage interest, even if it covers your full mortgage payment.

Real Estate Taxes:

1. You can deduct real estate taxes if they are based on the value of your home, are similar to others in your area, and are not used to provide you special benefits that others do not get.
2. They will generally be reported on the Form 1098 from your lender if they are paid through your escrow account via your monthly payment. If you pay through escrow and they are not reported on your 1098, you probably had your mortgage sold and the other bank handled them. Again, make sure you get all of your 1098 forms. If you don't have a mortgage, you will use your own records of paying them to determine the amount (if you don't have a mortgage you get a tax bill to pay just like other bills.)
3. When you buy your home, no matter who pays the real estate taxes, you only get to deduct the taxes based on the dates you owned the home. The HUD form will normally indicate which taxes were attributed to you. If they are not broken down on the HUD, you ratio them based on the days of ownership to the entire year.
4. You can only deduct taxes based on the value of your home. The transfer taxes and tax stamps that will be riddled through your HUD statement are not deductible.
5. If you receive a refund of real estate taxes in the same year you paid them, only include the amount that was actually kept by the government. If you receive a refund in a later year, you must include the refund as income in the year you get it, but only to extent they benefitted you. If your itemized deductions were only $100 above the standard deduction the year you deducted them, and you receive a rebate of $500, you only include $100 as income since you would have gotten the full standard deduction anyway.

Mortgage Insurance:

Mortgage insurance premiums (including VA, FHA and USDA funding fees) may be deductible. You can generally find these on the HUD or your 1098 Form. Here are the details:

1. The home must have been purchased after December 31, 2006.
2. The deduction is decreased by 10% for every $1000 AGI exceeds $100,000 ($500 and $50,000 for MFS).
3. Must be for first or second home.
4. Prepaid insurance premiums must be spread out over 7 years or the life of the loan, except for insurance provided by the VA or Rural Housing Authority.

Energy Efficient Home Improvements:

There are two credits for energy efficient home improvements and they are quite restrictive. I will cover each separately, but there are some common items to consider. They must be for your MAIN home, the one you live at most of the time, but that home can be a house, boat, RV, fifth wheel, condo or houseboat. You must own it (you can still be paying a mortgage). You must reduce your basis that we discussed above by the amount the credit lowers your taxes by. Costs are considered paid when the work is complete, or when you move back into the home if you had to leave while the work was completed. Most of the time, if you are having a home constructed, the builder will take any credits for energy efficiencies associated with the home, especially if you are buying a tract home from one of the major builders in a planned community. If you are having a custom house built, communicate with your builder, and your tax professional, to ensure it is clear who is qualified to take and who is taking any credits available.

Here are the details on the two credits:

Residential Energy Efficient Property:

1. This is the big one, and the hard one. To get this one, you need to have installed truly alternative energy sources as a part of your home. Examples are solar power, wind, geothermal, fuel cell, or solar hot water. Work with the installer and your tax professional to determine if you qualify, and get documentation from the installer. Taxes and government subsidies are a big part of determining the cost effectiveness of these type of projects, so you need to do more than just read this section.
2. The credit is up to 30% of the qualified costs, with each type of improvement having its own maximums.
3. This credit is available for new construction.
4. If you share the house with someone other than your spouse, you get the credit based on what you paid, and the maximum is applied based on the percentage paid by each occupant.

Nonbusiness Energy Property Credit:

1. This is the much more common credit, so I'm going to provide more details.
2. The credit is 10% of qualifying costs with a LIFETIME maximum credit for all costs of $500.
3. The LIFETIME maximum credit for windows is $200 (this is inclusive, not in addition to the $500 limit, so, if you take $200 for windows, you only have $300 for the rest of your life for other things).
4. They are subject to AGI limitations that were not available for 2014 at the time this book was being published.
5. The credit is available for insulation, exterior doors, windows, skylights and roofs that are SPECIFICALLY designed to reduce heat loss or gain.
6. It also applies to water heaters, heating systems, and air conditioners that are near the most efficient available at the time of installation.

7. The instructions for the current year form will identify the standards to be met, but the manufacturer or installer can also tell you. They must provide, and you must maintain, documentation to prove that it meets these standards. I recommend that you make the contractor or salesman SHOW you the documentation and proof that it meets the standards. Energy Star doesn't mean crap—these items have to be really high quality (and generally more expensive than non-qualified items).

8. If you share the house with someone other than your spouse, you get the credit based on what you paid, and the maximum is applied based on the percentage paid by each occupant.

9. If you and your spouse have separate main homes, there are extra hoops to jump through, and you will need a bit of professional help to be safe.

If you got the First-Time Homebuyer Credit:

The last big thing to discuss about your home is if you bought it in 2008 and took the First-Time Homebuyer Credit. If you did, you should have been paying it back at the rate of $500 per year as a part of your tax return. As long as you own and live in the home, you will pay the $500 each year until you pay the whole amount back. Here are a few more things to be aware of:

1. If you sell the home you have to pay back the remaining amount you hadn't paid, up to your gain on the sale. The gain is figured by taking the sales proceeds, minus expenses of the sale, and subtracting the basis. The basis is discussed above, but is reduced by the unpaid portion of the credit.

2. If the home is condemned or destroyed, you have two years to buy a new home. If you do, you continue to repay at $500 per year. If you don't, you pay back the remaining amount on the tax return in the year that the 2 years ends, up to gain as discussed in 1.

3. If the home is transferred in a divorce, the credit issues go to the spouse who gets the house.

4. You don't have to repay the credit if you die. If there is a surviving spouse who was on the return when the credit was taken, their repayment amount is cut in half (the spouse who died takes half the issue with them to the grave).

5. If the house ceases to be your main home, you must repay the remaining credit that tax year.

6. If you are transferred on PCS orders as a member of the military you don't have to repay the credit immediately, unless you sell the home. You just keep paying the $500 per year. This also applies to Foreign Service employees sent on extended official duty.

Military: BAH does not affect the deductibility of mortgage interest. VA Funding Fee counts as mortgage insurance and does not need to be spread over 7 years on an original mortgage. It can be deducted fully or spread over 7 years depending on your preference.

Areas not fully explored here that may require more research for you: A foreign home, mortgage assistance payments, divorce issues, short-term financing, gifts and transfers of houses other than arms length sale, reverse mortgages and if you cohabitate and share payments with someone other than your spouse.

26. I Made Home Improvements

Home improvements are not a tax deduction for your personal residence. Sorry. Now that doesn't mean you shouldn't track them. Let me first say that if they are energy efficient home improvements, they MIGHT qualify for a credit. Check out the next section to see if they do. If not, read on...

One of the goals of this book is to not talk in taxese, but, sometimes you have to talk some basic tax terms that most people have never heard of. One of those terms is "Basis." Basis, to put it in layman's terms, is how much you've put into something. Generally, we're talking about money. At its most simple, basis is what you pay for something. Everything you own has some sort of basis, and the IRS actually thinks you're going to track this for everything you own, just in case it ever comes up on a tax return. That said, there are a few things you really need to know, or be able to figure out, the basis of. One of these is your investments: stocks and bonds, but that's for a future discussion. The other is your house. Someday you will probably sell your house, give it away to your family, or convert it to business or rental use. You'll need to know the basis in that case.

Figuring out that basis can get VERY complex. For most people, it's what you paid for the house plus the cost of improvements that you make. A lot of other things might affect it, such as taking a home office deduction, having to pay special assessments for sewer improvements, or getting paid by the city so they can take part of your property and build a sidewalk on it. If these come up, or any other thing that appears to affect the value or money you have at stake in your property, either talk to an expert, or keep all the paperwork in your "home" file.

You do have a "home" file, right? If the answer is no, immediately find that big package of crap they gave you when you closed on the house, and put it in a file labeled "home." Into this file you will put all records of things we just discussed, as well as paperwork documenting the cost of any home improvements. Improvements raise the value of the home, and increase the basis. Repairs maintain the home, and don't increase the basis. Put repair receipts in the file anyway, just in case. The file isn't just for tax stuff. If you refinance or take out a home equity line of credit, put that paperwork in there, too.

Military: Not much different for you here.

27. I Made Energy Efficient Home Improvements

The two credits for energy efficient home improvements are quite restrictive. I will cover each credit separately, but there are some common items to consider. They must be for your MAIN home, the one you live at most of the time. That home can be a house, boat, RV, fifth wheel, condo or houseboat. You must own it (you can still be paying a mortgage). You must reduce your basis that we discussed in the I'm Buying a Home section by the amount the credit lowers your taxes. Costs are considered paid when the work is complete, or when you move back into the home if you had to leave while the work was completed. Most of the time, if you are having a home constructed, the builder will take any credits for energy efficiencies associated with the home, especially if you are buying a tract home from one of the major builders in a planned community. If you are having a custom house built, communicate with your builder, and your tax professional, to ensure it is clear who is qualified to take and who is taking any credits available.

Here are the details on the two credits:

Residential Energy Efficient Property Credit:

1. This credit is the big one, and the hard one. To get the Residential Energy Efficient Property Credit, you need to have installed truly alternative energy sources as a part of your home. Examples are solar power, wind, geothermal, fuel cell, or solar hot water. Work with the installer and your tax professional to determine if you qualify, and get documentation from the installer. Taxes and government subsidies make a big part of determining the cost effectiveness of these type of projects, so you need to do more than just read this section.
2. The credit is up to 30% of the qualified costs, with each type of improvement having its own maximum.
3. This credit is available for new construction.
4. If you share the house with someone other than your spouse, you get the credit based on what you paid, and the maximum is applied based on the percentage paid by each occupant.

Non-business Energy Property Credit:

1. This is the much more common credit, so I'm going to provide more details.
2. The Non-business Energy Property Credit is 10% of qualifying costs, with a LIFETIME maximum credit for all costs of $500.
3. The LIFETIME maximum credit for windows is $200 (this is inclusive, not in addition to the $500 limit; if you take $200 for windows, you only have $300 for the rest of your life for other things).
4. They are subject to AGI limitations for 2014 that were unavailable at the time this book was being published.
5. The credit is available for insulation, exterior doors, windows, skylights and roofs that are SPECIFICALLY designed to reduce heat loss or gain.

6. It also applies to water heaters, heating systems, and air conditioners that are near the most efficient available at the time of installation.

7. The instructions for the current year form will identify the standards to be met, but the manufacturer or installer can also tell you. They must provide, and you must maintain, documentation to prove that it meets these standards. I recommend that you make the contractor or salesman SHOW you the documentation and proof that it meets the standards. Energy Star doesn't mean crap—these items have to be really high quality (and generally more expensive than non-qualified items).

8. If you share the house with someone other than your spouse, you get the credit based on what you paid, and the maximum is applied based on the percentage paid by each occupant.

9. If you and your spouse have separate main homes, there are extra hoops to jump through and you will need a bit of professional help to be safe.

Military: Not much different for you here.

28. I Have to File Married Filing Separately

I hope that you're filing MFS because you want to, but let me open this section by saying that MFS should be avoided except in a few very specific circumstances. These are:

1. You have no choice (you are married, don't meet the HH requirements and can't convince your spouse to file jointly)
2. You don't want to be responsible for your spouse's taxes
3. You will get better refunds as a result of MFS (generally this means that one of you has job expenses and/or medical expenses and a lower income).

If you think the third reason applies, run your tax returns both ways and see which one works out better. If the first applies, but there's wiggle room on the part of your spouse, consider running your tax returns both ways and see if the change in results makes them change their mind (you might need to make a financial compromise if it improves yours and hurts theirs).

One other place where MFS might help is if you are using Income Based Repayment (IBR) for student loans. Filing separately means only your income counts toward the calculation. Make sure that the negative tax effects don't outweigh the lower student loan payments. Don't try MFS if both you and your spouse are on IBR.

One of the things that is sometimes hard about filing MFS is that you need your spouse's name (spelled right), SSN and often their birthday. If you don't have it, you will have to attempt to get it (awkward conversation, I know, I've listened to them a lot). If you can't get it, you will have to paper file the return, which will delay your refund.

I'm not going to discuss every detail of the differences between MFS and MFJ. You should review the sections of this book that apply to you in conjunction with this section to fully understand the effects (though if this section says you don't get some or other deduction or credit, there's not much point in reading the section on it).

One thing I want to make clear is that living in a community property state (AZ, CA, ID, LA, NV, NM, TX, WA, WI) can have dramatic effects on how you file— expert help should be sought if you are MFS in a community property state. Specific rules for the treatment of community property vary from state to state and are too detailed to cover here. To give an example, in most cases you include half of your income and half of their income, instead of just your own. Separation agreements only make it worse. Trust me, get professional tax help in these cases.

You can go from a MFS return to a joint return with no special restrictions under the usual rules for amending returns, but you generally can't file a MFS return after filing a MFJ return once the due date for the return has passed. The IRS really doesn't like MFS returns (my opinion). If you don't agree, see the following list of what happens:

1. If one spouse itemizes deductions, the other spouse must as well. This means if the other spouse has no deductions, they get zero for a standard deduction.
2. You get half the standard deduction ($6,300), home mortgage interest limitations ($500,000 of mortgage and $50,000 of home equity debt), capital loss limitation ($1,500), exclusion of gain on sale of main home ($250,000), and Alternative Minimum Tax (AMT) exemptions. The tax brackets shift at exactly half the income they would for MFJ.
3. The income thresholds for the phase-out of the following are cut in half from MFJ thresholds: Child Tax Credit, Retirement Savings Contribution Credit, Exemption and Itemized Deductions phase-out.
4. You are not allowed the Earned Income Credit, Elderly or Disabled Credit (unless you lived apart all year), Child and Dependent Care Credit, Adoption Credit, and neither Education Credit (Lifetime Learning and American Opportunity).
5. You cannot take deductions for student loans or tuition and fees.
6. You cannot exclude U.S. Savings Bond interest used for higher education.
7. You cannot make deductible or Roth IRA contributions if you have an AGI over $10,000, unless you and your spouse lived apart all year (you cannot have spent a single night with them).
8. Your Social Security benefits become taxable at $0 of income, unless you and your spouse lived apart all year.
9. If you and your spouse lived together at any time during the year, you cannot deduct any Rental Real Estate Losses using the exception for Active Participation. If you lived apart, the limit for deduction is $12,500 and starts phasing out at an income of $50,000. (This will make a lot more sense when you read the sections on renting out your home, former home or investment property.)
10. It is possible to claim the exemption for your spouse if they had no income, are not filing a return, cannot be claimed by someone else and you were still married on December 31 of the tax year.
11. When claiming deductions, the spouse claiming it must have paid it and meet the requirements for deducting it. If the payment is made from a joint account into which both spouses put earnings into, it is presumed to be paid half by each spouse, unless you can prove otherwise. If one spouse pays for something, but the other spouse is the one who meets the requirements for deducting it then NOBODY gets to deduct it.
12. Medical expenses for your children may be deducted even if you don't get to claim the exemption.
13. You can claim medical expenses for your spouse if you paid them or the services were provided while you were married.
14. If you file a separate state and/or local return, you deduct the taxes you paid. If you file a joint return, you ratio the taxes based upon your income (your

deduction is equal to your income, divided by the total income, multiplied by the tax paid).

15. If you own more than one house, you can only deduct interest from one of them, unless the other spouse consents in writing to allow you to deduct both.

16. If you made joint estimated payments, you can divide them any way you can agree on with your spouse. If you can't agree, you ratio them by income in the same manner discussed under 14. If you divide payments made, you write "DIV" under the word payments to the left of line 62 on your tax return. If your spouse is filing HH, they need to write your name and SSN on their return just like you had to as discussed above. If you make separate estimated payments you just include them as normal.

17. Dependent Care Benefits paid by your employer become taxable above $2,500, vice $5,000.

18. If you got an Affordable Care Act (Obamacare) subsidy you might have to pay the full amount back.

Military: Don't file MFS just because your military spouse is deployed. Either get a Power of Attorney or get an extension.

29. I Have Medical Expenses

Medical expenses are one of the itemized deductions you are allowed, though they are subject to limitations. You should review the general Itemized Deductions section as well as this section, since you might need other deductions to get over the standard deduction. The biggest questions about medical expenses are, what can I deduct, who can I deduct it for, and what stupid rules apply. I'll start with the first stupid rule, then tell you what's deductible, who it's deductible for, and the rest of the stupid rules. The first stupid rule is that you can only deduct medical expenses that exceed 10% of you AGI. (This number is 7.5% if you and/or your spouse were born before January 2nd, 1951.) You actually include all of your deductible expenses, but then you subtract 10% of your AGI from it, before deducting what's left (or nothing, if 10% of your AGI is more than your expenses). The theory behind this is, I believe, to prevent most people from having to track their expenses unless something catastrophic happens to them (though the Affordable Care act raising that number from 7.5% to 10% was just to get more tax revenue). As usual, this completely fails to accomplish its goal, since you don't know if something big will happen to you late in the year, so, to be safe, you need to track all your medical expenses that would suddenly be deductible once this happens. My advice is to apply the drawer system. Toss all your medical bills in a drawer, with the date paid. At the end of the year, find out what 10% of your AGI is and, if it's close, pull them out and add them up. Otherwise, empty the drawer out and start over with the New Year.

The idea of medical expenses is that they have to identify, prevent, cure, improve, or alleviate the symptoms of a SPECIFIC medical condition. They can't be just for general health, and they generally must be prescribed or supervised by a doctor or other qualified medical professional (I'll specify when they don't with an *). They include equipment, supplies and diagnostic devices. That said, many things that are or are not deductible will seem that they don't quite meet these criteria, or they may seem offensive or violate your political or moral standards (for example, the first on the list is abortion). If I list it one way or another, you can be pretty sure that it's been fought over and resolved to reasonable satisfaction one way or another. I'll list a ton of specific yes's and no's, but won't try to justify them (many times I can't because there is little rhyme or reason to them). If they are maybe's, I'll discuss circumstances that help or hurt your chances—you might want to enlist an expert to help you make the right choice.

After the yes, no and maybes, I'll go into more details, other deductions and general rules for medical deductions. The lists are long and sometimes repetitive to make it most likely that something you're looking for is discussed. More and more alternative therapies are becoming accepted every day, so if one isn't on this list, consult a professional just to make sure.

Yes:

Abortion
Acupuncture
Inpatient alcohol and drug treatment, including meals and lodging
Travel to and from AA meetings if attending based on medical advice
Ambulance
Artificial limbs and teeth
Autoette
Bandages*
Birth control pills
Braces
Braille books and magazines* (the amount above regular price)
Breast pumps and supplies*
Chiropractor
Christian Science Practitioner
Clinics
Contact lenses, including cleaning and storage supplies
Crutches*
Dental (except teeth whitening)
Diagnostic devices, such as blood pressure or sugar test supplies*
Prescribed drugs that are legal in the United States and legally imported
Prescription drugs taken in a foreign country if legal in that country and the U.S.
Insulin*
Eye doctor, glasses and eye surgery
Fertility treatments, including sterility procedure reversal
Sterilization
Service animal for PHYSICAL disability including costs to maintain the animal
Hearing aids
Hospital services, including meals (inpatient care) and lodging
Lab fees
Lead-based paint removal (if it is covered, see Maybe #7)
Medical exams
Medical information plan used to provide information to physicians
Doctor visits and services (includes most medical practitioners)
Halfway house from mental institution (not home of relative)
Occupational therapist
Operations (not cosmetic unless medically prescribed to treat something)
Organ donor medical expenses
Osteopath
Oxygen and associated equipment for medical problems
Physical therapist
Podiatrist
Prosthesis
Psychiatric care
Psychoanalysis

Psychologist
Sex reassignment for treatment of gender identity disorder (this means not elective)
Stop smoking programs (but not non-prescription gums or patches)
Surgery
Telephone and television specially designed for hearing impaired
Therapy as medical treatment
Transplants
Wheelchair
Whirlpool baths ordered by doctor
Wig advised by doctor for mental health of patient losing hair due to disease
X-rays

No:

Babysitting or nursing care for a healthy baby
Car medical insurance not specifically for you and your family (dependents)
Teeth whitening, except as discussed under Maybe #2.
Illegal operations or drugs
Drugs illegally imported into the U.S.
Drugs taken in another country that are illegal there or in the U.S.
Maternity clothes
Dancing or other lessons used to improve general health
Health club dues
Meals that are not paid to a hospital or other institution during inpatient care
Non-prescription drugs other than insulin
Swimming lessons
Travel that is merely beneficial to general health
Vet fees, except for a service animal discussed in the Yes section
Expenses reimbursed by insurance or other sources.
Funeral expenses
Household help, except as discussed under Maybe #12 and #14
Payroll deductions for Medicare Part A (the deductions shown on your W-2 box 6 or pay stub under Medicare)
Employer-provided health care, unless they include it as wages (odds are they are not)
Surrogate parenting expenses
Bottled water

Maybe (or detailed explanation required):

1. Car medical insurance is deductible if it is for you or your family (dependents) and is separately priced in the policy from other insurance.
2. Cosmetic surgery is only deductible if it fixes a deformity you are born with, or that is caused by an accident, injury, illness or the treatment of an illness.
Example 1: Breast enhancement for improvement of looks is not deductible, but

following breast cancer mastectomy it would be. Example 2: Scar removal would be deductible, but not skin treatments to correct common effects of old age.

3. Diaper service is deductible only if it is needed to relieve the effects of a disease.

4. Vitamins or supplements are only deductible if they are recommended by a medical professional for the treatment of a SPECIFIC disease. Never deductible for preventative care.

5. Personal use items are not generally deductible, but if you pay more than the normal price for something as a result of a specific disease, you can deduct the difference between regular price and the special price. An example would be the extra cost of Braille books over normal books.

6. Health insurance premiums are mostly deductible. If you take the self-employed health insurance deduction, you can't double deduct as an itemized deduction. Specifically deductible health insurances are medical and dental coverage, membership in associations that give cooperative medical care, long-term care insurance (subject to limits based on age), Medicare Part A (only if not enrolled in Social Security—payroll deductions for Medicare Part A are not deductible), Medicare Part B, and Medicare Part D. Prepaid medical care insurance has special limitations.

7. Modifications to your house to accommodate a medical condition are deductible if they are primarily for the medical condition. If they increase the value of your home, you must reduce the deduction by the increase in value. The classic example is an elevator that costs $10,000, but increases the home's value by $6,000. The deduction would be $4,000. Maintenance, repair and operation expenses (including electricity if you can account for how much is used by the device) are deductible even if you couldn't deduct the installation due to it increasing the value of the home. If lead paint was mitigated by covering instead of removal, you treat it just like a home improvement and deduct the cost minus the increase in home's value.

8. Improvements to plumbing and fixtures in a home or apartment you rent to accommodate your medical condition are deductible.

9. If your car is modified to accommodate your medical condition or disability (such as hand controls) the cost of the modification is deductible. If you purchase a specially equipped vehicle, such as a wheelchair lift equipped van, or a car that is already modified, the difference in price between the modified vehicle and the same, unmodified vehicle is deductible. Maintenance and upkeep costs are not deductible (though you get mileage similar to any other vehicle, which we will discuss later).

10. Lodging is deductible when provided by the hospital or similar facility. You can deduct $50 a night for lodging not at a medical facility if it is primarily for and essential to medical care, the care is provided by a qualified physician in a hospital or equivalent facility, the lodging is not fancy, and there is no element of pleasure or vacation in the travel. This disallows deductions for "medical tourism" and the like.

11. Meal expenses are only deductible if provided by and paid to a hospital or similar facility.

12. Long-term care services are deductible if they are medically necessary to treat a chronic condition and are under the plan of care prescribed by a medical professional. Chronically ill must be certified by a physician that within the prior 12 months either the person could not perform at least two essential activities of daily living for at least 90 days due to a medical condition (these activities are eating, toileting, bathing, dressing, transferring and continence) or they require substantial supervision to be protected due to severe cognitive impairment (think Alzheimer's, dementia and the like).

13. Nursing home care is deductible if the primary reason for being there is medical. If the primary reason is not medical, only the expenses specifically for medical care are deductible.

14. Nursing services are deductible even if not provided by a professional nurse. Their lodging and meals are also deductible if the nurse lives with the person requiring care. If the nurse provides non-medical household services, the cost must be separated from the medical services. Nursing services include medical care, grooming, bathing, providing medication and changing dressings. Some non-medical household services may qualify as long-term care under 12 above. They may also qualify for the Child and Dependent Care Credit, which I discuss under the children sections and sections about caring for parents, family members and others. If you pay the nurse as your employee, you can include Social Security and Medicare tax matching, as well as any state employment tax or unemployment insurance.

15. Special education for children with mental and physical handicaps is deductible, including attending special schools, as well as meals and lodging at the school, so long as the schooling is recommended by a doctor. The deduction is allowed even if non-special-needs education is provided as well.

16. Transportation for medical care is deductible. For a car, this is either gas and oil, or the standard medical mileage rate (23 cents a mile). Parking and tolls are deductible in addition to gas and oil, or the standard mileage rate. The travel must be primarily for medical care. Driving to and from work, even if by a medically special means, is never deductible as medical expense. Travel includes airfare, taxis, train, bus, rental cars, and other necessary means. Lodging is subject to the limits and restrictions discussed in 10, above. Travel to receive medical care for personal reasons, as opposed to medical (you want to get an operation in Las Vegas because you like the shows) is not deductible. Travel for improving your general health is not deductible. Travel expenses for a nurse travelling with you are deductible if you are travelling for care and can't travel alone. Transportation to visit a mentally ill relative are deductible if recommended as part of the treatment. The expenses of a parent travelling with a child who needs care is deductible.

17. Weight loss programs are deductible if they are for the treatment of a SPECIFIC medical condition diagnosed by a physician:
- Membership in weight loss groups and meetings
- Separate fees for weight loss programs at gyms (but not general membership)

- Food costs above those of a normal diet if they treat or improve a specific illness, are not part of normal nutritional needs, AND the need is substantiated by a physician.

You cannot deduct gym membership, weight loss costs to improve general health and appearance, and costs for replacement foods for normal foods (such as low-calorie, low-fat diet foods or nutritional supplements).

18. You can deduct costs of attending (including travel, but not meals and lodging) seminars and conferences if they are about a specific medical condition that you or your dependent has. You have to spend most of your time attending classes, seminars or workshops about the condition. Beware the vacation disguised as a conference!

19. If you buy a test to check for a disease or to self diagnose, they are deductible even if not suggested by a doctor.

20. Service dogs for mental disability or psychiatric treatment MAY be deductible. This one is very complex and should be discussed with a tax pro.

Here are the rest of the details:

1. You can deduct medical expenses in the year you pay them. If you pay by check or charge, the year is determined based on when you send the check, or charge the card. Payments made with credit cards count even if you don't pay the balance off. If you pay with loan proceeds independent of the medical provider, you can generally deduct the amount you pay. If you finance through the medical provider, you can only deduct the payments you make to them, not the full bill.

2. Don't deduct expenses paid by your insurance company, your employer, or paid for with proceeds from a tax advantaged medical account, such as a Health Savings Account or Medical Savings Account. Also don't deduct expenses that are reimbursed through a lawsuit or settlement.

3. If medical expenses are reimbursed in a later year than the one you deducted them in, they are added as income in that year, but only to the extent they improved your taxes in the year deducted. For example, if the reimbursement amount would have dropped your expenses below 10% of your AGI, only the part above 10% helped you. Similarly, if the reimbursement would have dropped your itemized deductions below your standard deduction, only the amount above your standard deduction helped you. This can be complicated if the numbers are close, so you might want to seek help if you are in this situation.

4. You can deduct medical expenses you paid for your spouse on your tax return as long as you were married to them either at the time the expenses were paid or the medical services provided. If you file MFS, there is a separate section for that.

5. You can deduct medical expenses you paid for your dependent included on your tax return as long as they were your dependent either at the time the expenses were paid, or the medical services provided.

6. You can claim expenses for someone who would be your dependent, and claimed on your tax return, but was not, as long as it was for one of the following reasons: They made more than $4,050, they filed a joint return, you waived the exemption to the child's other parent during divorce or separation, or someone else

claimed you or your spouse as a dependent. The $4,050 and the divorce one are the biggest reasons. I discuss waiving the exemption in the section on Divorce. The $4,050 comes up as your child gets older but continues to live at home. It comes into play if they turn 19 and don't go to school, or turn 24 regardless of school. In those situations, you lose the exemption when they make more than $4,050 (unless they are disabled), but you can still deduct medical expenses. They may also come up if you care for an aging parent who makes more than $4,050, even if they don't live with you. Make sure to review the specific sections on people who live with you or taking care of your parents to be sure you follow the right rules for claiming them.

7. One other item for divorced or separated parents: If you or the other child's parent have custody and one of you claims the child, and you are divorced, legally separated or lived apart the last six months of the year, each parent claims the medical expenses that they paid, regardless of who claims the child's exemption. If there is a third party who provides custody or support for the child who is not married to either parent, this may not apply and you should seek help in determining who claims what for the child.

Military: You can't deduct medical expenses if they would have been reimbursable, even if you elect to pay for service due to not wanting to wait for military or VA medical services. This means that most active military will have no deductible medical expenses, unless they pay for fertility treatments.

Discussed elsewhere or not discussed: MFS, non-citizen parents or children, third-party support or custody.

30. I have a High Deductible Health Plan and/or Health Savings Account through Work

Done right, a High Deductible Health Plan (HDHP) and Health Savings Account (HSA) through your employer should have no impact on your tax return bottom line, and should be simple to put on your tax return (unless you're doing it by hand on paper). This section provides an overview of how HDHP and HSA affect your taxes, then goes into more detail for more complicated situations.

The idea of High Deductible Health Plans and Health Savings Accounts is that they should go hand-in-hand to provide predictability, affordability and tax advantages with regard to health care and insurance costs. The basic idea is that you get a health insurance plan that has a high, relatively fixed deductible. In return for this, you get two main advantages: the plan should be cheaper than low deductible insurance, and you can save money in a tax advantaged account to pay for health care costs up to the deductible. All the complicated rules and limits are designed to align with these ideas.

For most people, these rules and limits will be handled at the employer level. The health plan will be purchased through your employer, the contributions to the HSA account will be either made by your employer, or done through payroll deduction, or both. Most will even provide a debit-type card that will only allow you to use it for allowed expenses. In this situation, everything you need to file your taxes is included on your W-2 (a code W in box 12), a Form 1099SA from the HSA account administrator, and a Form 5498 from the same place. If all of these apply to you, the only thing you need to be careful about is to make sure that you stay in the plan for at least a year. If you do, you just input your W-2 and 1099 into the software (or provide to your tax professional) and indicate that everything taken out of the HSA was used for appropriate medical expenses. If your plan doesn't provide a card that prevents you from using the HSA for unauthorized expenses, you will need to know what's allowed, and ensure you only take money out for those things (discussed later). Having done all these things, your tax return should show no deductions, additions or extra taxes due to your HDHP and HSA. You will have a Form 8889, but nothing should carry to the main tax return. This may make you wonder where the tax advantages are, which is a good question. The tax advantages occurred as you were paid, and as the HSA earned money. None of the money put into the HSA is included as taxable income, so nothing gets withheld from it, and it doesn't appear on your tax return. In addition, you don't include any earnings from the HSA account in income. You don't have to use all the money you put in in the same year. You can let it keep growing until you really need it. There's no limit on how much you take out, except that it must be used for allowable medical expenses.

That's where the easy part ends. The rest of this section will cover all the nitty gritty, and other requirements and rules. If the previous paragraph covered your situation, you're done, but feel free to keep reading, and definitely read it when you leave your job or cancel your plan.

In order to have an HSA you must be covered under a HDHP. Both will be defined in the details below, as well as other requirements.

HSA:

1. An HSA is an account set up with a custodian, such as a bank or financial institution. Contributions up to the annual limit are either not included in income (when contributed through your employer) or deducted off of your income when filing taxes if you make them yourself. Earnings are not taxed. Withdrawals can only be made (with a few exceptions) for qualified medical expenses (discussed later). These withdrawals are tax free.

2. Withdrawals that are not for qualified medical expenses are taxable and subject to an additional 20% penalty.

3. Contributions do not have to be used in any given year, and can be used for qualified medical expenses even after you no longer qualify to contribute.

4. Contributions can be made by the taxpayer, their employer, or anyone else, as long as they do not exceed the total allowed amount of contributions for the year.

5. There is a maximum amount that can be contributed in any given year. This limit for 2015 is $3,350 for a person covered by a plan for only him or herself (single plan), $6,750 for someone with coverage for them self and at least one other person (family plan). This number is increased by $1,000 if you are over 55.

6. If both you and your spouse have HSAs, the limit applies to the total amount contributed to the accounts, though if both of you are over 55 you get an extra $2,000 instead of just $1,000.

7. There are some provisions for rolling over money from IRA's and other tax advantaged health accounts, but you should talk to your tax professional before doing this.

8. Qualified medical expenses are those that are incurred after the account was set up, and would be deductible as a medical expense (see the chapter on I Have Medical Expenses for details). The same rules for who you can deduct expenses for (such as spouse or dependent) apply for these expenses. In addition, qualified medical expenses include non-prescription drugs that are prescribed by a doctor. Insurance premiums don't count unless you are over 65, unemployed or they are for long-term care. Medigap insurance does not count.

9. Medical expenses paid from your HSA that would have qualified except that they were incurred before the account was set up save you from the 20% penalty, but the withdrawal is still taxable.

10. When you die, you can leave your HSA to your spouse and it becomes his or her HSA. If you leave it to someone else, they must take the money out and pay taxes on it (but no penalty). If it is left to your estate, the money goes on your final return, and is taxable to the extent the amount in it exceeds any medical expenses you had in the year before your death—again, no penalty.

11. To qualify for an HSA, you must be covered under a HDHP (discussed below). You cannot have any other comprehensive health insurance except disability, dental, vision, or long-term care. You cannot be enrolled in Medicare. You can't qualify as someone else's dependent, even if they don't claim you. If your spouse has a non-HDHP plan, you can still have an HSA if you are not covered by your spouse's plan, and you have a HDHP.

12. If you are covered on the first day of December, you are considered covered for that whole year, as long as you maintain coverage for at least a year. If you don't maintain coverage for a full year, your contribution limit is 1/12 of the annual total, times the number of months in the year you were covered. If your coverage is ended before December 1st, you get to contribute an amount equal to your annual limit, divided by 12, times the number of months you were covered.

13. You cannot take a medical expense itemized deduction for expenses you paid with funds out of the HSA.

14. You cannot have an HSA and another active tax preferred medical account such as a Health Reimbursement Account or Flexible Spending Account (FSA). You can have an FSA if it is restricted from paying medical expenses.

15. You can make contributions for a previous year up to 4/15 of the next year.

16. Excess contributions are subject to a 6% penalty—take them and any earnings out by the due date of the return.

HDHP:

1. A HDHP is a plan that has minimum annual deductibles, and a minimum cap on annual out-of-pocket expenses for covered expenses. For a single person's plan, the deductible must be at least $1,300 and the annual cap at least $6,550. For a family plan (two or more people covered) the deductible is at least $2,600 and the cap at least $13,100.

2. The HDHP can have a prescription drug plan, as long as it doesn't start paying for drugs until the deductible is met.

3. If the plan is a family plan, but has separates deductibles for each individual, the individual deductibles must meet the requirements for a single plan, and the totals of the deductibles must meet the requirements for a family plan.

4. There are some other annoying rules on what does or does not qualify, but they are best handled by the insurance provider. They will generally be identifying HDHP's for you so you know what qualifies you for an HSA.

Military: Military medical care and Tricare are disqualifying from having an HSA.

31. I'm Donating to Charity

My favorite subject!

I've said before, and I'll say it again: Don't do anything just for the tax benefits! Usually this is because when you spend money to save on taxes, you save a lot less on taxes than you spend. Charity contains one of the few exceptions to this: Non-cash contributions (think Goodwill). It's a total win for everyone! You give away stuff you don't want, the charity uses it to accomplish its mission, and you get a tax deduction! That said, charity has a LOT of rules and recordkeeping requirements, so, before I get into those, I'm going to give some simple rules to follow that will make your charitable giving simple and easy. Most people will be able to tailor their giving to meet these requirements and won't have to read the encyclopedia volume that follows. Before I do that, let me remind you that charitable contributions are a part of itemized deductions, so if you don't meet the itemized deduction threshold, you don't get any benefit from charitable giving. Read the Itemized Deductions section for more details.

Here's the simple system:

1. Give to established, mainstream charities who can confirm that they are allowed to receive tax deductible contributions and will provide you with a receipt.
2. Give less than $250 by check or charge (no cash) to any given charity, on any given day. (This means you can give your church or charity over $90,000 in a year without needing a written acknowledgement, and you can give to as many different organizations as you want. You can even give over $12,000 in weekly donations via $249 checks in the church collection plate.)
3. If you want to donate more to your church, make sure they provide a written statement acknowledging the donation and that it specifies that no goods or services were provided by them to you (intangible religious benefits such as church services don't count). The acknowledgement will usually cover the entire year.
4. Don't make donations with strings attached, designated for a specific person, or in return for something provided by the charity.
5. If you make non-cash contributions, take a picture of the donated items (save it on your computer, no need to print), make a list of the donated items, and get a receipt (unless dropped at a drop box—see below).
6. Do not donate more than $5,000 worth of items in a single day.
7. Do not donate more than $5,000 of a category of items (such as books) in a single year.

Follow rules 1 through 4 above and your cash contributions will be simple and easy. Rules 5 through 7 will simplify non-cash donations. The next four items are special cases that tend to come up, and/or cool tricks you can use.

1. The drop box exception. I have called this the loophole you can drive a truck through. You need a receipt if you donate non-cash items, with the exception of places that don't normally provide a receipt. The publications specifically list drop boxes as an example. So you can donate non-cash items to a drop box, and make your own receipt. I still recommend taking pictures and making a list, and you may want to take a picture of the drop box. This exception is ripe for abuse, but don't lie to the IRS. Trust me. You will need the location of the drop box, the organization that placed it, their local address, the date you donated the items, the value of the items and a list of the items. From this, you can make your "receipt."

2. Garage sales. I like garage sales. What I don't like is when the vultures come around later in the day, offering you pennies for your items because they know you want to get rid of them. Don't do it! Sell your stuff for a reasonable price, then, while everything's on the table after the sale, take pictures of it all, load it into your car, and drop off at Goodwill or another place that takes non-cash contributions. Or take them to a drop box like we talked about above. If you itemize, you'll do better on your taxes than the pennies you'll get from the late-comers.

3. Auctions, dinners and shows. If you buy a ticket for an event from a charity, you only get to deduct the difference between what you paid for the ticket, and the value of what you receive. Good charities will provide this information. If the values are close, don't waste your time with the deduction, just be happy you're helping a good organization. Raffle tickets are not deductible.

4. Volunteering. Your time is not deductible. Your legitimate expenses in providing your time are. Don't try comingling vacations and volunteering, travel deductions for charity work are only deductible if charity is the sole purpose of the trip. If you travel for volunteering with no significant personal enjoyment involved (other than the joy of giving) you can deduct your travel expenses (airfare, lodging, mass transit). You can also deduct mileage (14 cents a mile), meals when away overnight, and uniforms that aren't suitable for everyday use.

If everything you do fits the above, you can stop reading; otherwise, here are the nasty details:

1. You have to donate to a qualified organization, for qualified purposes. Most major charities and churches qualify. You can verify that they qualify by going to www.irs.gov, click on tools, and then click Exempt Organizations Select Check. This has a search function, as well as the ability to download the full list of exempt organizations.

2. Civic leagues, homeowner's associations, labor unions, clubs, lobbying organizations, political groups and candidates are not organizations for which your donation would be tax deductible.

3. You cannot place strings on your donation such that it is directed to a specific individual or group.

4. Your time has no deductible value, nor does your blood.

5. The charities have to be U.S. charities, though Mexican, Israeli and Canadian charities may be deductible under certain very restrictive conditions.

6. You cannot receive benefits from your donation unless you subtract the value of the benefit from the amount you deduct (if you buy tickets to a $10 movie from an organization for $15, you deduct $5). Token benefits, such as pens or religious services, do not have to be deducted.

7. Lottery, raffle or bingo ticket costs are not deductible.

8. You can deduct 14 cents a mile for travel related to volunteering or gift giving.

9. Any single donation of $250 or more in cash requires a written acknowledgement from the organization. This acknowledgement needs to include the organization's name, amount of the donation, and a statement as to whether any goods or services were provided in return for the donation and the value of those services. This statement cannot be reproduced later for an audit. You must get it before you file your return, or the due date of your tax return (including extensions), whichever is earlier. For donations less than $250, a bank statement or cancelled check is sufficient.

10. Non-cash donations must be in good used or better condition. This is a bit of a nebulous term, so I recommend taking pictures of any non-cash donations you make.

11. You deduct the fair market value of the non cash donation. Fair Market Value is (standby for taxese) the amount that a willing buyer would pay a willing seller if both parties were knowledgeable of all facts and had no ulterior motives. This is NOT the price that Goodwill sells the item for (no profit motive) but really is the price a for-profit thrift store would sell it. You generally cannot deduct more than you paid for an item (or what it was worth when you inherited it).

12. You need a receipt for any non-cash donation, unless the drop box exception discussed above applies.

13. If you donate more than $5,000 worth of items at a single time, you will need a statement from a qualified appraiser as to the value of the items. This also applies if you donate more than $5,000 worth of similar items (such as books) in a year. You cannot deduct the cost of the appraisal.

14. You cannot deduct more than 50% of your AGI in a single year, but the excess is carried over to the next year. Certain unusual contributions may be further limited.

15. Non-cash donations exceeding $500 for the year require filing Form 8283 with your return. This form asks for additional information, such as how much you paid for the property and how you determined the value. I hate this form and think it is the perfect example of being completely unrealistic as to what the average taxpayer has the time or inclination to track.

16. If you donate a car, you get to deduct what the organization sold it for. They should provide a Form 1098-C with this value. If the charity uses the vehicle, makes improvements to it, or sells it to a needy individual below market value, you can deduct the Fair Market Value of the car at the time of the donation. Don't place strings on the use or disposition of the car.

17. Don't try to deduct a house donated to the fire department for them to burn down for training, especially if you retain title to the land.

Military: You can get a Year to Date charity amount from your LES for payroll deductions to CFC and the like. Dues to your officer or enlisted associations are not deductible. Many veterans groups are qualified organizations.

Not discussed: Donations of stock, investments, collectibles or IRA's.

32. I'm Living with Someone Who Helps Pay my Bills

If you are living with someone who helps pay your bills, the main thing we're concerned with is whether you are their dependent (or they're yours) and if they can file HH. We won't discuss if they are your dependent in this section; that's covered in the following sections. If you are paying more than half the bills, read those sections (as they apply). If they are paying more than half the bills, read this section. If it's close, read all the sections. The point for you is that if someone else can claim you, you can't claim yourself. I'm assuming they (and you for that matter) are an adult, who may or may not be related to you. I'm also assuming you are not their minor child or child attending college (if you are, read the sections on children—they're written from the parent's perspective, but they still apply. You should coordinate with your parents in filing when you live with them.). I'm also assuming you are not permanently disabled and unable to work. If you're married to the person you live with, this is the wrong section—you should be looking into MFJ or MFS. In many cases, there will be no effect on your taxes. I'm first going to cover situations where you cannot be claimed, then talk about other common situations, and lastly cover all the nit-picky rules. With luck, your situation will be covered before you have to read the detailed stuff.

Here are the simple situations where you cannot be claimed:

If you are married and file a joint return with your spouse, you cannot be claimed unless you are only filing to get 100% of your money back, and neither you nor your spouse would have owed any taxes (at all—not just getting a refund) if you filed separately. For the remainder of this section, this rule applies, and I'm assuming when I say you can be claimed that you aren't MFJ.

If they are not related to you (parent, child, sibling, niece, nephew, aunt, uncle [including grands- and greats-, and steps-] or parent, child or sibling in-law) and they did not live with you the entire year, you cannot be claimed. Temporary absences for school, medical treatment, business, vacations, etc. can be included in the year.

If you have gross income (wages, investment income, business income, taxable pensions or annuities) of more than $4,050, you cannot be claimed.

If you pay more than half of your support, you cannot be claimed (Appendix A Test 2). Support includes the rental value of your lodging (take what it would cost to rent the entire house or apartment and divide by the number of people sharing the place, including children), clothing, transportation, recreation, lodging, medical expenses, and other necessities. If what you earn from all sources, minus what you put away in savings, is more than half of this amount, you support yourself and cannot be claimed.

If you don't pay more than half of your support, but neither does the person you live with (there's a third person, someone sends you money for your support, or you receive support from the government or charity), you cannot be claimed as their dependent.

Here are some other common situations:

Roommate: If you live with a roommate, you would expect that you would share in the bills, however unequally they are shared. Having a roommate is generally not a dependent situation. In fact, depending on the situation, one of you might be the tenant of the other, if one owns or leases the property and makes the payments. Usually you just treat it as two people sharing the bills. If, however, you provide limited funds to the household, live there all year, make less than $4,050 from all sources (wages, investment income, business income, taxable pensions or annuities), and are unmarried, you need to determine if your roommate supports you (Appendix A Test 2). Support includes the rental value of your lodging (take what it would cost to rent the entire house or apartment and divide by the number of people sharing the place, including children), clothing, transportation, recreation, lodging, medical expenses, and other necessities. If what you earn from all sources, minus what you put away in savings, is more than half of this amount, you support yourself and cannot be claimed. Unrelated Roommates cannot use you to file HH.

Boyfriend, girlfriend or fiancée: This situation is actually almost identical to the roommate situation, discussed above, with two unusual exceptions. One is that in some states you may cross a line that makes you common-law married. This is actually pretty unlikely to happen accidentally, but you should be aware of the laws as they affect you in your state. You might actually be able to claim yourself as married, without a formal ceremony, but you should seek professional assistance, both in tax law and marriage law, before trying it. Second, it is also possible, though unlikely, that your living situation violates state law. The example given in the IRS publication is living with your girlfriend who is married to someone else—if this violates state law, you cannot claim or be claimed by them, regardless of whether you meet the other requirements. Unrelated Roommates cannot use you to file HH.

Adult child with parents: If you move back in with your parents, are older than 18 and not going to college, or are older than 23 regardless of college attendance, the usual rules for claiming a non-relative apply. If you live there six months or more, make less than $4,050 from any source and are supported by them (Appendix A Test 2), they can claim you as a dependent. Support includes the rental value of your lodging (take what it would cost to rent the entire house or apartment and divide by the number of people sharing the place, including children), clothing, transportation, recreation, lodging, medical expenses, and other necessities. If what you earn from all sources, minus what you put away in savings, is more than half of this amount, you support yourself and cannot be claimed. If the age and college situations apply, read the section on children and coordinate with your parents to file your taxes correctly. If your single parent can claim you, they may be able to file HH. (The determination of support for HH is different than the support test in that you do not include the fair rental value. Instead, you include actual rent, or mortgage interest and real estate taxes [not the whole mortgage payment]. You also include repairs, insurance, utilities and food eaten in the home.)

Living in a friend's house: Treat this the same as the roommate section discussed above.

Living with a family member: Again, treat this like the roommate section, except that if they are your parent, child, sibling, niece, nephew, aunt, uncle (including grands-, greats-, and steps-) or parent, child or sibling in-law, then you don't have to live with them for the entire year. If they meet this requirement, you live with them more than half the year, and they are unmarried, they may be able to file HH (the determination of support for HH is different than the support test in that you do not include the fair rental value. Instead, you include actual rent, or mortgage interest and real estate taxes (not the whole mortgage payment). You also include repairs, insurance, utilities and food eaten in the home.)

Here are the nit-picky details:

1. I don't include Social Security as gross income because it is only included as gross income if it is taxable. The amount of income required to make it taxable well exceeds the $4,050 we're concerned with. So if it's included, you are already above $4,050. I include this comment only because someone will read the book and point out that I "forgot" about Social Security.
2. If you live with more than one person, they determine if they can claim you independently of each other. Mathematically, the support test will either eliminate one or both such that it can't result in both being able to claim you, or neither will be able to claim you.
3. It is possible for the situation in 2 above to result in no one paying more than half your support, even though together they do provide more than half. There is something called a Multiple Support Agreement (Form 2120) that would allow them to agree to combine support to allow one of them to claim the exemption. Seek professional help if this applies.
4. If there are divorced or separated parents involved in this, read the I'm Getting Divorced section in addition to this section, though if you are 18 or older it is unlikely to affect this.

Military: If a person lives with you at the time you are deployed they continue to count as living with you during the deployment. Some people might debate this, but a good rule of thumb is that a non-permanent deployment or assignment does not change the living situation for taxes so long as the intention is for the dependent to return to the pre-deployment living situation when the deployment or temporary assignment ends. Geographical bachelor or Permanent Change of Station orders would not count for as "temporary".

33. I'm Supporting my Parents

NOTE: Support is discussed periodically below, and is usually obvious and straightforward. I have included a Support Worksheet in Appendix A if you need more details.

The first thing we need to establish is whether you are truly (in accordance with IRS definitions) supporting your parents (Appendix A Test 2). Support includes the rental value of their lodging (take what it would cost to rent the entire house or apartment they are living in and divide by the number of people sharing the place, including children), clothing, transportation, recreation, lodging, medical expenses, and other necessities. If what they earn from all sources (including savings withdrawals), minus what they put away in savings, is more than half of this amount, they support themselves and cannot be claimed. Once you establish that, you need to check some other tests. I'm going to run down the normal situations that would allow you to claim them. There aren't a lot of additional details and tricks for this section, so I'm covering everything in the straightforward section. Included in the discussion is the potential for HH filing status, which has some unique aspects with regard to parents.

To claim HH, you must pay at least half the cost to maintain the place they are living for at least half the year, be that their home, a nursing home, or other arrangements. This determination is different than the support test in that you do not include the fair rental value. Instead, you include actual rent, or mortgage interest and real estate taxes (not the whole mortgage payment). You also include repairs, insurance, utilities and food eaten in the home. Assuming this applies, and you meet the other tests to claim them, you would meet the requirements to claim HH (assuming you are unmarried).

If your parents are married, they must not file a joint tax return, or, if they do, they must file only to get ALL their money back, and, if they had filed separately, they both would have gotten ALL their money back. It's useful to run all three tax returns using MFJ and MFS with and without you claiming the exemption to determine the best way for all of you to file.

Your parent's gross income must be less than $4,050. This includes wages, investment income, business income, and taxable pensions or annuities.

If you meet all the above, you can claim your parents as dependents.

If you and other family members share the support of your parents but no one pays more than half, you might be able to file a Multiple Support Agreement that would allow one of you to claim them (but not get HH). You file Form 2120, but I would seek professional help if this applies.

Military: Not much different here for you.

34. I'm Supporting an Adult Relative or Friend

NOTE: Support is discussed periodically below, and is usually obvious and straightforward. I have included a Support Worksheet in Appendix A if you need more details.

Two big things need to be established before we can decide whether you can claim this person, and whether you can use the HH filing status.

The first thing we need to establish is whether you are truly (in accordance with IRS definitions) supporting this person (Appendix A Test 2). Support includes the rental value of their lodging (take what it would cost to rent the entire house or apartment they are living in and divide by the number of people sharing the place, including children), clothing, transportation, recreation, lodging, medical expenses, and other necessities. If what they earn from all sources (including savings withdrawals), minus what they put away in savings, is more than half of this amount, they support themselves and cannot be claimed.

The second thing you need to establish is if they are a certain kind of relative. These are parent (previous section), child (have their own section), sibling, niece, nephew, aunt, uncle (including grands-, greats-, and steps-) or parent-, child- or sibling in-law. If it is one of these, the person does not need to live with you all year, and HH is a possibility. Otherwise, they must live with you the entire year, and HH is not possible. Temporary absences for school, treatment, business, vacations, etc. can be included in the year.

To claim HH, you must pay at least half the cost to maintain the place they are living for at least half the year, and that must also be your home. This determination is different than the support test in that you do not include the fair rental value. Instead, you include actual rent, or mortgage interest and real estate taxes (not the whole mortgage payment). You also include repairs, insurance, utilities and food eaten in the home. Assuming this applies, and you meet the other tests to claim them, you would meet the requirements to claim HH (assuming you are unmarried).

If they are married, they must not file a joint tax return, or, if they do, they must file only to get ALL their money back, and, if they had filed separately, they both would have gotten ALL their money back. It's useful to run all three tax returns using MFJ and MFS with and without you claiming the exemption to determine the best way for all of you to file.

Their gross income must be less than $4,050. This includes wages, investment income, business income, and taxable pensions or annuities.

If you meet all the above, you can claim them as a dependent.

If you and other persons share their support, but no one pays more than half, you might be able to file a Multiple Support Agreement that would allow one of you to claim them (but not get HH). You file Form 2120, but I would seek professional help if this applies.

Military: If a person lives with you at the time you are deployed they continue to count as living with you during the deployment. Some people might debate this, but a good rule of thumb is that a non-permanent deployment or assignment does not change the living situation for taxes so long as the intention is for the dependent to return to the pre-deployment living situation when the deployment or temporary assignment ends. Geographical bachelor or Permanent Change of Station orders would not count as "temporary".

35. I'm Supporting a Minor who is not my Child

NOTE: Support is discussed periodically below, and is usually obvious and straightforward. I have included a Support Worksheet in Appendix A if you need more details.

This is a very complicated situation. Most people think it's obvious and fall back on the: "I support them so I must be able to claim them!" argument. But the rules are messy. The first thing I'm going to assume is that this is not a foster child placed with you by an authorized placement agency—that's a whole other situation. You should also be aware that if you are or were married to the mother or father of the child, you are the step-parent, regardless of if you were subsequently divorced (see I'm Having a Child and I'm Getting Divorced). If you live with and are married to the parent of the child, you should be filing MFJ and reading the I'm Having a Child section. Just a reminder that a child that is born or died during the year is presumed to have lived with the person with whom they were living at the time of birth or death for the whole year.

I'm going to break down some basic situations and scenarios, then go over the nitty gritty details. There are going to be a lot of scenarios, so standby:

You are related to the child in the following ways: Sibling or step-sibling, grandchild, niece or nephew or any of their descendents, and their parent lives with you.

First off, in this scenario, the child's parent wins in a fight over claiming the child, period. If, however, the parent does not plan to claim the child, you can claim them if you meet some criteria. The child must have lived with you as a member of your household for more than six months (temporary absences for school, illness, etc. still count as living with you). The child can't provide more than half their own support (Appendix A Test 1). Support includes the rental value of their lodging (take what it would cost to rent the entire house or apartment they are living in and divide by the number of people sharing the place, including children), clothing, transportation, recreation, lodging, medical expenses, and other necessities. If what they earn from all sources (including savings withdrawals), minus what they put away in savings, is more than half of this amount, they support themselves and cannot be claimed. They cannot file a MFJ return unless they are only filing to get ALL their withholding back and the couple would both get ALL their money back if they filed separately. The child must be under age 19, or under 24 if a full-time student during at least 5 months, or permanently and totally disabled (doctor's statement must be provided). If you meet all those tests, you can claim the child as a dependent. The child will also qualify you for Earned Income Credit, Child Tax Credit, Dependent Care Credit and HH if you meet the other criteria for them. I'm not going to rehash these here, but they are included in the I'm Having a Child section.

You are related to the child in the following ways: Sibling or step-sibling, grandchild, niece or nephew or any of their descendents, and their parent does not live with you.

You can claim them if you meet some criteria. The child must have lived with you as a member of your household for more than six months (temporary absences for school, illness, etc. still count as living with you). The child can't provide more than half their own support (Appendix A Test 1). Support includes the rental value of their lodging (take what it would cost to rent the entire house or apartment they are living in and divide by the number of people sharing the place, including children), clothing, transportation, recreation, lodging, medical expenses, and other necessities. If what they earn from all sources (including savings withdrawals), minus what they put away in savings, is more than half of this amount, they support themselves and cannot be claimed. They cannot file a MFJ return unless they are only filing to get ALL their withholding back and the couple would both get ALL their money back if they filed separately. The child must be under age 19, or under 24 if a full-time student during at least 5 months, or permanently and totally disabled (doctor's statement must be provided). If you meet all those tests, you can claim the child as a dependent. The child will also qualify you for Earned Income Credit, Child Tax Credit, Dependent Care Credit and HH if you meet the other criteria for them. I'm not going to rehash these here, but they are included in the I'm Having a Child section.

You are not related to the child as discussed above and their parent lives with you:

First off, in this scenario, the child's parent wins in a fight over claiming the child, period. If, however, the parent does not meet the criteria to claim the child, you can claim them if you meet some criteria. The child must have lived with you as a member of your household for the entire year (temporary absences for school, illness, etc. still count as living with you). You must provide over half the child's support (Appendix A Test 2). Support includes the rental value of their lodging (take what it would cost to rent the entire house or apartment they are living in and divide by the number of people sharing the place, including children), clothing, transportation, recreation, lodging, medical expenses, and other necessities. If you pay more than half of this amount, you support them. They cannot file a MFJ return unless they are only filing to get ALL their withholding back and the couple would both get ALL their money back if they filed separately. The child cannot have gross income of more than $4,050 from any source. This includes wages, investment income, business income, and taxable pensions or annuities. If you meet all the above, you can claim the child as a dependent. You cannot get Earned Income Credit, HH or Dependent Care Credit.

You are not related to the child as discussed above and their parent does not live with you:

You can claim them if you meet some criteria. The child must have lived with you as a member of your household for the entire year (temporary absences for school, illness, etc. still count as living with you). You must provide over half the child's support (Appendix A Test 2). Support includes the rental value of their lodging (take what it would cost to rent the entire house or apartment they are living in and divide by the number of people sharing the place, including children), clothing, transportation, recreation, lodging, medical expenses, and other necessities. If you pay more than half of this amount, you support them. They cannot file a MFJ return unless they are only filing to get ALL their withholding back and the couple would both get ALL their money back if they filed separately. The child cannot have gross income of more than $4,050 from any source. This includes wages, investment income, business income, and taxable pensions or annuities. If you meet all the above, you can claim the child as a dependent. You cannot get Earned Income Credit, HH or Dependent Care Credit.

For any of the above scenarios, if someone else (other than the child's parent) lives with the child and wants to claim them, you can either agree ahead of time who claims them, or apply tie-breaker rules. If you don't agree, and two people try to claim the child, the first electronically filed return will go through. The second return will be rejected, requiring the child to be removed, or the return filed on paper. When the IRS gets the second, paper-filed return, they will send letters attempting to determine who gets the child in accordance with the tie-breaker rules. They will award the child to the one who wins, and demand money back from the incorrect filer, if they already received it. The tie breaker rules are: Parent wins over non-parent. Higher AGI wins between two non-parents. If two *parents* are fighting over a child, the parent with whom the child spends more nights during the year wins, before applying the AGI test.

Military: If a child lives with you at the time you are deployed they continue to count as living with you during the deployment, even if you send them to another household (such as your parents) for the time you are deployed. Some people might debate this, but a good rule of thumb is that a non-permanent deployment or assignment does not change the living situation for taxes so long as the intention is for the dependent to return to the pre-deployment living situation when the deployment or temporary assignment ends (sending the child to live with their other parent might be trouble). Geographical bachelor or Permanent Change of Station orders would not count as "temporary".

Not discussed: Foster children.

36. Someone Claimed my Child!

I assume when you say someone claimed your child that, you either know from someone that it happened, or your tax return was rejected due to the child already being claimed. In either case, if you have the proper rights to claim the child, you can still claim the child AND YOU SHOULD!

I see it all the time, where people don't want to cause trouble and just leave the child off their tax return when someone else claims them (see Note 1 below). This is a mistake! Guess what's going to happen next year. Follow a few simple steps and you will eventually get your money. The person who claimed the child incorrectly will have to pay their extra money back, likely preventing this from happening again. The IRS also has some things that will help in the future if Earned Income Credit is involved, but you don't need to worry about that.

Here are the steps:

1. Make sure you are the proper person to claim the child. Reread the I'm Having a Child and I'm Getting Divorced sections, and be sure. Talk to your tax professional and be completely honest and upfront about the situation. Once you are sure you are in the right...

2. Gather documentation that shows the child's relationship to you, the fact that they live with you, their age, and their student status. Birth certificates, marriage certificates, school and medical records, statements from daycare and neighbors will all help.

3. Print and mail in your tax return. You can do this before you have all your documentation from step 2, and you can send copies or not send copies of the documentation. I've seen it suggested both ways and can't honestly say if one way is better or not. The main problem you might run across with this is if you are using a professional and having your fees withheld from the refund. The pro may want to be paid upfront now, since your refund will be delayed and not e-filed. Make this happen! Do not let the cost stop you from filing!

Your refund may be significantly delayed, and you may get a letter from the IRS asking for the documentation we talked about in step 2. Keep at it, and you will win. There is no ambiguity on claiming children. Only one person has the right to claim a child and if that's you, you should have only minor speed bumps between you and your refund.

Note 1: If it was a family member or even your child claiming themselves, and you want to avoid trouble, you can run the numbers with and without the child and see how much money is involved compared to the hassle. Particularly if it is your own child (maybe a college or high school age child claiming themselves) have a pointed conversation with them about the next year - I always tell clients to tell their children that as long as they live at home, their tax documents go through YOU! Particularly when your child claims them self, you can usually still file Head of Household (if you are a single parent) using them as a non-dependent. It's possible in this scenario that you don't lose too much.

Military: No real differences for you here.

37. My Tax Return got Rejected by the IRS!

First thing to do here is relax. Very often the fix for this is simple. Oftentimes your software or Tax Pro will be able to walk you through fixing the problem and resubmitting the return.

Second thing to understand is that the return has been rejected for ELECTRONIC FILING ONLY. It hasn't been audited. The IRS is not coming to get you. This doesn't mean you can't file. E-file rejection is simply the IRS way of preventing certain kinds of fraud, ensuring only one return per person has been submitted and a few other things. A rejected return isn't even considered filed yet, so, no matter how bad you buggered it up, you aren't in any trouble at all. Worst case, if you have filed an accurate return, you might have to mail it in and wait a while to get your refund (if you owe, pay by April 15th even if you are still having trouble getting the return accepted!)

All the above said, there are some very common reasons for rejected tax returns, and I'm going to cover a lot of them, and some advice on correcting them. Your software or tax professional is the first resource for information, but it can be confusing. I'll try to use the verbiage the IRS will use when informing you, but, since I'm lumping things together, they may not match exactly. You should be able to figure out what I'm talking about. I'm not going to use the code numbers (mostly) for the same reason. Once you correct the error causing the reject, you just resend the return. You can keep resending as many times as needed.

Prior Year AGI or PIN incorrect: As one step to prevent tax ID theft, the IRS requires tax software users to provide information from their prior years return to help ensure they are who they say they are. You must provide your prior year's AGI or the PIN (5 digit code that you probably didn't even enter yourself) you used. This is a good reason to use the same software every year, since it grabs this information automatically. If you have your prior year return, fixing this is easy - get your AGI (1040EZ line 4, 1040A line 21, 1040 line 37) or your PIN (form 8879 next to your signature) and input it into the software and resend. If you don't have a copy of your tax return, things get hard. You can try 1 followed by the last 4 of your SSN as a PIN, you can pay a professional to file it (since they see you and your forms face to face they don't need this extra step), or you can paper file. You can also get a copy of your return from the IRS, or the professional who filed it.

Name, SSN or Birthday do not match IRS records: There are numerous rejects involving wrong personal information. Your software or tax pro should tell you which one is wrong (primary SSN is first name on return, Secondary is the spouse, and dependents are numbered in the order they appear on the tax return). Generally this is as simple as checking the information and correcting it to match the Social Security Card and Birth Certificate. Sometimes, in the case of names with more than just first, middle, and last names, the Social Security

Administration inputs what you consider to be their second middle name as their last name (just one example of many). If there are more than three names on the Social Security Card, you can try changing the information and resending (keeping in mind that the ORDER of the names stay the same - Joe Bob Billy Smith might be first name Joe, middle name Bob Billy, last name Smith, or could be first name Joe, middle name Bob and last name Billy Smith, but wouldn't be first name Smith, middle name Joe Bob, last name Billy.)

Primary or Secondary SSN has already filed: This is generally caused by one of four things:
1. You filed and forgot you filed (not likely, but I've seen it)
2. Your spouse (or girlfriend, or ex spouse) already filed a return with you as their spouse.
3. The preparer you used filed your return when you hadn't (or believed you hadn't) approved it.
4. Tax ID theft.

I'm going to cover 4 (Tax ID theft) at the very end of this section, and 2 might also qualify as 4 if they did this behind your back and you didn't plan to file with them. If that's the case read the Tax ID theft part at the end of this section.
If 1 is the case, and the return you filed isn't right, you'll need to amend (Note 1) the original tax return (wait until the first one's processed, but make sure to get done before April 15th.)
For 2, if it's not fraud or ID theft, what you do depends on your personal relationship with the person, and whether you are actually married. It could be a misunderstanding, manipulation, or a lot of other things. If you aren't married to the person, don't know the person, and/or did not intend to file jointly, you should paper file your own, accurate tax return and include an explanation as to what happened (to the best of your knowledge.) If you are married to the person and intended to file jointly, verify the return is accurate and amend (Note 1) it if it isn't.
For 3, you will have to deal with the preparer. I can't really tell you what to do, since it depends on if it's a mistake, a misunderstanding, or fraud. Your action will depend on how long you've dealt with them and the level of trust you have. You might have to deal with the preparer, their boss, the corporation or a lawyer. I will say that one thing I see, not often, but also not too rarely, is people who see a preparer and are unsatisfied with the results, so they walk out with or without their paperwork. The preparer then files the return and has their fees withheld, so they get paid for the work they did. This is ILLEGAL! If they don't have a signed 8879 (or equivalent) from you, they CANNOT file the return. I can't tell you what exactly to do, but I can tell you not to accept this and raise whatever hell you need to get it fixed. At the very least report them to the IRS.

SSN has already been claimed as a dependent on another tax return: If it's your child that's already been claimed, read the section: Someone Claimed my Child. If it's you or your spouse (primary or secondary SSN) you have some sleuthing to do. If you recently moved out from your parents (or other person) who may have been supporting you, contact them and see if they did it and work out what the proper thing to do was. Based on that, either fix your return to identify that you were claimed, or paper file your tax return as is (in this case the other party should amend (Note 1) their return to remove you as a dependent - but that's their problem, not yours.) If you have no idea who did it (or you know, and you know it's fraudulent) see the last part of this section on Tax ID theft.

Records say Form 8862 required: If you improperly claimed Earned Income Credit (EIC) in the past, the IRS requires you to file Form 8862 to provide additional information before allowing you to claim EIC. Simply fill out the form in the software and resend the return.

Records indicate person deceased: This can be bad...real bad...especially if the indicated person is still alive. How to fix things when the IRS and Social Security Administration have decided you're dead is VERY hard, and way beyond the scope of this book. In either case, whether the person is actually dead or not is irrelevant to filing this tax return. You will need to send the return in on paper.

F???-502, Employer Identification Number is incorrect: This means the Employer Identification Number (EIN) for the specified form is incorrect. The ??? will have the form type, either W2, W2G, 1099R or 2439. Simply find the specified form (or forms) and verify that the EIN you entered matches the form. Correct any errors and resend. Some forms, W-2's in particular, can have the number in a weird place (Boeing is one I see all the time). Make sure you don't use the State EIN for the federal.

ID theft PIN not entered or incorrect: If your tax identity was stolen or at risk, the IRS may issue an ID theft PIN to ensure that you are protected from future fraud. You should know this happened and have a letter with the PIN. If you have it, add it to the return and resend. If you don't...use the IRS "Get an IP PIN" tool at irs.gov to recover it. If that doesn't work, call (800) 908-4490 between 7am and 7pm, Monday through Friday.

Tax ID Theft: If your return was rejected because you, your spouse or children were filed as taxpayers or dependents on a return you don't know about, or that you know was fraudulent, that's tax ID theft. There's a bit of a line between outright tax ID theft (stranger or someone you know steals your information and uses it to claim a refund) and dependency disputes (ex spouse claims child you were entitled to). ID theft requires a police report and ID theft affidavit (Form 14039). Disputes just require paper filing an accurate return with documentation submitted or available proving your claim. If it's ID theft, go to IRS.gov and search for "ID theft" and follow their instructions (during tax season there is often a very prominent link posted right on the IRS front page about ID theft, so you can click it without searching.) The basic steps will involve filing a police report, filling out Form 14039 (ID theft affidavit), and sending your tax return in with the affidavit and copies of identification cards. There are also other steps to take for future protection, including getting an ID theft PIN, checking credit reports and reporting to the FTC. Your refund will be significantly delayed.

Note 1: Amending a tax return means filing form 1040X, where you report the original numbers, the correct numbers, and the difference, and include an explanation for the changes. It has to be mailed in, and takes a LOOOOOOONG time to be processed.

38. I (or my Spouse or Child) am Going to College

This is a HUGE section with lots of possibilities, so I'm going to try to break it down as much as possible. Start reading with the very first part and then stop when you have your situation covered. Make sure that you don't use the same expenses for more than one credit or deduction. That's a serious no-no.

1. Determine who you can claim expenses for:

You can claim education expenses and credits for yourself and your spouse if you are MFJ. You can also claim them for someone who you claim as a dependent on your tax return. You can claim the credits for a dependent even if they pay the expenses themselves, but you should revisit dependency in the appropriate sections to make sure you can still claim them. Age and support start becoming issues at this point. In addition, student loans taken out by your dependent that they are obligated to repay count as funds available for their own support, so these can knock you out of dependency through non-support.

2. Gather your information and documents:

The school is going to (or should) send you a Form 1098T that details what they think you paid. This form is useful for a lot of things, but don't rely on it solely to determine what you paid. Verify that it matches what you think you paid, and you should get an account transcript from the school showing what was charged, what was paid, and how it was paid. The one nice thing about the 1098T is that it will tell you if you were more than half-time, if you were a graduate student, and it has the data needed to fill out your tax forms. Using the 1098T, your payment receipts and other documentation, get the following information for the student:
    a. Total tuition charged
    b. Total course-required books and fees—these have to be specifically required as a condition of enrollment in the college or a course. They can't be general study supplies, athletic fees and other things unless they are required by the school as a condition of attendance.
    c. Total charges for room and board
    d. Total amount of scholarships and grants
    e. Status of at least half-time (from 1098T)
    f. Year of college as determined by the school (freshman, sophomore, junior, senior or graduate as of the beginning of the tax year)
    g. Whether the student has ever been convicted of a felony drug offense
    h. Total amount of U.S. Savings Bond interest used to pay for college
    i. Total amount of money from tax advantaged tuition plans, such as Coverdell Educational Savings Accounts, Qualified Tuition Plans, Prepaid College Plans, 529 plans or other state-sponsored plans used for education.

You'll notice we don't talk about student loans because the expenses are considered paid even if you use student loans or a credit card.

3. Determine if college expenses exceed scholarships and tax advantaged plan sources:

Take the total of a and b from above (your college expenses), and compare it to the total of d, h and i (your tax advantaged funding sources and scholarships). If your expenses exceed your tax advantaged funding sources and scholarships, you have the potential for a credit or deduction. If they do not, then you have a problem. You need to make sure you can take advantage of the tax advantages of the funding sources, and determine if you have taxable income from scholarships. This will be discussed in later steps.

4. See if you can use the American Opportunity Credit (AOC):

This is the best credit available because you get up to $2,500 of credit, with $1,000 refundable (you get it even after your tax is reduced to zero) on only $4,000 of expenses. Generally, you should always shoot for this one. I'm going to refer to the letters from 2, above, to move things along when available. This credit is the one that will come up for a student attending a standard two- or four-year college with the intention of getting a degree or other certificate. You get it for the first four years of education (freshman, sophomore, junior, senior, as determined by the college, even if it takes you more than four years to progress through them). However, each student gets a maximum of 4 tax years worth of AOC in their life (even if it's their parents taking the credit). For the normal student, they will have 4 years of schooling spanning 5 tax years. Most students begin college in Fall of the same year they graduate high school; half of their college senior year will be in the spring of their fourth year—the fifth tax year of college. This means that you can take the AOC for any four of those five years. If the student takes 6 years to graduate, you still get any four of those six years. Many tax professionals will spend a lot of time trying to anticipate the best four years to take. My recommendation is to take it the first four years the credit is available—you never know what's going to happen in the future. The only caveat is that if you only have a couple hundred dollars of expenses in the first year, you might want to wait to start taking the credit the following tax year. Otherwise, you won't get much out of the AOC and one of your 4 years is wasted.

One other point: you can take as many AOCs as you have students on your tax return. If you, your wife and your three children all qualify, you can get FIVE separate AOCs. Here are the rules once you've figured out that the year qualifies:

 a. If college expenses determined in 3 (above) do not exceed scholarships and tax advantaged sources, you get nothing.

 b. If the answer to 2e is not at least half-time, you cannot get AOC.

 c. If the student has been convicted of a felony drug offense, you don't get AOC.

 d. The student has to be attending an eligible school with the intention of getting a degree or other recognized educational credential, which includes virtually every accredited postsecondary (post high school) institution. This can even include colleges outside the U.S. if they are eligible to participate in the U.S. Federal Student Aid program. The college can tell you if they are eligible.

     e. You cannot be filing MFS.

     f. If your AGI exceeds $180,000 (MFJ) or $90,000 (HH or Single) you cannot get AOC.

     g. If your AGI exceeds $160,000 (MFJ) or $80,000 (HH or Single) your credit will be limited. In this case, you should figure out the AOC, the Lifetime Learning Credit (LLC, next) and the Tuition and Fees Deduction (after LLC) to see which gets you the most money. If it is very close, save the AOC for a later year, since you only get 4 years of AOC, unless this is your final year as an undergraduate.

     h. Calculate your expenses for Form 8863. This number will be a + b - d - h - i (tuition plus course-related fees, minus scholarships, grants and tax advantaged funding sources). This is the number you will use when filling out Form 8863 or entering data in your software program (though software may ask for a, b, d, h and i through separate questions).

5. If you don't get AOC, see if you can get the Lifetime Learning Credit (LLC):

The LLC is a nice credit, but not as lucrative as the AOC. You get 20% of eligible expenses, up to $2,000 of credit. The expenses are more limited, but the rules for qualifying are less restrictive. This is the credit you would use if the student had already used 4 years of AOC, wasn't attending half-time, wasn't in a degree or credential program, was a graduate student, or already has a four year degree. Another major difference is that while you can get an AOC for as many students as appear on the tax return, you can get a maximum of $2,000 of LLC, per tax return, regardless of how many students are on the tax return. Here's how we work the LLC:

     a. If college expenses determined in 3 (above) do not exceed scholarships and tax advantaged sources, you get nothing.

     b. If the answer to 2e is not at least half-time, you can still get LLC.

     c. If the student has been convicted of a felony drug offense, you don't get LLC.

     d. The student has to be attending an eligible school with or without the intention of getting a degree or credential, which includes virtually every accredited postsecondary (post high school) institution. This can even include colleges outside the U.S. if they are eligible to participate in the U.S. Federal Student Aid program. The college can tell you if they are eligible. This includes truck driving school, welding school and other non-degree attaining schools.

     e. You cannot be filing MFS.

     f. If your AGI exceeds $131,000 (MFJ) or $65,000 (HH or Single) you cannot get LLC.

     g. If your AGI exceeds $111,000 (MFJ) or $55,000 (HH or Single) your credit will be limited, you should check to see if the Tuition and Fees deduction will provide you with more benefit.

h. Calculate your expenses for Form 8863. This number will be a - d - h - i (tuition without course-related fees, minus scholarships, grants and tax advantaged funding sources). This is the number you will use when filling out Form 8863 or entering data in your software program (though software may ask for a, d, h and i through separate questions).

6. If you don't get AOC or LLC, see if the Tuition and Fees Deduction will benefit you:

The tuition and fees deduction is the least beneficial of the education benefits; you get a deduction from income instead of a tax credit. It is an "above the line" deduction, which means it improves your taxes whether you itemize or not, and may reduce your AGI for figuring other limitations. The expenses that you can deduct for this deduction are virtually the same as the AOC, except that books and course-related fees are only included if they MUST be paid directly to the education institution as a condition of enrollment. One big caveat on all this education stuff is that the AOC and the LLC have no effect on state taxes. This deduction often does, so when determining whether this is better than the LLC or AOC, make sure to check your state taxes as well. Here are the details:

a. If college expenses determined in 3 (above) do not exceed scholarships and tax advantaged sources, you get nothing.

b. If the answer to 2e is not at least half-time, you can still get this deduction.

c. If the student has been convicted of a felony drug offense, you still get this deduction.

d. The student has to be attending an eligible school with or without the intention of getting a degree or credential, which includes virtually every accredited postsecondary (post high school) institution. This can even include colleges outside the U.S. if they are eligible to participate in the U.S. Federal Student Aid program. The college can tell you if they are eligible. This includes truck driving school, welding school and other non-degree attaining schools.

e. You cannot be filing MFS.

f. If your AGI exceeds $160,000 (MFJ) or $80,000 (HH or Single) you cannot get this deduction.

g. You can deduct a maximum of $4,000 if your income is less than $130,000 (MFJ) or $65,000 (Single or HH). If your income is between $130,000 and $160,000 (MFJ) or between $65,000 and $80,000 (HH or Single) you can deduct $2,000. This is per tax return, not per person.

h. Calculate your expenses for Form 8917. This number will be a + b (if required to be paid to the institution as discussed above) - d - h - i (tuition with required course-related fees minus scholarships, grants and tax advantaged funding sources). This is the number you will use when filling out Form 8917 or entering data in your software program (though software may ask for a, b, d, h and i through separate questions).

7. If you have QTPs, ESAs, 529s, or other tax advantaged education savings, account for them:

Bottom line, do not withdraw more from these accounts than your educational expenses. These are tuition, fees, and room and board (does not have to be paid through the college, but cannot exceed what the college would have charged). Make sure your student is enrolled at least half-time. Lastly, make sure you don't include expenses paid with these funds when calculating any of the credits or deductions above.

8. If you use Savings Bond proceeds to pay for education, figure out what's tax free:

When you cash in U.S. Savings Bonds, you normally pay federal tax on the interest (difference between what you paid for the bond and how much they pay you when cashing in), but no state tax. When you use it for education, however, you can exclude the interest from income. That said, it's actually one of the more complicated subjects with regard to education expenses, because the exclusion is limited by how much cash you get, and not just by the interest you received. I would suggest talking to a tax professional before cashing in bonds for education, but here are a few simple tips to keep you out of trouble:
    a. Make sure your AGI is below $116,300 (MFJ) or $77,550 (Single or HH) before you cash in savings bonds for education. Above this income your deduction starts phasing out (Completely gone at $146,300 (MFJ) and $92,550 (S/HH.)
    b. Make sure that you don't cash in more in bonds (not just interest) than the tuition you have to pay, less any other scholarships or tax advantaged education savings you are using. Room and board does not count.
    If you follow these rules, you should be safe.

9. If you get more in scholarships and grants than tuition, prepare to pay taxes on it:

Did that scare you? Good. Now we can determine if you need to pay taxes on it, but, before that, let me say one thing. If you can find a way to get scholarships and grants that exceed the cost of your tuition, you win. Seriously. You will have to pay taxes on the excess (maybe), but it's free money! Pay the taxes and be happy! First, take the amount from 2d (scholarships and grants) and subtract a and b from it. If the number is positive, it's taxable, and you add it to line 7 of Form 1040 (the same line as your wages from your W-2s). If it's negative, you do not need to include anything as income.

10. VA benefits. If you use VA benefits (or GI Bill) to pay for school, none of the benefits are taxable, including any housing allowances you get. However, you can't get deductions or credits for expenses paid by the VA or with VA money.

The benefits can interact weirdly with the credits and deductions, so I would check with an expert before filing.

Military: See 10 above about GI Bill and VA benefits. Also, if you use Tuition Assistance (TA) to pay for schooling, you cannot use that expense for a deduction or credit. Think of TA, VA benefits and GI Bill as scholarships except that they won't be taxable income if they exceed expenses. The 1098-T you get from many schools will not note the TA or GI Bill payments, making it look like you have valid expenses. Don't fall for this. The IRS will eventually catch on and it can get ugly. Use the calculations I talked about, including military education benefits as if they were scholarships and you will be okay.

39. I Have to Pay Things for my Job

Let's start by saving the majority of you a whole bunch of trouble. Employee expenses are a part of itemizing, so if you have just a few expenses and not a lot of other itemizing, you probably can skip this section. In addition, these expenses are subject to a floor of 2% of your AGI; if you have a high income, or few expenses, you can probably skip this section. To be honest, not a lot of people get a big advantage out of these deductions, but some people do VERY well.

Here are some examples of expenses that many people have: mileage expenses for travelling not involving to and from your home to work (commuting is not deductible), travel expenses for travelling away from your home area overnight, expenses for working out of your home office, tools and supplies you need to do your job, safety equipment and uniforms that are not suitable for wear away from work, entertainment expenses for clients, licensing and continuing education, liability insurance, and union dues. There are a ton more, but these are the big ones. If they sound like they apply to you, read on.

I'm going to start with some general rules that apply to the majority of deductions, and then I'm simply going to run down a laundry list of deductible items and discuss how they might apply.

General Rules:

1. In order to deduct job-related expenses, they have to be ordinary and necessary (IRS words). This basically means that they have to be necessary in order for you to accomplish your job under the rules and requirements of your employer. They can't be something you do simply to make the job easier on you. The ordinary part means they have to be an accepted part of your line of work. They can't be some crazy rules or plan set up by you or your employer that don't have a good business purpose.
2. You have to know some things in order to do this right. The only way to get the information you need is from your employer, through your understanding of your employer's reimbursement system. You need to know how the plan works for you to claim and be reimbursed for your expenses:

- If you get no reimbursement, you can itemize the expense. You will need to keep accurate records of your expenses, including receipts. I recommend using a notebook, and a box or envelope. You write the date, description and amount of the expense in the notebook, and throw the receipt in the box or envelope. Use the notebook for preparing your taxes, and save the box/envelope in case you get audited.
- If you report your expenses to your employer, they reimburse you in your paycheck, and they include the reimbursement on your W-2 in box 1 then it is easy to simply deduct your allowed expenses, since you paid taxes on them through your paycheck.

- If your employer reimburses you and does not include them on your W-2 you will need to report BOTH your expenses, AND the amount your employer reimbursed you. You will need to keep accurate records of your expenses, including receipts. I always recommend using a notebook, and a box or envelope. You write the date, description and amount of the expense in the notebook, and throw the receipt in the box or envelope. Use the notebook for preparing your taxes, and save the box/envelope in case you get audited.

If you are entitled to be reimbursed, but don't submit the paperwork, causing you not to be reimbursed, you cannot deduct the expense.

3. As far as including on your tax return, your software or preparer will help you get things in the right place. Beware of relying on the software questions to keep you from messing up—you have to read all the fine print and pop-ups to stay out of trouble. If you prepare your return yourself, you can include the expenses directly on Schedule A if all of the following apply:

- The expenses are not reimbursed outside of your W-2,
- You don't claim travel, vehicle, meal or entertainment expenses, and
- You aren't claiming military reservist, fee-based government employee, performance artist or impairment-related expenses.

Otherwise, you have to use Form 2106.

Deductible Expenses:

1. Vehicle expenses: There is a LOT to this, so I'm going to simplify it a bit. If your situation is more complicated than this, seek professional help. This part of the discussion is about travelling during your work day. If the vehicle expense is for overnight travel, we will discuss that later. As a general rule, you can deduct mileage between work locations and between jobs, but not to or from your home. For example, if you go to the main office of your job, you cannot deduct the mileage to get there. You can deduct mileage from the main office to and between the various work locations you go to. You cannot deduct the mileage to go home, even if you don't go back to the main office before going home. If you have two or more jobs, you can deduct the mileage between the two or more jobs, but not to or from your home (regardless of which job you finish at).

2. Uniforms. Sigh. This is the one no one gets right. You can deduct uniforms that are not appropriate for wear outside of work. This doesn't mean what YOU would wear, but what a normal person would wear.

Coveralls	Not deductible
Suits	Not deductible
Logo polo shirts	Not deductible
Scrubs	Deductible
Military uniforms*	Mostly not deductible
Military insignia**	Deductible if it exceeds your reimbursement
Safety wear	Deductible

* Usually not deductible because you can wear them away from work and you get reimbursed

** Reservist's uniforms are usually deductible

*** Such as steel-toe boots, gloves and fire-retardant clothing

3. Safety equipment, such as goggles, face shield, gloves and other similar equipment, is deductible.

4. Tools that you need for your job and that are not provided by your employer are generally deductible. If your employer provides tools, but you purchase better ones, they are not deductible. Big, expensive tools that last more than a year must be depreciated—get help if this applies. Most small hand tools, small power tools and such are deductible immediately. Big tools, like table saws, are usually depreciated. Consumables like paint brushes, rollers and razor blades are deducted immediately.

5. Insurance that you are required to have, such as errors and omissions insurance or other liability insurance, is deductible. Car insurance is not deductible unless you have a SPECIFIC rider that is required in order to use your car for business.

6. Professional accreditation fees other than your initial licensing fees, such as your law license, CPA license or nursing license, are deductible.

7. Professional publications or books to maintain your skill and knowledge are deductible, as well as membership dues for professional organizations.

8. Union dues are deductible.

9. Phone charges for a second home phone line are deductible (never try to deduct your primary home phone line). Cell phones are troublesome, though you are allowed to deduct the portion that is used for business. Better to have a second, dedicated work cell phone—that would be deductible.

10. If you maintain an office in your home for performing work duties, and the ONLY thing you do there is employment-related work AND you regularly use it for that, you might be able to deduct an office in home. You also have to be using it because your employer wants you to work from home, not just because you do. This gets complicated, so you may want to seek assistance. You can deduct a percentage of the household bills based on the square footage of the office, ratioed to the square footage of your home. You would add up rent, utilities and maintenance, and multiply it by the office square footage, and divide by the house square footage. If you own your home you can also take depreciation of the home, but you should DEFINETELY seek professional help due to complex issues that arise affecting the future of your home. The IRS tried to "simplify" this by allowing you to take $5 times the square footage of your office, up to $1,500. Most professionals want to run the numbers both ways to ensure you get the best deal.

11. Separate from an office in home, if you have utilities that are SPECIFIC to your job, such as a dedicated high-speed Local Area Network line, you can deduct this expense.

12. Medical examinations, inoculations or other procedures required for your line of work are deductible.

13. Legal fees required for your line of work or needed to collect taxable compensation are deductible.

14. Overnight travel outside of the area you normally work is deductible. You should try to ensure that the trips you take are 100% for business, and that ensures that they are 100% deductible. You can deduct airfare, lodging (you must claim actual expenses for lodging), meals (you'll only get 50% of the meals, but you can use a standard meal rate provided by the government instead of tracking the actual expense), tips, car rental, taxis, trains, busses, and other normal travel expenses.
15. Education: You can deduct work-related education so long as it maintains your skills for your current line of work. You cannot deduct education expenses that qualify you for a new line of work. The education must either be required by law, or required by your employer to maintain your current job status or position, or improve your skills in your current position. It CANNOT qualify you for a new career or more senior position. There are some grey areas in this, and recent court cases have loosened up what qualifies. If you are unsure, see a tax specialist. If it qualifies you for a new career, it may qualify for the Lifetime Learning Credit or other deduction. The education also cannot be that required to meet the minimum standards for your job, such as taking the bar exam to be a lawyer. Deductible expenses are tuition, fees, books, transportation, and other similar items. You can take travel TO education, if it is necessary for your job, but not travel AS education (travel agents be aware of this!) A foreign language interpreter can deduct travel to a school to improve language skills, but not travel to the country that speaks the language just to get better at it.

Military: Most military members are fully reimbursed for their expenses so generally your only deduction will be for professional publications if you pay for them. Two exceptions are the Boomer Deduction (not covered in this book - google it) and reservists whose drill location is more than 100 miles from their home (details below):

National Guard or Reserves:

Members of the National Guard or Reserves, who travel more than 100 miles from home to their drilling or service location can deduct these travel expenses directly on Form 1040 rather than as an itemized deduction. This is a BIG difference that is great for the tax return! They are still accounted for on the same form as other job expenses (Form 2106 in their own column) but they carry directly to the 1040, reducing your AGI and improving many aspects of your tax return.

Deductible expenses are mileage, tolls, parking, ferry travel, lodging (must be actual expense and cannot exceed the federal per diem rate), meals and incidental expenses (can take the standard federal per diem amount for the area rather than keeping records).

You should have a mileage log for this and save receipts and records that prove your expenses and document the days you were required to travel.

Many states have benefits similar to this. Some states do not tax reserve pay and in this case, you cannot deduct these expenses on those states (or must add them back for the state).

Not discussed: Boomer Deduction, performing artist expenses, impairment-related expenses or fee-based government official expenses. No main place of business and travel outside your metro area during the workday. Actual vehicle expenses.

40. I Tele-Commute

Let's start with the simple stuff. If you work mostly at a place of work, and only occasionally tele-commute, you don't really qualify for this section and should read the previous section.

This section applies to the person who does the majority of their work out of their home (spends more time working from home than at an office). This would also apply if a person works at a lot of different locations, and does most of their planning, organizing, and office work out of their home. It also assumes that you are doing this for the convenience of your employer. In other words, they asked or told you to work from home, or asked for volunteers to work from home. It would not apply if you are working from home because it was easier for you, or you are unable to work away from home.

This section is basically a rehash of the last section, but tailored to someone working from home, so you don't need to read the previous section on paying for things for your job (employee expenses). They go together with tele-commuting so will all be covered here.

Let's start by saving the majority of you a whole bunch of trouble. Employee expenses are a part of itemizing, so if you have just a few expenses and not a lot of other itemizing, you probably can skip this section. In addition, these expenses are subject to a floor of 2% of your AGI; if you have a high income, or few expenses, you can probably skip this section. To be honest, not a lot of people get a big advantage out of these deductions, but some people do VERY well.

Here are some examples of expenses that many people have: mileage expenses for travelling not involving to and from your home to work (commuting is not deductible), travel expenses for travelling away from your home area overnight, expenses for working out of your home office, tools and supplies you need to do your job, safety equipment and uniforms that are not suitable for wear away from work, entertainment expenses for clients, licensing and continuing education, liability insurance, and union dues. There are a ton more, but these are the big ones. If they sound like they apply to you, read on.

I'm going to start with some general rules that apply to the majority of deductions, and then I'm simply going to run down a laundry list of deductible items and discuss how they might apply.

General Rules:

1. In order to deduct job-related expenses, they have to be ordinary and necessary (IRS words). This basically means that they have to be necessary in order for you to accomplish your job under the rules and requirements of your employer (hence the rules on convenience of the employer discussed earlier). They can't be

something you do simply to make the job easier on you. The ordinary part means they have to be an accepted part of your line of work. They can't be some crazy rules or plan set up by you or your employer that don't have a good business purpose.

2. You have to know some things in order to do this right. The only way to get the information you need is from your employer, through your understanding of your employer's reimbursement system. You need to know how the plan works for you to claim and be reimbursed for your expenses:

- If you get no reimbursement, you can itemize the expense. You will need to keep accurate records of your expenses, including receipts. I recommend using a notebook, and a box or envelope. You write the date, description and amount of the expense in the notebook, and throw the receipt in the box or envelope. Use the notebook for preparing your taxes, and save the box/envelope in case you get audited.
- If you report your expenses to your employer, they reimburse you in your paycheck, and they include the reimbursement on your W-2 in box 1, then it is easy to simply deduct your allowed expenses, since you paid taxes on them through your paycheck.
- If your employer reimburses you and does not include them on your W-2, you will need to report BOTH your expenses AND the amount your employer reimbursed you. You will need to keep accurate records of your expenses, including receipts. I always recommend using a notebook, and a box or envelope. You write the date, description and amount of the expense in the notebook, and throw the receipt in the box or envelope. Use the notebook for preparing your taxes, and save the box/envelope in case you get audited.

If you are entitled to be reimbursed, but don't submit the paperwork and are therefore not reimbursed, you cannot deduct the expense.

3. As far as including on your tax return, your software or preparer will help you get things in the right place. Beware of relying on the software questions to keep you from messing up—you have to read all the fine print and pop-ups to stay out of trouble. If you prepare your return yourself, you can include the expenses directly on Schedule A if all of the following apply:

- The expenses are not reimbursed outside of your W-2,
- You don't claim travel, vehicle, meal or entertainment expenses, and
- You aren't claiming military reservist, fee-based government employee, performance artist or impairment-related expenses.

Otherwise, you have to use Form 2106.

Deductible Expenses:

1. Vehicle expenses: There is a LOT to this, so I'm going to simplify it a bit. If your situation is more complicated than this, seek professional help. This part of the discussion is about travelling during your work day. If the vehicle expense is for overnight travel, we will discuss that later. As a general rule, you can deduct

mileage between work locations and between jobs, but not to or from your home. For example, if you go to the main office of your job, you cannot deduct the mileage to get there. You can deduct mileage from the main office to and between the various work locations you go to. You cannot deduct the mileage to go home, even if you don't go back to the main office before going home. If you have two or more jobs, you can deduct the mileage between the two or more jobs, but not to or from your home (regardless of which job you finish at). For a tele-commuter, you **would** generally deduct any mileage between your house and your main work office if you had an office in home and any mileage from your work office to work locations, or from your home to temporary work locations would generally be deductible.

2. Uniforms. Sigh. This is the one no one gets right. You can deduct uniforms that are not appropriate for wear outside of work. This doesn't mean what YOU would wear, but what a normal person would wear.

Coveralls	Not deductible
Suits	Not deductible
Logo polo shirts	Not deductible
Scrubs	Deductible
Military uniforms*	Mostly not deductible
Military insignia**	Deductible if it exceeds your reimbursement
Safety wear	Deductible

* Usually not deductible because you can wear them away from work and you get reimbursed
** Reservist's uniforms are usually deductible
*** Such as steel-toe boots, gloves and fire-retardant clothing

3. Safety equipment, such as goggles, face shield, gloves and other similar equipment, is deductible.

4. Tools that you need for your job and that are not provided by your employer are generally deductible. If your employer provides tools, but you purchase better ones, they are not deductible. Big, expensive tools that last more than a year must be depreciated—get help if this applies. Most small hand tools, small power tools and such are deductible immediately. Big tools, like table saws, are usually depreciated. Consumables like paint brushes, rollers and razor blades are deducted immediately. The computer in your home office that is exclusively for business use (have a separate one for personal use) can be depreciated, along with any furniture or other equipment.

5. Insurance that you are required to have, such as errors and omissions insurance or other liability insurance, is deductible. Car insurance is not deductible unless you have a SPECIFIC rider that is required in order to use your car for business.

6. Professional accreditation fees other than your initial licensing fees, such as your law license, CPA license or nursing license, are deductible.

7. Professional publications or books to maintain your skill and knowledge are deductible, as well as membership dues for professional organizations.

8. Union dues are deductible.

9. Phone charges for a second home phone line are deductible (never try to deduct your primary home phone line). Cell phones are troublesome, though you are allowed to deduct the portion that is used for business. Better to have a second, dedicated work cell phone—that would be deductible.

10. If you maintain an office in your home for performing work duties, and the ONLY thing you do there is employment-related work AND you regularly use it for that, you might be able to deduct an office in home (have an area that is exclusively business—please). This gets complicated, so you may want to seek assistance. You can deduct a percentage of the household bills based on the square footage of the office, ratioed to the square footage of your home. You would add up rent, utilities and maintenance, and multiply it by the office square footage, and divide by the house square footage. If you own your home you can also take depreciation of the home, but you should DEFINETELY seek professional help due to complex issues that arise affecting the future of your home. The IRS tried to "simplify" this by allowing you to take $5 times the square footage of your office, up to $1,500. Most professionals want to run the numbers both ways to ensure you get the best deal. Your software should work this out for you, or you can find a worksheet on the Internet (the IRS has one) that will help you with the numbers.

11. Separate from an office in home, if you have utilities that are SPECIFIC to your job, such as a dedicated high-speed Local Area Network line, you can deduct this expense.

12. Medical examinations, inoculations or other procedures required for your line of work are deductible.

13. Legal fees required for your line of work or needed to collect taxable compensation are deductible.

14. Overnight travel outside of the area you normally work is deductible. You should try to ensure that the trips you take are 100% for business, and that ensures that they are 100% deductible. You can deduct airfare, lodging (you must claim actual expenses for lodging), meals (you'll only get 50% of the meals, but you can use a standard meal rate provided by the government instead of tracking the actual expense), tips, car rental, taxis, trains, busses, and other normal travel expenses.

15. Education: You can deduct work-related education so long as it maintains your skills for your current line of work. You cannot deduct education expenses that qualify you for a new line of work. The education must either be required by law, or required by your employer to maintain your current job status or position, or improve your skills in your current position. It CANNOT qualify you for a new career or more senior position. There are some grey areas in this, and recent court cases have loosened up what qualifies. If you are unsure, see a tax specialist. If it qualifies you for a new career, it may qualify for the Lifetime Learning Credit or other deduction. The education also cannot be that required to meet the minimum standards for your job, such as taking the bar exam to be a lawyer. Deductible expenses are tuition, fees, books, transportation, and other similar items. You can take travel TO education, if it is necessary for your job, but not travel AS education (travel agents be aware of this!). A foreign language interpreter can

deduct travel to a school to improve language skills, but not travel to the country that speaks the language just to get better at it.

Military: Most military members are fully reimbursed for their expenses and also rarely tele-commute, so generally your only deduction will be for professional publications if you pay for them. Two exceptions are the Boomer Deduction (not covered in this book—google it) and reservists whose drill location is more than 100 miles from their home (details in previous section).

41. I Work Overseas

This is not really a fully instructional section. It really is a "get a tax professional" section and a "don't listen to the too good to be true stories from your friends (or tax pro or employer)" section.

Essentially, there are a lot of ways in which the tax system is set up to avoid you paying taxes on your income to both the United States and a foreign country. The U.S. is unique in that it is one of the only countries that taxes **worldwide income**, regardless of source. Most other countries only tax income from sources within said country. This necessitates systems to avoid double taxation. The methods used to prevent double taxation depend on whether your employer is U.S. or foreign, what country you are in, how long you are there, whether you are a bona fide resident of the foreign country (not the easiest of questions), tax treaties in effect between us and them, and who's social security system is responsible for you. There are TONS of other factors, but these are the big ones.

Point is, get professional help for this, from someone who specializes in foreign taxes.

That said, many people, including your employer, co-workers, and overly aggressive tax professionals, will tout not necessarily true things about working tax-free in a foreign country. The gist is that if you work overseas for over a year, you don't pay U.S. taxes. This is true, with a BUNCH of caveats. The biggest of which is that you need stronger ties to the foreign country than to the U.S. If you go overseas on a 1-year contract (these are often sold as tax-free contracts) you probably don't qualify, especially if you left behind a spouse, kids and/or home. Many people have been taking advantage of this and not getting caught, but the IRS is cracking down. In addition, it has a maximum to be excluded, and the remaining part is taxed at the rate it would have been if the other income is excluded.

There are a myriad of complexities to this! Get professional help!

One piece of advice I give in ALL these situations is to try to withhold from your taxes as if you were working in the United States. Worst case you get a huge refund.

Military: This pretty much doesn't apply to you, no matter how much time you spend overseas—though it might apply to your working spouse.

42. I Lost my Job

That sucks. I'm sorry to hear that you lost your job. This loss brings up a lot of tax issues, many of which will seem like adding insult to injury. For example, almost any money you get to help you get through the unemployment period, like, say, unemployment compensation, will be taxable. I'm going to go over several things, but I want to say, loudly and emphatically, DON'T TOUCH YOUR PENSION PLAN! Accessing your pension plan should be an absolute last resort. Taking money out of your 401k (I'm going to say 401k to cover all the various retirement accounts that follow the standard rules for tax advantaged plans) should be done only if it's the difference between eating and not eating, keeping the lights on, or saving your mortgage (and sometimes not even then). We'll talk about what to do with the 401k that doesn't involve taking it out, but trust me, you don't want to just liquidate it. This also applies to personal retirement accounts, such as Individual Retirement Accounts.

The first thing to know is that almost any money you get is going to be taxable, within reasonable limits. This includes disability, third-party sick pay, severance, unemployment compensation or any other lump sum or periodic payments. Generally you'll get a W-2, a 1099R or other formal tax form in January or February of the following year. This is a perfect sign that they belong on your tax return. An example I give is Social Security: even Social Security Disability is taxable. Supplemental Security Income (SSI) is from the same agency, but is not taxable. The sure way of knowing the difference is the receipt of the 1099SSA. To keep the nit-pickers at bay, when I say taxable, it doesn't necessarily mean you'll pay taxes on it, but you'll report it on your tax return and calculate the potential taxability. You can't absolutely rely on getting these forms as a way of knowing what to report, mainly because they may not make it to you if you have to move or they get the wrong address. The best way to be sure is to communicate with the agencies giving you money, and ensure you know what forms to expect. You should also have them withhold taxes if possible. They often will under-withhold, so you need to be prepared for a tax bill. Life can really suck when you've been scraping by for a year, depleting your savings, and then you get a big tax bill at the end of the year. Preparation is key to staying ahead of this. You'll need to calculate your income from when you had a job, other sources of income while unemployed, and estimate your tax liability to ensure you have enough withheld. Otherwise, you need to set enough aside for Uncle Sam and his bastard step-children from the state you live in. Professional help can be useful.

While you're unemployed, job searching expenses are potentially deductible as an itemized deduction. If you didn't itemize before losing your job, you probably won't start now. If you already itemize, these can be a bit of help. You can deduct travel, placement services, resume writing, and fees for job search training.

If you take money out of CDs, the early withdrawal penalties are deductible against the interest earned. I'm not talking about retirement accounts here, just savings accounts that have a specified term for which you are supposed to keep them.

If you have to relocate for a job, read the next section on moving for a job.

For your 401k, you will need to do something with it, though you are sometimes allowed to leave it with your former employer. I'm not a financial advisor, but my non-professional suggestion is to roll it over to an Individual Retirement Account with a financial services company. Seek professional assistance from a licensed financial advisor, or if you are good at handling your investments, do it yourself, but DON'T HAVE THEM SEND THE MONEY TO YOU! Do a trustee to trustee transfer, where you tell the destination financial institution to go get the money from your old employer. You don't have to do it this way, but trust me, this is the safe and easy way to do it.

If you absolutely have to take money out of your 401k or Individual Retirement Accounts (IRAs), take the absolute minimum out that you need to SURVIVE. Make sure they withhold the maximum (generally 20%) and realize that this probably won't be enough. You will probably pay a 10% penalty, plus your regular tax rate (probably AT LEAST another 15%). If you have a Roth IRA, you can look into taking some out of there first. You can actually take the amount you put into a Roth IRA out tax-free, but I would seek advice from both your tax professional, and your financial professional before doing this.

Military: See the next section for moving information.

If you retired, see the section titled: I Retired from the Military.

The discussion above about 401k's applies to your Thrift Savings Plan.

If you were kicked out and they recouped bonuses or pay, you may have a Claim of Right repayment deduction or credit. If you are making periodic payments on these, and you have control and can afford it, it is to your advantage to ensure that the total payments for a year exceed $3000. If the payment is less than or equal to $3000, your only option is to take it as an Itemized Deduction subject to a 2% of income limitation. In this case, if you don't itemize, you're out of luck. If it's over $3000 you can deduct it (like the <$3000) or take a refundable credit equal to the taxes you originally paid on it. This is quite complex, but can be lucrative. You basically redo the tax return for the year you received the money, and see what the difference is. This is the credit you get, dollar for dollar, on the current year's tax return.

43. I Had to Move

Moving expenses should be simple, but the IRS insists on making them complicated. I'll try to simplify the rules you need to qualify, go over the usual expenses, and then talk about reimbursement and other complicated crap.

Here are the rules to see if your move qualifies:

You have to be moving to get or maintain a job. You don't actually have to have a job in the place you move to, but if not, you need to get one within a year. If you start a new job in a new place, you need to move yourself and your family within a year. If you move within a year but your family doesn't, you can deduct your moving expenses, but not theirs. If you have a good reason for not moving within a year, such as you wait to move your family for 18 months so your kids can finish school, that's okay, and you can deduct the expenses. The idea of all these rules is that you really have to be moving for job reasons, and not other reasons.

You need to be moving a decent distance. Just moving from house to house to lower your commute is not enough. Simple test, take your old commute from home to work and add 50 miles to it. If your new job is at least this distance from your old house, you're good. It's not really a tough test to meet. If you are military moving on Permanent Change of Station orders, you don't need to meet this test.

There's one more test that's complicated, but rarely comes into play. The gist of it is that you have to be moving near your new place of work. This is generally a no brainer. You basically can't move from Georgia to Texas when your job is in California. Duh. Ask a professional for help if this doesn't apply to you in an obvious way.

You have to work full-time in your new location for at least 39 of the first 52 weeks after the move. Full-time is that which is typical for your job type. If you are self-employed the requirements are more restrictive—seek professional assistance. If your job is seasonal, you can consider yourself to have worked the full year if you work the normal season in the first 52 weeks, and the "off-season" is less than six months. This most commonly applies to teachers who are good if they work full-time for the normal school schedule for the first 52 weeks. Seasonal tax pros who work 4 out of 12 months can't use that exception. If you lose your new job due to employer's convenience and not for willful misconduct, you don't have to meet the test. Obviously, it's possible to need to file a tax return before you have met these tests. There are a number of ways to handle this. My recommendation, if you're pretty sure you'll be staying at the job for a year, is to take the deduction assuming you'll meet the test (this is allowed). If you end up not meeting the test, amend the tax return to remove the deduction. You can also not take the deduction, and then amend to add it on when you do meet the test.

That's pretty much it for qualifying to deduct expenses.

Here's what you can deduct:

You can deduct only reasonable expenses for moving you, your family and your household goods. You must move by the most direct route and not take side trips or excess vacations. If you have some of your household at a different location, you can deduct the moving expenses for them, but not any more than it would have cost to move them by the direct route from your old home to new home. Make sure to save all receipts.

If you drive you can deduct 19 cents a mile, or actual costs for oil and gas ONLY. In addition to that, you can deduct parking and tolls.

You can deduct lodging, but not meals for you and your family members. You get lodging for the day you have to leave your old house, up to the day you get ANY lodging (including hotel) in the area of your new job. You can't deduct meals. You can deduct plane, rail or train fare for you and your family. You don't have to travel together, but you only get one trip per person. (You can't go back and forth moving kids and keep deducting your travel, but you can deduct each kid's plane ticket.)

You can deduct expenses for moving your household goods, if you pay them. This includes truck rental and supplies, or professional moving services.

You can deduct thirty days of storage either before or after the move (or combination of before and after, but not more than 30 days).

You can deduct the cost of connecting and disconnecting utilities (but not deposits or regular monthly charges).

Here's how to handle reimbursements:

First of all, if your company uses a professional relocation services company to move you, you probably got more reimbursement than you could have deducted. Relocation service companies also tend to cover any additional taxes you might pay for extras they throw in. Refer to the information packet provided by the relocation company to see how it should be handled tax-wise. The good companies will actually provide a sample tax form with numbers filled in for your move.

Outside of that, you need to know how your employer reimbursed you. You probably need to contact them to see what happened, as they can handle reimbursement in a number of ways. Obviously, if they did not reimburse, report all your allowed expenses and you're good to go. If you have a W-2 with a Code P in Box 12, or your employer reimbursed you and you have no code P in Box 12, read on...

Determine from your employer if all reimbursements are in Box 12 with Code P, Box 1 with your wages, or a combination. Reimbursements in Box 12 get reported by you on your return unless they exactly match your expenses. Reimbursements in Box 1 do not get reported (they are included as income and already taxed). Here are specific situations:

- If all reimbursements are in Box 12 with Code P, and they exactly match your expenses, don't report anything about the move.

- If all reimbursements are in Box 12 with Code P, and the allowable expenses are different, report all expenses and reimbursements (the number from Box 12 with Code P)

- If all reimbursements are in Box 1 with your wages, report your allowed expenses, but no reimbursement.

- If there is a combination of reimbursements between Box 1 and Box 12 with Code P, report all allowed expenses and only the reimbursement from Box 12 with Code P.

These are reported on Form 3903

Military: If the military moves you by contracting someone to move your stuff, you generally won't have moving expenses unless you have to pay to move things the military won't move for you (excess weight, hazardous material, second vehicle, etc.) If you do the move and get reimbursed, you will get a second W-2 for the reimbursement, and your moving expenses are deductible as discussed previously. The only difference is that you don't have to meet the distance tests since a PCS (permanent change of station) move automatically qualifies. These rules also apply to the final move you make upon discharge or retirement, even if it occurs after you become a civilian (you get up to a year after discharge to make your final move - this is a DOD rule not a tax rule, but you can see why I would mention it.)

Not discussed: Self employed moves, International Moves.

44. I Sold my Home

There's good news and bad news in this section. The good news is, you probably won't have to pay income taxes on the gain you might have. The bad news is, you probably won't be able to take the loss if you sold the home for less than you paid for it. Also if the property wasn't your main home (say it was a vacation home or you rented it out) you're in the wrong section. You want I Sold my Rental Property or I Sold a Home that Wasn't my Principal Residence section. You'll need to know some information about the house, and one piece of taxese that is almost as important as AGI. The information is the date purchased, price paid, cost of any improvements, date sold, sales price and expenses of sale. The taxese is Basis. Basis is basically your investment in something. It comes up all the time in taxes. Simply put, it's what you put into a property minus what you took out. For a house, it's generally the price you paid, plus any improvements you made to it. Other things that can affect the basis are casualties (such as fire or flooding), payments for easements (a sidewalk or right of way), using the property for business purposes (results in a deduction called depreciation, which we will discuss later), First-Time Homebuyer Credit that hasn't been paid back, the bank wrote off some of your debt, and parts of the property have been sold off (such as part of the land). Some of these will require you to seek professional tax help. There are a lot of other things, but we won't cover most of them because they rarely come up. Maybe in a later edition...

Let's start with the easy scenario...

If you (and your spouse, if filing MFJ) owned your home for at least two of the last five years, lived in it for two of the last five years, never ran a business out of it, never rented it to someone else, and haven't excluded the gain on a principal residence in the two years prior to the sale, you can exclude up to $250,000 of gain ($500,000 if MFJ). In fact, you probably signed a form during closing that attested to these facts. If so, the home sale won't even be reported to the IRS and you don't need to do ANYTHING! If it is reported to the IRS, you'll receive a Form 1099-S and you'll need to report the sale on your tax return (Schedule D). You will need to back out any gain or loss with another line entry that cancels it out. To figure your gain, you take the price you sold it for, minus expenses of sale, minus your basis. Here are the details on calculating the gain and taking the exclusion (assumes you meet all exclusion requirements discussed above):

1. Figure out your BASIS: Using the HUD settlement statement from when you bought the home (the long form with columns that identifies expenses paid by the buyer and paid by the seller), figure out the price you paid for the home. If the seller paid points for you, subtract that amount from the basis. Add (from the HUD) settlement fees, title fees, legal fees, recording fees, survey fees, transfer or tax stamps that you paid. Also add any amounts that the seller owed, but you paid. Now add any amounts you paid to improve the home. This is your BASIS. If any

other weirdness occurred that affected the basis, seek professional help. Also seek help if you received the house as a gift or inheritance.

2. Now figure out the proceeds from the sale. To do this you use the HUD settlement statement from the sale of the home. Take the sales price and subtract any expenses you paid. Make sure to include the agent's commission since that usually makes a big difference. This is the SALE PROCEEDS.

3. Subtract the BASIS from the SALES PROCEEDS and you have the GAIN (if negative this is a LOSS, which you cannot deduct).

4. Report, on Schedule D in the Long Term section, the date purchased, date sold, BASIS, SALES PROCEEDS and GAIN (or zero for gain if it was a loss).

5. On the next line of Schedule D, write "Section 121 Exclusion" in the description, and a negative number in the Gain/Loss column. This negative number is the SMALLER of the GAIN discussed above, and $250,000 if you are not filing MFJ and $500,000 if you are filing MFJ. Essentially, if the gain exceeds your exclusion ($500K MFJ, $250K not MFJ), you pay taxes on the amount that exceeds the exclusion. Otherwise, these lines should zero out.

6. If there is a gain that is not excluded, you'll pay taxes at a lower rate than normal (maximum 23.8), depending on your tax bracket. When you sell the home and get the check from closing, you should run these numbers and see how much of the money to set aside from closing. Basically, saving 23.8% of the amount from line 5 above will cover you safely.

Steps 3 through 6 may be handled by your software, but you want to make sure the results are as I discussed by reviewing the tax return before filing.

What if you don't meet the 2 of 5 year rules and non-business/non-rental use rules? Let's talk some scenarios...

If one of you (you or your spouse) does not meet the 2 out of 5 year USE rule (don't worry about ownership if at least one of you meets it), figure out the exclusion for EACH of you, as if you weren't married, and take the total of that amount as your maximum exclusion for line 5 in the discussion above.

If you rented the property out, check out the next section: I Sold my Rental Property. If you used the property for business, seek out some professional help.

Let's say you have to move out before you have owned and lived in the home for two years, do you get an exclusion? Yes, if you meet certain circumstances:

1. If you move due to a change in employment (you or your spouse), and the new employer is at least 50 miles further from the home than the previous employer was, you can take a reduced exclusion.

2. If you move and the primary purpose was for medical care for you, your spouse, parent (step and in-law included), child, foster child, adopted child, grandchild (including in-laws), sibling (including half-siblings, in-laws and step-siblings), uncle, aunt, niece or cousin, you may qualify for a reduced exclusion.

This has to be to treat an illness, disease or injury and can't just be for improving the well-being of the individual.

3. If you move due to unforeseen circumstances that essentially FORCE you to move, you are eligible for a reduced exclusion. This can't simply be a move that improves your life, it needs to seriously affect your ability to live. Examples include divorce, death, unemployment, casualty to the home, loss of the home, multiple births from the same pregnancy or natural or man-made disasters.

If you qualify for the reduced exclusion, you calculate it this way:

1. Figure out your BASIS: Using the HUD settlement statement from when you bought the home (the long form with columns that identifies expenses paid by the buyer and paid by the seller), figure out the price you paid for the home. If the seller paid points for you, subtract that amount from the basis. Add (from the HUD) settlement fees, title fees, legal fees, recording fees, survey fees, transfer or tax stamps that you paid. Also add any amounts that the seller owed, but you paid. Now add any amounts you paid to improve the home. This is your BASIS. If any other weirdness occurred that affected the basis, seek professional help. Also seek help if you received the house as a gift or inheritance.

2. Now figure out the proceeds from the sale. To do this you use the HUD settlement statement from the sale of the home. Take the sales price and subtract any expenses you paid. Make sure to include the agent's commission since that usually makes a big difference. This is the SALE PROCEEDS.

3. Subtract the BASIS from the SALES PROCEEDS and you have the GAIN (if negative this is a LOSS, which you cannot deduct).

4. Report, on Schedule D in the Long Term section, the date purchased, date sold, BASIS, SALES PROCEEDS and GAIN (or zero for gain if it was a loss).

5. Calculate your reduced exclusion: this is the days you met ALL tests divided by 730, multiplied by $500,000 if you are MFJ and $250,000 if you are not.

6. On the next line of Schedule D, write "Section 121 Exclusion" in the description, and a negative number in the Gain/Loss column. This negative number is the SMALLER of the GAIN discussed on line 4 above and the reduced exclusion from line 5 above. You pay taxes on the amount that exceeds the exclusion. Otherwise, these lines should zero out.

7. If there is a gain that is not excluded, you'll pay taxes at a lower rate than normal (maximum 23.8%), depending on your tax bracket. When you sell the home and get the check from closing, you should run these numbers and see how much of the money to set aside from closing. Basically, saving 23.8% of the amount from line 5 above will cover you safely.

Steps 3 through 7 may be handled by your software, but you want to make sure the results are as I discussed by reviewing the tax return before filing.

Military: If you are on active duty for greater than 90 days and stationed greater than 50 miles from the principle residence in question, you can extend the 5 year test period for the ownership and residence tests for up to 10 years. What this means is that when you buy a home in the military and live in it for at least two years, if they transfer you more than 50 miles away, you can exclude the gain as long as you sell it within 13 years of moving out (or 3 years after you get out of the military, whichever is sooner) and still exclude up to $500,000 of gain if MFJ and $250,000 if you are not. This applies even if you buy and move into a new house! If you convert the house to rental, this exception still applies, but see the next section, I Sold my Rental Property, for some other caveats.

For the purposes of the reduced exclusion for when you own and live in it for less than two years due to unforeseen circumstances, a PCS move counts as an unforeseen circumstance for the purposes of the reduced exclusion.

Not discussed: Inherited or gifted homes. Vacant land adjacent to residence sale. Business or rental use of residence. Physically or mentally disabled persons. Deceased spouse home sale. Divorced person not living in home. Home co-owned by taxpayer and a non-spouse.

45. I Sold my Rental Property

Now we're starting to get complicated. First of all, if you converted your personal residence to rental use, and then sold it within 3 years of conversion to rental, you might be able to get the personal residence exclusion for some of the gain. If this is the case, seek a tax professional to help you out. If not, read on...

This is a VERY complex situation, and, in general, I'm not a fan of doing it yourself or with software. You can get away with doing rental property with software, if you're very careful. However, the sale of the property can get pretty messy. If you insist on doing it yourself, please have a professional review the return before filing it. If you've had rental property for any length of time, most of the terms I'm using should be familiar to you; this section is going to be a bit over the head of the typical taxpayer. If you own rental property, and this still goes over your head, get professional help, and bring your past few years of taxes for a review.

The first thing you need to do is closeout the rental portion of your tax return, recording the income and expenses on Schedule E. You note the date of sale, and figure out the depreciation of the property, and any other assets that you've been depreciating. If, in the past, you have disallowed losses from the rental property due to income limitations, or not being an active participant, you will net these losses with the gain or loss from the current year, and take that as a rental gain or loss on your Form 1040.

Now figure the gain or loss on the rental property:

1. Figure out your BASIS: Using the HUD settlement statement from when you bought the home (the long form with columns that identifies expenses paid by the buyer and paid by the seller), figure out the price you paid for the home. If the seller paid points for you, subtract that amount from the basis. Add (from the HUD) settlement fees, title fees, legal fees, recording fees, survey fees, transfer or tax stamps that you paid. Also add any amounts that the seller owed, but you paid. Now add any amounts you paid to improve the home. This is your BASIS. If any other weirdness occurred that affected the basis, seek professional help. Also seek help if you received the house as a gift or inheritance. Now subtract the depreciation taken on the property through the years, including the current year (note the total amount of depreciation for later as well).
2. Now figure out the proceeds from the sale. To do this you use the HUD settlement statement from the Sale of the home. Take the sales price and subtract any expenses you paid. Make sure to include the agent's commission since that usually makes a big difference. This is the SALE PROCEEDS.
3. Subtract the BASIS from the SALES PROCEEDS and you have the GAIN (if negative this is a LOSS).

4. Report, on Form 4797 in the Long Term or Short Term section (Long Term if owned more than 1 year), the date purchased, date sold, BASIS, SALES PROCEEDS and GAIN (or LOSS).
5. If there is a gain, you'll pay taxes at a higher rate up to the amount of depreciation we discussed in step 1. Above that, you'll pay taxes at a lower rate than normal (maximum 23.8%) depending on your tax bracket (if the sale was Long Term). When you sell the home and get the check from closing, you should run these numbers and see how much of the money to set aside from closing. Steps 3 through 5 may be handled by your software, but you want to make sure the results are as I discussed by reviewing the tax return before filing.

If the home qualified as a personal residence (discussed in the previous section) the depreciation portion of the gain will ALWAYS be taxed as depreciation recapture (the higher rate) even if you can exclude the gain as personal residence.

Military: The above caveat is more likely to apply to you due to the extended period of time for which you can qualify for the exclusion (as discussed in the previous section).

46. I Sold a Home that Wasn't my Primary Residence

In this case I'm assuming that this is either investment property that you've held, but not rented out, or property that you acquired through inheritance. If the property is an inheritance, and was investment property held by the person you inherited it from, it remains investment property. If it was the residence of the person you inherited it from (even if they didn't live in it at the time of death), it remains personal use property, unless you take action to convert it to investment or rental property (talk to a tax dude to help you understand what makes this happen - it's not as clear cut as we might like). The reason this matters is that you can't take a loss on personal property, but you can on investment property. I'll cover both scenarios below, as I tell you how to calculate your gain or loss.

1. Figure out your BASIS: Using the HUD settlement statement from when you bought the home (the long form with columns that identifies expenses paid by the buyer and paid by the seller), figure out the price you paid for the home. If the seller paid points for you, subtract that amount from the basis. Add (from the HUD) settlement fees, title fees, legal fees, recording fees, survey fees, transfer or tax stamps that you paid. Also add any amounts that the seller owed, but you paid. Now add any amounts you paid to improve the home. This is your BASIS. If any other weirdness occurred that affected the basis, seek professional help. If you inherited the home, it should be appraised and the appraisal value plus the cost of any improvements you make is your BASIS.
2. Now figure out the proceeds from the sale. To do this you use the HUD settlement statement from the Sale of the home. Take the sales price and subtract any expenses you paid. Make sure to include the agent's commission since that usually makes a big difference. This is the SALE PROCEEDS.
3. Subtract the BASIS from the SALES PROCEEDS and you have the GAIN (if negative this is a LOSS).
4. Report, on Schedule D in the Long Term or Short Term section (Long Term if owned more than 1 year or inherited), the date purchased (or inherited), date sold, BASIS, SALES PROCEEDS and GAIN (or LOSS—zero if inherited or not investment property).
5. If there is a gain and it's long-term, you'll pay taxes at a lower rate than normal (maximum 23.8%), depending on your tax bracket. When you sell the home and get the check from closing, you should run these numbers and see how much of the money to set aside from closing. Save 23.8% of the gain just to be safe. If short-term, it will be taxed as if it were regular wages. That could be much higher, so set aside a BIG chunk of the proceeds.
Steps 3 through 5 may be handled by your software, but you want to make sure the results are as I discussed by reviewing the tax return before filing.

Military: Not a lot of differences for you here.

Not discussed: Other forms of property other than investment homes or inherited homes.

47. I Get Tips at Work

Tips. Fricken tips. I have to say that these are the bane of a tax professional's existence. The IRS has very straightforward and very specific rules for how to handle tip income. The problem is that literally no one does it the right way. The other problem is that the lack of compliance is driven by employers not understanding and/or not caring about the rules. Now who's going to fight their employer over proper tip reporting? I guess the good news is that the IRS doesn't really seem to be focused on proper tip reporting. I hate to ascribe bad motives to employers, since I think most of it is pure ignorance, but the methods I see used mostly save the employer a lot of money in Social Security and Medicare matching payments. I'm going to go over the right way to do tips, as well as some rationale for doing it correctly. I don't expect you to fight your employer over these, since for most people having a job is more important than fighting over tax technicalities.

The right way to handle tips is to maintain a tip record. You don't have to record every individual tip, but you need to track it well enough to have a daily total of tips received. Your employer may provide an electronic way to do this, and that's okay, but you need to accurately record your total tips, both cash and credit. If you have to give some of your tips to other employees as a result of a tip sharing arrangement, record the amount you pay out to them. You only pay taxes on tips you keep. Separate cash, credit and non-cash tips. You need to report these tips to your employer by the 10th of the following month, if there is not an arrangement to report more often. By reporting tips to your employer, they should include all of them on your W-2, and you don't need to do any special reporting on your tax return. Check your W-2 to ensure it matches your records. If your employer reported a different amount, you can make an adjustment on your tax return to correct it to the right amount.

If you fail to report accurate tip numbers to your employer, you can be charged a penalty of 50% of the amount of taxes (including Social Security and Medicare) that you would have paid if you fully reported your tips.

Employers can be a pain on this because many employers withhold Social Security and Medicare taxes from your wages and credit card tips, and then they match that amount of taxes out of their own pocket. Any cash tips that are reported cause them to have to withhold Social Security and Medicare taxes from your regular wages, and then match from their own pocket. This is at a rate of 7.65%, so there's a motivation by your employer to report the lowest tips possible.

Sorry that this section sucks, but reality, rules and practicality just don't line up very well in this area.

Military: You should not be getting tips unless you work another job.

48. I Receive Benefits from the Government

There are many different programs that will get you money from the government, and some of them have tax implications. I'll list the ones that come up most often.

Aid to Families with Dependent Children, Food Stamps, WIC (Women, Infants, and Children) and other programs similar to these are not taxable and have no impact on your tax return (since most are state-run, they may have different names). In fact, the IRS makes it a point to state that receiving Earned Income Credit (EIC) has no impact on these programs, nor do they on EIC. The only time they tend to come up is during EIC due diligence (which is how the IRS ensures professionals do not ignore things that indicate EIC fraud). One of the indicators of potential fraud is claiming EIC when you do not appear to have sufficient income to support a child. This doesn't mean you can't get EIC—support is not a requirement for EIC, but it does bring up questions that need answered. So you may be asked about other forms of support that you have that allow you to care for your child, and these programs would be included. Don't worry about disclosing this information, it will not be used against you.

SSI and Social Security. I bring these up together because they are very often confused due to both being sourced from the Social Security Administration. SSI is a program to provide assistance to the low income, the disabled, the elderly and children with limited financial resources. It is not based upon contributions to the Social Security program that are withheld from your paycheck. SSI is not taxable and is treated similarly to the programs in the preceding paragraph. Social Security is paid based upon contributions to the Social Security program by a taxpayer, and those contributions generally must meet certain thresholds in order to receive benefits. It is paid to people who have met contribution requirements and who have reached at least 62 years of age, or are disabled. It may also be paid to survivors of contributors. Social Security is potentially taxable to the person receiving it. If your children receive Social Security due to a deceased parent, it is unearned income to them, and may impact tests for you claiming them as a dependent (see chapters on claiming children). Children's Social Security income may require them to file a tax return (if all they receive is Social Security they generally will not need to file). If you receive Social Security in your name, you must report it on your tax return, and a calculation based on your other income will determine if it's taxable. Here are the fine points:

1. SSI is never taxable and does not need to be reported.
2. Social Security is unearned income to the person who receives it.
3. Social Security should always be reported if you are required to file a tax return.
4. If you are not sure if you are receiving SSI or Social Security, you can tell because you will get a Form 1099-SSA for Social Security. The 1099-SSA can come quite a bit later than your W-2s, so make sure you wait for it.

5. Even if Social Security is not taxable, it can impact other areas of your tax return. In particular, Social Security will lower EIC, but not increase it.

6. Determining how much of Social Security is taxable:

a. The first thing you have to do is figure out your income that will be used to calculate the taxability of Social Security. This number is all your taxable income, plus any tax exempt interest, plus HALF of your Social Security income for the year (from your 1099-SSA).

b. Figure out your "base amount" for comparison. This is $25,000 if you are Single, HH, or QW filing status, $32,000 if you are MFJ, $25,000 if you are MFS and didn't live with your spouse for EVEN ONE NIGHT during the year, $0 if you are MFS and lived with your spouse anytime during the year. MFS sucks, as we've discussed.

c. Compare the income from 1 (above) to the base amount from 2. If the income exceeds the base amount, some of your benefits are taxable. There is a complex worksheet to determine how much is taxable, but it will generally be between 50% and 85% of your Social Security income if your income exceeds the base amount. It gets to 85% pretty fast, so if you are above the base amount you can expect to pay a decent amount of taxes.

Military: No differences for you here. Military pay and allowances are not benefits from the government in the way we are discussing them here.

Things not covered just yet: Housing/Rent Assistance, HAMP and HARP (foreclosure prevention programs). Probably a lot more programs that I've never heard of and/or don't affect taxes.

49. I Have Investments Outside of Work

This is going to be a LOOOOOOONG section, covering a ton of information about investments. As usual, I will try to cover the more common situations early, so that you don't have to read the whole section if you don't need to. To be clear, this section is not about investments through your job, or investments in tax advantaged accounts such as IRAs. The next couple sections cover some of those. Even with this section being quite long, I can't cover every detail of every investment. I'll list the things I didn't cover at the end. I will also provide some quick hit information to provide some direction regarding more complex issues, or simply to direct you to seek professional help when applicable. One last thing before I go too far, I am not a financial adviser. None of the information in this chapter is meant as investment advice or advocacy of any particular strategy, except to the extent that it impacts your taxes. Investing should be done with thorough research on your part or the assistance of a reputable financial advisor— and that is not me.

A note for everyone: Your tax information will be reported to you on various forms of 1099s, many of which will be different from each other. Be very careful that you get all the data from your 1099s into your tax software or onto your tax return. If you have any doubts, have it checked by a professional, especially if you are new to investing.

Mutual Fund Investor:

If you have an account where all you do is put money in mutual funds and generally leave it there long-term (even if you shuffle it around once or twice a year) you really don't have a lot to worry about here. If you don't already know, mutual funds are one of the most common ways that we ordinary people invest our money. They pool our money with millions of other people's money and then invest it based on the criteria disclosed to us in the prospectus (you did read that, right). Generally, you pay taxes on the dividends and capital gains that the mutual fund makes on your behalf, even if the money gets reinvested. Dividends are the income that the mutual fund gets when the stocks they hold distribute some of their profits to their shareholders as cash. Capital Gains distributions are the gains the mutual fund has when it sells some stock it owns at a profit (these are netted with stocks they sell at a loss, but if the net is negative there's no money to be distributed). Both Dividends and Capital Gains Distributions are yours. You can have the money sent to you on a quarterly basis, though most people simply have the money reinvested automatically in new shares of the mutual fund. Either way, you have to report and pay taxes on these on your return. Your investment company will send you a 1099-DIV (though they may send you a combined 1099 if you have other investments besides mutual funds, or you sell or exchange funds, but it will have the same information). The 1099 will report your dividends, qualified dividends (dividends that get a lower tax rate), and capital gain distributions. These are all reported directly into your software or directly on your

Form 1040, Schedule B and/or Schedule D, and are fairly straightforward and easy to handle.

If you sold one mutual fund, even if just to move the money into a different mutual fund, they will send you a 1099-B. This will list your "proceeds from broker or barter transactions." This is a complicated way of saying, "how much you got for selling something." The key is that you need to report this, even if you sold it for EXACTLY (or less) than what you paid for it. Many times, the IRS gets just the amount you sold it for, not the amount you paid for it. You only pay taxes on what you made (difference between price paid and price sold), but the IRS may not know what you paid for it, so if you don't report it, they'll send a letter demanding an amount of taxes based on the full proceeds. This wrinkle is the source of many a jaw-droppingly scary letter from the IRS. The biggest problem for some people is figuring out just what you paid for it, especially if you only sold a portion. The good news is that many brokers are providing this information (it's required to be on the form they send you if you purchased it in the last couple years, so this is getting easier every year). If the information is not on the 1099, you can either get it by reviewing the statements from when you purchased it (and every statement between then and the sale, since you add dividends and capital gain distributions to basis), contact your broker for help, or bring your records to your tax professional. I will add that if you are paying a full service broker, they should be doing this for you. They may need records from a previous broker, but I would demand this from them.

The last couple of things you might see on your 1099 are "Non-dividend Distributions" and "Foreign Taxes Paid." Non-dividend distributions are essentially a return of the money you invested in a company. They are tax neutral, but they reduce the amount you "paid" for a mutual fund, and will increase your gain when you sell. Hopefully your investment company is tracking this for you. You will generally see Foreign Taxes Paid when you invest in a fund that invests outside of the United States. This represents your portion of the taxes the mutual fund paid to foreign governments. You can get these taxes back on your tax return as a Foreign Tax Credit. If they are from mainstream mutual funds, you generally file a simplified version of Form 1116 and the taxes come back to you.

Individual Stock Investor:

The first warning I'll give you is to either make sure the companies you are buying are actually corporations, or be prepared for the craziness that ensues from investing in non-corporations. What I'm talking about are Real Estate Investment Trusts, Limited Liability Partnerships and the like. Thanks to technology, you can pop onto an investment web site and buy these just like a regular stock from a corporation. The old classic example would be Kinder Morgan Energy Partnership. You could buy a share in the partnership just like it was a stock, but late in the tax season (sometimes after filing your taxes) you get a Schedule K-1 representing your share of the various items from the partnership's tax return. This quite complicated form can drive you crazy and almost certainly requires a tax professional to file. This is not to say that these aren't great investments, many are, but you need to know what you are getting into. For the record, I believe Kinder Morgan has converted itself to a traditional corporation.

Having said that, the main differences between a mutual fund investor and an individual stock investor is that you won't have capital gain distributions, and you might get 1099-DIVs and 1099-Bs individually for your stocks, or combined depending upon your investment company. When you invest in individual stocks, you only pay capital gains when you sell the individual stocks. It's also a lot easier to track basis since you don't have to track capital gain distributions. The separate or combined forms for 1099-DIV and 1099-B don't significantly impact how they're reported, other than using more lines on Schedule B, Schedule D or form 8949. Do be aware that anytime you sell an individual stock, you will have to report it on your tax return and pay taxes on the gain (or deduct some or all of the loss—capital loss deduction is discussed below).

Day-Trader:

I'm not really interested in going into a huge amount of details on this, but the big thing to point out is that usually, EVERY single stock transaction needs to be reported on your Form 8949. As a guy whose done tax returns for day traders with thousands of transactions, this sucks. What you can do now is, if the investment company reports the basis to the IRS, you can do one line for combined short-term sales (less than one year from purchase to sale) and one line for long-term sales. You can tell the basis has been reported to the IRS because those transactions will be separated from the other transactions on the 1099-B. The form will specifically say that the transaction's basis is reported to the IRS. You will need to send a copy of the 1099-B to the IRS, either with your mailed-in tax return, or attached to Form 8453 if you are electronically filing.

Read if you sold ANYTHING (or you get a 1099-B):

I kind of talked about this already, but it's important enough to reinforce. If you sell or exchange a mutual fund or stock, you should get a 1099-B. If you get a 1099-B, you absolutely MUST report it on your tax return, even if you broke even or lost money. Tons of terrifying IRS letters are generated from people not reporting transactions because "I didn't make any money." The problem is that the IRS may not know you didn't make any money. You need to TELL them you didn't make any money, by reporting the transaction on your tax return.

Capital Gains and Losses:

As discussed above, when you sell a stock or a mutual fund, you may have a gain or a loss. On tax returns, you need to separate these gains and losses based on "holding period." Basically, if you bought the stock or fund more than a year before selling it, it's long-term. Less than a year ago, it's short-term. The capital gain distributions we talked about from mutual funds are assumed to be long-term. Later I will clarify holding periods for weird situations. So now what you do is net your long-term gains and losses and your short-term gains and losses. If you have short-term gains that exceed your losses, you pay taxes at your normal rate. If you have long-term gains that exceed your losses, you pay taxes at a lower rate, depending on your income. If they net to a loss, you can deduct some of that loss, and carry over the rest to your future tax returns. It will then be your starting point for long-term or short-term capital gains or losses. The amount of loss you can deduct in the current year is $3,000 ($1,500 if you are MFS). If your gains are long-term, they are taxed at a maximum rate of 23.8%. The great news is that if you are in the 10% or 15% tax bracket, they are taxed at ZERO! Keep in mind that your tax bracket is based on your income including your capital gain, so don't go overboard selling stock because you think you will be in the 15% tax bracket.

Wash Sales:

A wash sale is an IRS term that is specifically designed to prevent you from selling a stock that is currently losing money, solely for the purpose of generating a taxable loss. As long as you sell the stock and don't re-buy it, you're good. If you buy it back within 30 days of selling it, you essentially ignore the sale for tax purposes. You report it, but don't take the loss; your basis (purchase price) remains the amount you originally paid for it. This only applies to assets sold at a LOSS.

Reverse wash sale (not a real term):

A reverse wash is my made-up term for selling and buying stock back to eliminate gains from potential taxation. First and foremost, if you are not in the 15% tax bracket or below, stop reading. This won't work for you.

If you are, then you can cash in appreciated stock or mutual funds at a 0% tax rate so long as the gains do not put your taxable income above the 15% tax bracket. You can then immediately buy the same stock back (if you want) and the new price will be what is later used to figure gain when you sell it again. You can do this every year and effectively eliminate gains from potential taxation! This is why I call it the reverse wash sale. Wash sales only apply to losses, not gains.

Here is a list of things to consider when determining if it's worth contacting your tax professional for help on this:

1. For 2016, your taxable income should be several thousand dollars below: $37,651 if filing Single, $75,301 if filing MFJ, $50,401 if filing HH (taxable income is basically your income after all adjustments for deductions and exemptions).

2. You have unrealized gains in taxable brokerage accounts or mutual funds that you have held for more than a year (in most cases this means you have stocks or mutual funds that are worth more than you originally paid for them)

3. You're not under age 19 (24 if in school).

4. You're not receiving Earned Income Credit on your tax return.

5. You're not receiving Social Security payments (if this is most of your income you might still benefit).

6. You don't have a capital loss that you are carrying over.

7. Buying and selling stocks or mutual funds in your taxable accounts doesn't cost too much in commissions

Much of the above involves over-simplifications, but it gives you a starting point to see if you might be close.

If the above apply to you, wait until mid-November, and contact your tax professional. Provide them with copies of your recent pay-stubs from all your jobs, as well as amounts of any other taxable income you have or expect to receive before the end of the year (interest, dividends, capital gains, etc.) They should be able to calculate how much gain you can have and still pay 0 taxes on it. Don't worry if it's not perfect, even if you go over a little, only the portion above the 15% tax rate gets taxed, and this at a favorable rate. Once you have this number, review your unrealized gains and losses information from your brokerage account and determine what to sell to stay below the number they provided.

You can do this every year you are in the 15% tax bracket!

The rest of the details:

Municipal Bonds: When you buy bonds from states, cities or other municipalities, they are exempt from federal taxation. Most states exempt their own bonds from taxes, but tax other states.

Schedule K-1: These look very complicated, but the principal is that everything from a Schedule K-1 has a place on a regular tax return. They come with instructions that tell you where to put them. The most confusing part is that the information can carry to some incredibly complex tax returns, which means that often the most confusing part is realizing that some of the information doesn't actually carry to your tax return.

Original Issue Discount (1099-OID): As long as you don't buy bonds on the secondary market, OID (original issue discount) interest is just interest. What makes it weird is that you buy a bond at a discount to its ultimate price, and the difference between what you paid and the final price is interest, or OID. You pay taxes on the interest as it accrues, not when you finally cash in the bond. The 1099-OID gives you the right amount of interest to report on your return.

United States Savings Bonds: These differ from normal bonds in that you are allowed to wait to pay taxes on the interest until you cash the bonds in. There are also exclusions on taxability of interest if you use the proceeds for education (see the I'm Going to College section for details). Also, all US Treasury bonds and bills are exempt from taxation by the states.

Inherited and Gifted Investments: The only real change between inherited or gifted assets is how we determine your basis (cost) in the investment for gain purposes. For inherited assets, your basis is the basis on the date of death (and the assets are assumed to be held long-term). For gifted assets, the person who gave them to you has a basis, and that basis transfers to you. The long-term or short-term determination begins on the date it is given to you.

Puts and Calls: These are advanced investment vehicles where you're buying the right to buy or sell a given security at a later date at a specified price. The main effect of these instruments is on basis and proceeds amounts. If your investment company doesn't provide this information, you should seek help in determining it until you fully understand its effects.

Short Sales: Short sales are investments where you are betting that an asset's price is going to decrease. You borrow the asset from your broker and sell it, hoping to buy it back at a lower price to return it. If you buy it back at a lower price, the difference between the borrowed price and bought back price is a gain. If you are forced to pay more money for it than the price you sold it for, the difference is a loss.

Specified Private Activity Bonds: These are strange bonds that straddle the line between private and government. They are specifically identified and are generally tax free. If you are subject to Alternative Minimum Tax (see that section) they are taxable.

You receive income that's not really yours (nominee dividends): If for some reason you receive a 1099 reporting interest or dividends as your income, but it's really someone else's, seek professional help to unravel this.

Affordable Care Act Net Investment Income Tax: If you make above certain income thresholds, your total net investment income (income = gains – losses) is subject to an extra 3.8% tax above and beyond income and capital gains taxes. The thresholds are: $250,000 for MFJ and QW, $200,000 for HH and Single, $125,000 for MFS. The 23.8% maximum rate discussed previously in this section includes this potential 3.8% addition.

Military: No big differences for you.

Not discussed: Bond purchases on the secondary market that require allocation of interest between bonds.

50. I Have (or Want to Have) Tax Sheltered Investments (IRAs)

This section is about both Roth and Traditional Individual Retirement Accounts (IRAs). There are other tax sheltered investments and tax preferred investments, like municipal bonds discussed in the previous section. There are also SIMPLE IRAs, Simplified Employee Pensions and other types, but I won't be covering those here. The new myRA accounts you may have heard of work almost exactly like Roth IRAs that we will be discussing here (they have different contribution limits and investment choices).

I want to reiterate that I am not a financial advisor, so any advice I give is from a pure tax perspective. You should do your own research when starting to invest, or seek the advice of a licensed financial advisor. More importantly, just like I'm not an investment expert, your investment expert won't be a tax expert. You should get tax advice from a tax professional, not from your financial advisor. (Your bank, insurance company and others are also not tax experts.)

That said, I love IRAs. They are a phenomenal way to grow your retirement assets while postponing or avoiding taxation, so long as you understand the restrictions on them. I am going to give some general advice based on my experience that I think applies to the majority of people. I encourage you to seek additional advice to ensure that your situation isn't different.

One other thing to make clear, IRAs are not investments, they are shelters for your investments. You can invest IRA contributions in a wide variety of investment types, so don't just throw money in an IRA at your bank and think that's it. Talk to a financial advisor and make sure your investments are well thought out.

There is a credit that applies for lower income taxpayers called the Saver's Credit (technically retirement savings contributions credit) that gives you a credit of up to 50% of IRA or 401k contributions back on your tax return. Your AGI needs to be below $61,500 (MFJ), $46,125 (HH) or $30,750 for the others. The percentages are 10, 20 and 50 (lower AGI, higher percentage). Make sure to take this into account if you have a lower income and are considering IRA contributions—it can make a huge difference.

General Advice for Most People:

Most advisors agree on this general order for most people, especially if you are a long way from retirement age. There is some argument on which is better, Roth IRAs or Traditional IRAs, so check out the rules below to see how they impact your life. My general advice (from a tax perspective) is to invest in your companies 401k (or similar plan) to the extent that they match your contributions. Free money from the boss beats any tax benefits. Once you've done this, maximize contributions to Roth IRAs or Traditional IRAs. I like the Roth more than the Traditional, even though you don't get an immediate tax deduction (see details of the accounts later). Your Roth IRA earnings will never be taxed if you do it right, and these earnings should be much larger than your investment over the long-term.

Traditional IRAs become more desirable as your age and tax bracket increase. I think a young person with average incomes will benefit from a Roth more than a Traditional. Roth's also tend to have more flexibility regarding withdrawals. If you max out your IRAs, or have too much income to invest in them, shift back to your company's 401k, contributing to the Roth version if they offer it, for the same reasons the Roth IRA is preferred.

One piece of advice that is an exception to the above is if you don't have a Roth already, open a small one now. There is a 5 year rule for Roth withdrawals that starts with the date you first put money in any Roth IRA. It usually doesn't come in to play, but opening a small Roth when you first start retirement investing is a simple way to start the clock.

Very important: Don't put money into IRAs or 401ks unless you are nearly certain that you won't touch the money until retirement. There are weird exceptions for college, buying houses and other things, but, as a tax professional, I strongly encourage that you focus IRA and 401k contributions towards retirement. There are other ways to save for college, houses, etc. In addition, taking money out of your 401k or IRA before retirement can have SERIOUS tax consequences. Read the section on I Want to Take Money out of my IRA or 401k before you even THINK about taking the money out (unless you are retired.)

Rules for both Roth and Traditional IRAs:

Basics:
1. Your earnings grow without you having to pay taxes on them.
2. You generally have to wait until you are 59 and half to take the money out without a 10% penalty (in addition to any taxes due).
3. You have to have taxable compensation (basically income from a job or business) in order to contribute to IRAs.
4. There are income limitations that affect your ability to contribute to Roth IRAs and deduct Traditional IRA contributions. These limits are affected by whether you have a retirement plan through your work. Your W-2 has a check box that will indicate if you are covered by a retirement plan.
5. The investments available to an IRA owner are slightly limited, but you can generally invest in most stocks, bonds, mutual funds, Publically Traded Partnerships, Real Estate Investment Trusts, and certificates of deposit. Talk to your financial advisor if you want to invest in something obscure like currency, gold or collectibles.

Details:

1. Your contribution limit is the SMALLER of your (or your spouse's if MFJ) taxable compensation and $5,500 ($6,500 if over age 50). These are individual limits that apply separately to you and your spouse. If you accidentally contribute too much, contact your IRA custodian and your tax professional.
2. You can withdraw assets before 59 and a half if:

    a. You buy a house when you haven't owned one for the last 2 years ($10,000 maximum).

    b. You withdraw for certain college expenses (get help if you want to do this).

    c. You withdraw in equal annual installments based on your life expectancy (this is how you retire before age 59 and a half).

    d. You are permanently and totally disabled (talk to a tax professional: you can be receiving disability payments and still not qualify for this).

    e. You have unreimbursed medical expenses that exceed 10% of your AGI.

    f. If you are unemployed and use the withdrawal to pay for health insurance (check with tax professional for details).

    g. The IRS places a levy on the plan (they take it to pay your back taxes).

    h. You are a reservist called to active duty for at least 180 days.

    i. You withdraw due to divorce and the judge issues a Qualified Domestic Relations Order (see your tax professional).
3. You can't invest in collectibles like artwork, rugs, antiques, metals, gems, stamps, coins (except certain investment-grade precious metal coins), alcohol or other tangible personal property.
4. You can contribute to your 2016 IRA through April 15, 2017.

The main difference between a Traditional and Roth IRA is that you get to deduct the Traditional IRA contribution from current year's income, but you pay taxes on the withdrawals when you retire. You don't get to deduct Roth IRA contributions, but the withdrawals are tax-free (assuming you meet the requirements discussed below). Other differences between Traditional and Roth IRAs are discussed below.

Traditional IRA Rules:

Basics:
1. A traditional IRA contribution is deductible if you meet certain income limitations. You subtract the contribution from income before calculating your AGI.
2. Withdrawals from a Traditional IRA after you meet retirement age (generally 59 and a half) are taxable income in the year you withdraw them.
3. You can't contribute to a Traditional IRA in the year you turn 70 and a half or any subsequent year. You also must start withdrawing Traditional IRA assets in the year after you turn 70 and a half. I generally recommend you start these withdrawals in the year you turn 70 and a half. Your IRA custodian will help you calculate these withdrawals.

4. If you make too much money to deduct your Traditional IRA contribution, you can make a non-deductible contribution that will still grow tax deferred (earnings won't be taxed until they are withdrawn. If you make non-deductible contributions, make sure to keep track of them, since they affect the taxability of withdrawals).

Details:
1. If you or your spouse are covered by a retirement plan at your work, the amount of Traditional IRA contributions you can deduct is limited by your AGI.
2. If YOU are covered by a retirement plan at your work, your IRA deduction phases out between the following AGI's:
- MFJ or QW: $98,000 to $118,000
- Single or HH: $61,000 to $71,000
- MFS (and lived with spouse anytime during year): $0 to $10,000.

Use Single rates for MFS if you didn't spend even one night with your spouse. As an example, if you were HH and made less than $61,000, you get the full deduction. Between $61,000 and $71,000 the deduction starts to go down. Above $71,000 you get no deduction.
3. If your SPOUSE is covered by a retirement plan at your work and you are not, your IRA deduction phases out between the following AGI's: $184,000 to $194,000 if MFJ, $0 to $10,000 if MFS (and lived with spouse anytime during year). If you filed MFS but didn't spend even one night with your spouse, your deduction is unlimited.
4. Depending on which half of the year your birthday is, if you wait until the year AFTER you turn 70 and a half to take your required withdrawals, you could end up having to take two annual withdrawals in the same year, which can screw up your tax bracket and also make more of your social security taxable. This is why I recommend taking your first withdrawal in the year you turn 70 and a half.

Roth IRA Rules:

Basics:
1. You can continue to contribute to a Roth IRA at any age and there is no age at which you have to start taking withdrawals.
2. You do not get a current year deduction for contributions to a Roth IRA.
3. In addition to other rules for avoiding tax penalties on Roth IRA withdrawals, you must have had a Roth IRA open for at least 5 years.
4. Qualified withdrawals from a Roth IRA are tax-free (after age 59 and a half and at least 5 years since first Roth IRA contribution).
5. You can withdraw the money you put into a Roth IRA (but not the earnings) at any time, with no tax consequences. This is why you need to track and report your Roth IRA contributions on your tax returns.
6. There are income limitations above which you cannot make Roth IRA contributions. If you make contributions and later determine you made too much money, contact your IRA custodian and your tax professional BEFORE you file the tax return for the year in question (and before 4/15 of that year).

Details:

1. The income limitations at which Roth IRA contributions are phased out are: $184,000 to $194,000 if MFJ or QW, $117,000 to $132,000 if Single or HH, 0 to $10,000 if MFS and spent even one night with your spouse. Use Single rates if you file MFS and did not spend any nights with your spouse during the year.

Military: If you have so much combat zone time that you have little or no taxable income, you can count the non-taxable combat zone income as compensation to allow you to contribute to either type of IRA.

If you are on active duty you are considered covered by a retirement plan for the purposes of IRA contribution limits.

For early withdrawals from IRA's, a reservist called to active duty for more than 180 days counts for an exception to the 10% penalty. The exception code for form 5329 is 11.

Not discussed: Rollovers, conversions, and re-characterizations. SEP's and SIMPLE plans. Backdoor Roth contribution for high income earners.

51. I Want to Take Money out of my 401k or IRA

DON'T DO IT!

Okay, now that I've got your attention, you can touch it, just talk to your tax professional first. Really.

Your financial advisor is not a tax professional. Your banker is not a tax professional. Your insurance representative is not a tax professional. Talk to a tax professional first! There are a LOT of rules about taking money out of tax advantaged accounts. These accounts include SEP's, SIMPLE's, IRA's 401k's TSP's, 457's, 403b's and more. There are some exceptions that get you out of taxes and penalties, but they are complicated!

I'm not even going to go into them in this section. Talk to your tax professional!

I will say that the withholding is not, "paying the taxes already." The withholding is rarely enough. Meeting an exception to the penalty does not prevent taxation, just the penalty. Some exceptions only count for IRA's, but not 401k's. Some count for 401k's, but not IRA's. Only your tax professional can give you the right advice.

Two examples of bad advice:

1. A client recently took $10,000 out of his 401k to purchase a home. His banker told him that was an exception to taxes. WRONG! It's an exception to penalties, not taxes, and, oops, that exception only applies to IRAs, not 401k's. Unhappy client!

2. Another client, age 59, left her job. She was going to use her 401k to buy a house. A big house. Her financial advisor told her to roll it over to an IRA to avoid taxes while looking for a house. She knew she would pay taxes, but thought she could avoid the penalty. Her financial advisor told her she could. WRONG! Having it in an IRA when buying the house avoids the penalty on the FIRST $10,000. The other part of nearly $200,000 was fully penalized at 10%. To add insult to injury, because she was older than 55 and left her job, she could have taken it out of the 401k without penalty, for ANY reason. Once it hit the IRA, she had to wait until 59 and a half, or meet an exception. That's right, even with the bad rollover, 6 months would have saved her THOUSANDS! Unhappy client!

Talk to the tax experts, not the banking/insurance/financial experts. I won't give you investment advice, don't take tax advice from the wrong person.

Military: We're talking about the Thrift Savings Plan here!

52. I Had Debt Written Off by the Company I Owed Money To

If this has happened to you, the chances are that the company who wrote the debt off has or will issue you a 1099-C. This represents debt owed by the taxpayer that is written off by the lender as non-collectable. If you haven't received a 1099-C, they either have not written the debt off, or they sent it to an incorrect address. If you know that a credit card company or other debtor wrote off debt, but haven't received a 1099-C, you should gather your records as discussed below, but don't do anything until you receive the 1099-C (except communicate with the company to find out if they're sending one and get it if you can.) If you don't qualify for an exclusion, the debt written off is taxable to you, and should be reported on Form 1040, Line 21 as "Cancelled Debt". If an exclusion applies, you will use Form 982 to determine any exclusion from income and any non-excluded income is reported on Line 21 of Form 1040 as "Cancelled Debt."

The following exceptions MAY apply:

Bankruptcy
To the extent insolvent (liabilities exceed assets - Appendix B)
Certain Farm debts
Non-recourse loans (box 5 of Form 1099-C not checked)
Qualified personal residence debt (see next section on house foreclosure)
Qualified real property business debt

I'm only going to talk about one of those exceptions, since it applies to most situations (and the personal residence exclusion is in the next section). If you declared bankruptcy, own a farm, have a non-recourse loan, or have business real property, talk to a professional.

Insolvency:

I have added details on how to fill out the IRS Insolvency Worksheet in Appendix B.

Okay, so now let's talk about how to find out if you're insolvent. First look at the 1099C, box 1 and note the date. If you don't have the 1099C, use the date the debt was forgiven (you can call the lender to figure this out.) You will use this date and figure out, as of that date, how much your assets were, and how much your liabilities were. Your assets are everything you own, your liabilities are everything you owe.

We'll start with liabilities first. Start with the debt that was cancelled: the debt they cancelled counts as a liability, so that's your first number. Go to your credit cards, mortgages, car loans and any other money that you owe. Print out the first statement after the date in question. Now review the statement and determine what you owed as of that date. You can do this by highlighting the beginning balance and any charges or payments up to our date. Add the balance and charges, subtract any payments, and write this number on the statement. Repeat for all of your debts, and then add them up to get a total amount of liabilities. SAVE each of the statements! The IRS can ask you to prove how insolvent you were.

Now assets. Start with your bank accounts, brokerage statements, investments, etc. Print out each statement and highlight the value on the date in question. For checking accounts, they usually keep a running total. For brokerages, they may only give you a monthly balance. If you can, go online and get the actual balance on the date in question. Print the screen with this balance and keep it with the statement for that account. If you can't get an exact amount, use the balance closest to our date. Make sure to do this for your retirement plan at work (401k, 403B, TSP, etc.), as well as any Individual Retirement Accounts.

Now it gets harder. For any vehicles you have, go to kbb.com or edmunds.com and determine the value of them. You can use some judgment to get the best value (lower is better), but be reasonable. If your car is truly a piece of crap and you are using that to drop the value, take pictures to justify this assessment. It's also not a bad idea to take a picture of the odometer reading. Print the page from the website and highlight the value and attach it to any pictures you took.

Now you have to value everything else you own. This is difficult. Take pictures of big, valuable items and try to get a value off the internet—print any pages with values you use. For your general household, pictures and video can be useful to prove you don't have fancy, expensive furniture. Talk to a few people who know about values and try to get a good estimate. I wouldn't do an appraisal unless you're really unsure; just make sure your values aren't ridiculous.

For your house (or houses) get a real estate agent to run comps and give you a written value estimate for them. Save this paperwork.

Now the kicker. If you are receiving a pension such as military retirement, state or federal retirement, union retirement, VA disability or Social Security (even if it is not taxable) you must figure out the value of your payments as a lump sum based on your life expectancy. This is hard to figure out, and the number is usually an insolvency killer. (I did several checks of my military retirement from various sources and found values between $800,000 and $1.7 million.) If you're close with everything else, this will probably prevent you being insolvent and is probably not worth the effort.

Now take all your liabilities and add them up. Do the same with your assets. Subtract assets from liabilities and if you get a positive number, you're insolvent! This generally means you can avoid paying taxes on your cancelled debt up to the amount of your insolvency.

A couple words of warning:

1) Save all the paperwork.

2) Make sure to include the value of anything they repossessed in the asset column.

3) If the debt cancelled was in your name (or your spouse's) and not in the other's name, you have to calculate insolvency for the individual, not both of you (in this case include the full amount of anything in only the debtor's name, and split everything in both of your names).

4) If the numbers are close, make sure you have your ducks in a row. If you lowballed the value of your household, or forgot to include your $3,000 engagement ring, things can get ugly, and you could owe money back. Conversely, if your liabilities are enormous, and you have tens of thousands of dollars of insolvency above your cancelled debt, you can probably relax and not be quite as anal about household contents values (still do all the cars, house, big toys and bank accounts just like we said).

5) Insolvency affects tax attributes for future tax years. This is way beyond the scope of this book. You should seek professional assistance to determine the effect, especially if you have a business, investments, or rental property.

Keep Reading:

You may also receive a Form 1099-A if the debt collector took property that was secured by the debt—usually your car for a car loan or your house for a house loan. If it was your house, see the next section on foreclosure. Otherwise, the item is considered sold on the date reported on the 1099-A. Many banks totally suck at sending this paperwork, and often you will get a 1099-C and not the 1099-A. The good news is that as long as you don't use the property for business, it's generally a tax neutral situation. You report the property as sold on Schedule D, as personal property. You will include the date purchased, date sold (from the 1099-A, the price you paid (basis) and the price sold (Fair Market Value from the 1099-A). Make sure you indicate it as personal property. It should result in a negative number unless the property has increased in value. You cannot deduct the negative number, but if it's increased in value, you pay taxes on that increase—this is rare for repossessed property other than real estate.

Military: Your Thrift Savings Plan balance counts as an asset. If you are on active duty, the traditional military retirement that your service entitles you to does not count as an asset, even if you have been in more than 20 years. If you are retired, you must include an amount that would produce your retirement income if you had invested it in an annuity (bottom line is that retired military are rarely insolvent for the purposes of cancelled debt exclusion.) Some of these interpretations are not written in stone so consider getting professional help if you get a 1099-C and think you might be insolvent.

53. I Lost my House (Foreclosure, Short Sale or Bankruptcy)

If this has happened to you, the chances are that the company who foreclosed wrote the debt off and has or will issue you a Form 1099-C. This represents debt owed by the taxpayer that is written off by the lender as non-collectable. If you haven't received a 1099-C, they either have not written the debt off yet, they sent it to an incorrect address, or the amount not paid was covered by mortgage insurance (the lender might also be incompetent.) If your house was foreclosed, but you haven't received a 1099-C, you should gather your records as discussed below, but don't do anything until you receive the 1099-C (except communicate with your mortgage company to find out if they're sending one and get it if you can.) If you don't qualify for an exclusion, the debt written off is taxable to you, and should be reported on form 1040 Line 21 as "Cancelled Debt". If an exclusion applies, you will use Form 982 to determine any exclusion from income and any non-excluded income is reported on Line 21 of Form 1040 as "Cancelled Debt."

The following exceptions MAY apply:

Bankruptcy
To the extent insolvent (liabilities exceed assets - Appendix B)
Non-recourse loans (box 5 of 1099-C not checked)
Qualified personal residence debt

I'm only going to talk about two of those exceptions, since they apply to most situations. If you declared bankruptcy or have a non-recourse loan, talk to a professional.

Insolvency:

I have added details on how to fill out the IRS Insolvency Worksheet in Appendix B.

Okay, so now let's talk about how to find out if you're insolvent. First look at the 1099C, box 1 and note the date. If you don't have the 1099C, use the date the debt was forgiven (you can call the lender to figure this out). You will use this date and figure out, as of that date, how much your assets were, and how much your liabilities were. Your assets are everything you own, your liabilities are everything you owe.

We'll start with liabilities first. Start with the debt that was cancelled based on the 1099-C. This counts as a liability, so that's your first number. Go to your credit cards, mortgages, car loans and any other money that you owe. Print out the first statement after the date in question. Now review the statement and determine what you owed as of that date. You can do this by highlighting the beginning balance and any charges or payments up to that date. Add the balance and charges, subtract any payments, and write this number on the statement. Repeat for all of your debts, and then add them up to get a total amount of liabilities. SAVE each of the statements! The IRS can ask you to prove how insolvent you were.

Now assets. Start with your bank accounts, brokerage statements, investments etc. Print out each statement and highlight the value on the date in question. For checking accounts, they usually keep a running total. For brokerages, they may only give you a monthly balance. If you can, go online and get the actual balance on our date. Print the screen with this balance and keep it with the statement for that account. If you can't get an exact amount, use the balance closest to the date. Make sure to do this for your retirement plan at work (401k, 403B, TSP, etc.), as well as any Individual Retirement Accounts. Include the Fair Market Value of the foreclosed house from the 1099-C.

Now it gets harder. For any vehicles you have, go to kbb.com or edmunds.com and determine the value of them. You can use some judgment to get the best value (lower is better), but be reasonable. If your car is truly a piece of crap and you are using that to drop the value, take pictures to justify this assessment. It's also not a bad idea to take a picture of the odometer reading. Print the web pages and highlight the value and attach it to any pictures you took.

Now you have to value everything else you own. This is difficult. Take pictures of big, valuable items and try to get a value off the internet—print any pages with values you use. For your general household, pictures and video can be useful to prove you don't have fancy, expensive furniture. Talk to a few people who know about values and try to get a good estimate. I wouldn't do an appraisal unless you're really unsure, just make sure your values aren't ridiculous.

For your house (or houses) get a real estate agent to run comps and give you a written value estimate for them. Save this paperwork.

Now the kicker. If you are receiving a pension such as military retirement, state or federal retirement, union retirement, VA disability or Social Security (even if it is not taxable) you must figure out the value of your payments as a lump sum based on your life expectancy. This is hard to figure out, and the number is usually an insolvency killer. (I did several checks of my military retirement from various sources and found values between $800,000 and $1.7 million.) If you're close with everything else, this will probably prevent you from being insolvent and is probably not worth the effort.

Now take all your liabilities and add them up. Do the same with your assets. Subtract assets from liabilities and if you get a positive number, you're insolvent! This generally means you can avoid paying taxes on your cancelled debt up to the amount of your insolvency.

A couple words of warning:

1) Save all the paperwork.

2) Make sure to include the value of anything they repossessed in the asset column.

3) If the debt cancelled was in your name (or your spouse's) and not in the other's name, you have to calculate insolvency for the individual, not both of you (in this case include the full amount of anything in only the debtor's name, and split everything in both of your names).

4) If the numbers are close, make sure you have your ducks in a row. If you lowballed the value of your household, or forgot to include your $3,000 engagement ring, things can get ugly, and you could owe money back. Conversely, if your liabilities are enormous, and you have tens of thousands of dollars of insolvency above your cancelled debt, you can probably relax and not be quite as anal about household contents values (still do all the cars, house, big toys and bank accounts just like we said).

5) Insolvency affects tax attributes for future tax years. This is way beyond the scope of this book. You should seek professional assistance to determine the effect, especially if you have a business, investments, or rental property.

Personal Residence Exclusion:

This exclusion is set to expire January 1st of 2017. I suspect they will renew it, but if foreclosure is inevitable, it might be smart to make sure it happens before this date.

You can exclude canceled debt on the foreclosure of your primary home. It has to be your personal residence at the time of foreclosure. There is some debate on this as to whether you need to be living in the home the day of foreclosure, but most take the reasonable position that if you leave the home due to imminence of foreclosure, you can exclude it as personal residence. The 2 out of 5 year rule for excluding gain does not apply here, though the code can make you think it does. The definition of "personal residence" from that part of the code applies, not the time rules, so make sure you can defend the position that it was your residence at the time of foreclosure. If you moved out and stopped making the payments for a year, or converted it to a rental for a while, this probably does not apply, but talk to a professional just to make sure. There are detailed restrictions and limitations on this so it makes sense to check with a tax professional in any case.

Keep Reading:

You may also receive a Form 1099-A, but not always. The 1099-A represents the transfer of your house to the mortgage company, and is treated as if you sold it. Many banks totally suck at sending this paperwork, and often you will get a 1099-C and not the 1099-A, but you should report the sale. The good news is that as long as you don't use the property for business, it's generally a tax neutral situation. You report the property as sold on Schedule D, as a personal residence. If you owned and lived in the home for 2 of the last 5 years, never rented it to someone, and never used it for business, you can exclude $250,000 of gain ($500,000 if MFJ). You will include the date purchased, date sold (from the 1099-A or 1099-C, the price you paid [basis] and the price sold [Fair Market Value from the 1099-A or 1099-C]). Make sure you indicate it as personal residence property. Your software should exclude the gain as appropriate, and not allow a loss if that's the result. You may need to see a professional for help on this.

Military: As discussed, the 2 out of 5 year rule does not apply for the personal residence exclusion and thus the 10 year extension for the military does not apply either.

54. I am Retired (or Thinking About It)

This is a BIG topic for life, and a pretty big one for taxes. I am not a financial advisor, so I'm going to avoid giving advice on how to manage your retirement assets. I will tell you what happens as you utilize retirement assets and give advice based on the tax implications. I am going to make a few assumptions. First of all, this is not written for a military retiree (there will be a section, copied from my blog, on warnings for military retirees). Second, I'm assuming you are really retiring, and not still working (though I will talk about small jobs and their impact). I'm also not going to talk significantly about seriously early retirement. I will cover the key ages that matter with tax advantaged accounts. You should read this whole section, I will be jumping around and covering a wide variety of topics. As usual, I will use 401k to describe the whole gamut of the tax advantaged employee accounts such as 457, 403b, TSP, etc. that share the same basic withdrawal limits and tax advantages.

General Withdrawal Strategies:

Even though you are retired, your tax advantaged accounts, such as your 401k and IRA's retain a significant advantage. When planning your retirement, these accounts should be used later than your taxable accounts, because they will grow faster due to the tax advantages.

Ages that Matter:

These are the big ages that matter for the various retirement accounts:

50: The age at which a qualified public safety employee who has separated from that job can withdraw that employer's plan assets without paying the 10% early withdrawal penalty. A qualified public safety employee is a state, county or city employed police officer, firefighter or EMS worker.
55: The age at which a regular employee who has separated from that job can withdraw that employer's plan assets without paying the 10% early withdrawal penalty.
59 and a half: The age at which all tax advantaged retirement plan assets can be withdrawn without paying the 10% early withdrawal penalty, regardless of employment status.
62: Earliest age at which you can start collecting Social Security.
65 to 67: depending on your age, full Social Security retirement age. This is the age at which you get your full Social Security benefit. It is also the age at which having another job cannot force you to have to repay Social Security benefits. Go to www.ssa.gov for more details.
70 and a half: Age at which you must start withdrawing traditional IRA and traditional 401k assets based on your life expectancy. There is a wrinkle depending on your birthday, so I always recommend starting during the year you turn 70 and a half, to avoid having to make two withdrawals in one year. If you

want more details, talk to your tax professional. Your tax professional will probably need to use a calendar and some note paper to figure out which category applies to you.

Early Withdrawals:

If you don't meet the age requirements discussed above for 401k's and IRA's, your withdrawals from these accounts will have an additional 10% penalty, above and beyond the taxability of the accounts. Roth IRA's and Roth 401k's have the additional requirement that you must have had a Roth account from any source for at least five years to avoid the penalty (even if you meet the exceptions). In addition, the amount you put into a Roth account is NEVER subject to tax or penalty. There are a few exceptions:

1. You are permanently and totally disabled (which doesn't mean what it sounds like, so ask your tax pro and get a doctor's statement).
2. You withdraw in equal annual installments based on your life expectancy (your financial advisor can help set this up).
3. You have significant medical expenses such that they exceed 10% of your AGI.
4. You are dead :)
5. A judge provides a very specific order (a qualified domestic relations order) directing the assets to be distributed because of a divorce :(
6. You are withdrawing because the IRS has levied the plan to pay for your back taxes :(
7. For IRA's, your withdrawal does not exceed qualified education expenses.
8. For IRA's, you can exclude up to $10,000 from penalty if used to buy a first-time home (which actually means you haven't owned a home in the two years prior to the withdrawal).

Social Security:

Be aware that if you take Social Security before full retirement age (discussed above) you may have to pay it back if you work a second job. Since this is not a tax issue, I'll refer you to www.ssa.gov for more information. Social Security is taxable in a weird way. If it is your ONLY source of income, you probably won't pay taxes on it. It is also not subject to state income taxes in many states. If you have other sources of income, jobs, other retirement income, investment returns, then it can be up to 85% taxable. It is not taxed at 85%, but up to 85% of the Social Security will be subject to ordinary income tax rates. This greatly complicates decision making with regard to other sources of income, so it will serve you well to discuss major income-changing decisions with your tax pro to avoid big surprises in Social Security taxability. But I'll cover the basics (if you can call it that, here):

1. The first thing you have to do is figure out your income that will be used to calculate the taxability of Social Security. This number is all your taxable income,

plus any tax exempt interest, plus HALF of your Social Security income for the year (from your Form 1099-SSA).

2. Figure out your "base amount" for comparison. This is $25,000 if you are Single, HH, or QW filing status; $32,000 if you are MFJ; $25,000 if you are MFS and didn't live with your spouse for EVEN ONE NIGHT during the year; $0 if you are MFS and lived with your spouse anytime during the year. MFS sucks, as we've discussed.

3. Compare the income from 1 above, to the base amount from 2. If income exceeds base amount, some of your benefits are taxable. There is a complex worksheet to determine how much is taxable, but it will generally be between 50% and 85% of your Social Security income if your income exceeds the base amount. It gets to 85% pretty fast, so if you are above the base amount you can expect to pay a decent amount of taxes.

Annuities:

Annuities used to be amazingly complicated for taxes, but they've gotten easier (for taxes). They're still complicated overall. You usually end up with an annuity either from an employee retirement plan, life insurance contracts, direct annuity investment, or IRA rollover. Basically, you convert a large lump sum into a lifetime of payments. These payments are taxable, except to the extent that you invested money into the plan that you paid taxes on. If you rolled completely tax deducted amounts, such as from a traditional IRA or 401k into the annuity, the annuity is fully taxable. If you invested non-tax advantaged money into the account (for example, you bought an annuity for $30,000 with regular cash 20 years ago, and now it's worth $300,000) the original investment is non-taxable, and you get to exclude it from your withdrawals a little bit at a time, based on your life expectancy. To greatly simplify, if your life expectancy is 30 years, then the $30,000 we just talked about would be deducted from your taxable withdrawals at a rate of $1,000 per year, until it is used up. The bad news is that this is a very complicated calculation. The good news is that if you know basic information (most of which is provided on the 1099-R you'll get during tax season, just like a W-2) your software will handle it for you. Make sure you know the annuity starting date (the date of your first check received from it). The even better news is that, more and more, the annuity provider is doing the calculation for you, and giving you everything, including the taxable amount, right on the 1099-R.

For state purposes, an annuity or pension is taxable to the state you are a resident of, regardless of the source of the pension. If you are a resident of say, South Carolina, a CA Teachers or NY Firefighters pension is taxable to SC and NOT to CA or NY. Make sure to update your provider as to your state of residence so they can update the 1099-R you receive, and withhold as appropriate. Even if the 1099-R has the state you are not a residence of, you want to make sure to apply the income to the state you are a residence of at the time of receipt. If you move during the year, the payments are taxable to the state you were a resident of as you receive them, so keep track. You only have one state of residence, and it is generally moved at the time you establish yourself in the new state. As a basic rule, the date you move in your new house, or start your new job, are good indications that your residency shifted. Talk to a professional if this date is unclear.

Working a Job:

As discussed above, working a second job can cause you to have to pay back Social Security, or make it more taxable. The important thing about working a second job is that, in a normal retirement, with pension, Social Security and investments, this is another source of taxable income. The biggest problem is that none of these sources knows about the other. Therefore, when you appropriately indicate Married and 2 on the W-4 you get when you are hired (for example), they withhold assuming it's your ONLY income. If you make less than $20,000, they're going to think none of it is taxable and grossly under-withhold. I always recommend going Single and 0 on retirement jobs unless you have very limited income other than Social Security. Keep reading for more details.

Withholding:

As we just discussed, withholding can be an issue. None of your income sources will know about each other, and thus will tend to under-withhold. This is not something you want to be cavalier about. I highly recommend being aggressive on withholding in the first couple of years of retirement. Getting a couple thousand dollar tax bill at the end of the year can make a huge mess of your retirement plans. Start most of your withholding at Single and zero, and make sure to have state withholding as well. I also recommend saving a decent chuck of money in the first year, just in case. A tax pro can really help with this, but even the best of us have trouble figuring things out exactly right. As you progress through your retirement years, you can tweak the withholding as necessary to ease back off your early aggressiveness. For Social Security, you have to use a different method of withholding. They pull out based on percentages, usually 7, 10, 15 or 25. Start with at least 15, and ease off if necessary.

Military: This section, combined with the next section: I'm Retiring from the Military has pretty much everything you need.

55. I am Retiring from the Military

Retiring from the military can be a wonderful time of life, but it is also a time of uncertainty about jobs, residence, moving and other significant changes. Once all these are settled, retirement can seem like everything you dreamed it could be— until that first tax return. I've prepared dozens tax returns for newly retired military, and not one has had a happy outcome. I'll grant that some people are ready for it, but most times they are not. I've seen reactions that vary from, "That's all I'm getting back?" to "I owe $25,000! Are you kidding me?" It would not be an exaggeration to say that the several thousand dollar balance due is the most common result.

With this section I hope to provide information to mitigate the effects of retirement on your taxes (you can't prevent taxes, only minimize and prepare.) I'll start by explaining the changes you'll see, and then talk about what you can do.

Problem #1

ALL your income is taxable now. That's right, no non-taxable allowances, combat pay or other benefits. You might have the same salary as when you were on active duty, but at least 20 to 30% more will be taxable. While in the military, this had the effect of keeping most of your income out of the 25% tax bracket. To dispel a common misconception, only the portion of income that is in the 25% tax bracket is taxed at 25%, the rest at lower tax rates, but we'll see why this matters as we discuss things in more detail...

Problem #2

Your new job doesn't know about your retirement income, and your retirement income doesn't know about your job. This means that your wages and retirement will under-withhold in almost all circumstances. For an example, let's say you're married with two kids. You put Married 4 on your W-4 form, and, while on active duty, this would be fine. Now however, your job might put you a little into the 25% tax bracket, but they withhold just a little more than 15%. Your retirement sees you in the 10 to 15% tax bracket, so they withhold just over 10%. Together, you're thoroughly into the 25% tax bracket. If you make $20,000 more than the bottom of the 25% tax bracket, that's $5,000 that should be withheld...but maybe $3,000 actually gets withheld. Those numbers add up! This also is made worse if your spouse works. (Now don't think about lowering your income - big tax bills result from big income - and that's good.)

Problem #3

Did you get a great relocation package? They may have even covered the taxes for you (much of the package is taxable income). The problem is that the relocation package drove you right THROUGH the 25% tax bracket and into the 28% tax bracket. Your retirement should be taxed at 25%, but they're withholding 15%. Say you get $40,000 in retirement. The withholding will be less than

$6,000, but you should have $10,000 withheld. Do the math: $10,000 − $6,000 = my tax bill is how much?!?

Problem #4

What happened to my $1,000 Child Tax Credit? What about my Education Credit? And just what the hell is the Alternative Minimum Tax? Military allowances tend to keep you from the income limitations that many people face. If you have a kid in college, you could get a $2,500 American Opportunity Credit. If you have kids under 17, you should get $1,000 each on your taxes, but both of those have income limitations that you might face at your new income. The Alternative Minimum Tax is a tax designed to make everyone pay their fair share, but more and more people face it every year. A detailed analysis is beyond the scope of this section, but let's just say this—it's BAD.

Problem #5

Wait, state taxes? I never paid them before. I know a lot of you are "residents" of tax free states, or are from states that don't tax military, but now, you reside where you work. Most of those states are going to want their share of your money. DFAS tends to not withhold state taxes unless you make them (though many states don't tax military retirement). You should talk to your tax professional about the specifics of your state.

Problem #6

What do you mean I owe? They withheld the tax on my Thrift Savings Plan early distribution. DON'T DO IT—IT's A TRAP! Seriously, unless you're over 55 and not planning on working LEAVE IT ALONE! Now is not the time to get clever about using it to buy a house and not having a payment. Here's the deal: They will withhold 20%. 10% of this will cover the early withdrawal penalty. That leaves 10% in taxes. I believe we covered your new tax rate above (hint: at least 25%). That means you are AT LEAST 15% under-withheld. Take too much out and you could be a ton more under-withheld. Think "I'm going to OWE at least $1,500 for every $10,000 taken out (not counting the $2,000 they already kept)." That means, ignoring state taxes, you get less than $6,500 of every $10,000 you take out. I don't care what the interest rate on your house would be—you're not making that back! DON'T DO IT!!!!!

What to do:

So, besides not taking money out of your Thrift Savings Plan, what do you do? You have several options:

1: Over-withhold from your pension and your job.
2: Make estimated tax payments (I'm not a big fan of this one).
3: Save a large amount of money in the event that you have a large balance due.
4: Do a combination of the first three (another is ignore and hope, but I can tell you that doesn't work).

You should continue to treat taxes very conservatively until at least the end of your first full retired year. Also, no matter which method you use, you should ensure that your withholding and/or estimated tax payments at least equal your tax liability from the previous year. This will ensure you don't owe a penalty for underpayment.

To increase your withholding, you submit a W4 form. The IRS likes to pretend that if you follow the instructions, everything will be fine. This is bunk. The W4 instructions are the most useless instructions of any IRS form. My advice is to simply select Single and 0 for each and every job you have, as well as your retirement (you can do this online via Mypay for retirement.) After your first full year of retirement, if you get a big refund, you can readjust your withholding. I must warn you that even this might not be enough. You should strongly consider having a very conservative budget until you are sure what your tax situation will be. Set aside lots of money just in case you owe.

My best advice is to call your tax professional after you start the new job. Give them detailed information about your new income (retiree statement and pay stubs are best) and they can run the numbers for you.

56. I am Receiving Social Security (or Thinking About It)

Be aware that if you take Social Security before full retirement age (65 to 67 depending on your age) you may have to pay it back if you work a second job. Since this is not a tax issue, I'll refer you to www.ssa.gov for more information. Social Security is taxable in a weird way. If it is your ONLY source of income, you probably won't pay taxes on it. It is also not subject to state income taxes in many states. If you have other sources of income, jobs, other retirement or investment returns, then it can be up to 85% taxable. It is not taxed at 85%, but up to 85% of the Social Security will be subject to ordinary income tax rates. This greatly complicates decision making with regard to other sources of income, so it will serve you well to discuss major income changing decisions with your tax pro to avoid big surprises in Social Security taxability. I'll cover the basics (if you can call it that) here:

1. The first thing you have to do is figure out your income that will be used to calculate the taxability of Social Security. This number is all your taxable income, plus any tax exempt interest, plus HALF of your Social Security income for the year (from your Form 1099-SSA).
2. Figure out your "base amount" for comparison. This is $25,000 if you are Single, HH, or QW filing status, $32,000 if you are MFJ, $25,000 if you are MFS and didn't live with your spouse for EVEN ONE NIGHT during the year, $0 if you are MFS and lived with your spouse anytime during the year. MFS sucks, as we've discussed.
3. Compare the income from 1 above to the base amount from 2. If income exceeds the base amount, some of your benefits are taxable. There is a complex worksheet to determine how much is taxable, but it will generally be between 50% and 85% of your Social Security income if your income exceeds the base amount. It gets to 85% pretty fast, so if you are above the base amount you can expect to pay a decent amount of taxes.

Military: Not much different here.

57. I am Receiving an Annuity or Pension

The first thing I want to say is that, generally, if you are receiving an annuity or pension, the majority of it will be taxable to the federal government, and some or all of it may be taxed to the state. For state purposes, an annuity or pension is taxable to the state you are a resident of, regardless of the source of the pension. If you are a resident of say, South Carolina, a CA Teachers or NY Firefighters pension is taxable to SC and NOT to CA or NY. Make sure to update your provider as to your state of residence so they can update the Form 1099-R you receive, and withhold as appropriate. Even if the 1099-R has the state you are not a residence of, you want to make sure to apply the income to the state you are a residence of at the time of receipt. If you move during the year, the payments are taxable to the state you were a resident of as you receive them, so keep track. You only have one state of residence, and it is generally moved at the time you establish yourself in the new state. As a basic rule, the date you move in your new house, or start your new job, are good indications that your residency shifted. Talk to a professional if this date is unclear.

I also want to talk about disability. For the most part, disability pensions and annuities are taxable. Notable exceptions are Veteran's disability and SSI from Social Security. A good indication that your pension or annuity is at least partially taxable is the receipt of a 1099-R or 1099-SSA, even if it has the code for disability (Code 3).

Annuities used to be amazingly complicated for taxes, but they've gotten easier (for taxes). They're still complicated overall. You usually end up with an annuity either from an employee retirement plan, life insurance contracts, direct annuity investment, or IRA rollover. Basically, you convert a large lump sum into a lifetime of payments. These payments are taxable, except to the extent that you invested money into the plan that you paid taxes on. If you rolled completely tax deducted amounts, such as from a traditional IRA or 401k into the annuity, the annuity is fully taxable. If you invested non-tax advantaged money into the account (for example you bought an annuity for $30,000 with regular cash 20 years ago, and now it's worth $300,000) the original investment is non-taxable, and you get to exclude it from your withdrawals a little bit at a time, based on your life expectancy. To greatly simplify, if your life expectancy is 30 years, then the $30,000 we just talked about would be deducted from your taxable withdrawals at a rate of $1,000 per year, until it is used up. The bad news is that this is a very complicated calculation. The good news is that if you know basic information (most of which is provided on the 1099-R you'll get during tax season, just like a W-2) your software will handle it for you. Make sure you know the annuity starting date (the date you first received a check). The even better news is that, more and more, the annuity provider is doing the calculation for you, and giving you everything, including the taxable amount, right on the 1099-R.

Military: Military retirement is fully taxable at the Federal level. VA disability is fully tax free. State taxation of military retirement varies by state.

58. I am Paying on Student Loans

If you are paying off student loans that you received to pay for higher education, you may be able to deduct the interest on your tax return. The determination of if it is an eligible loan is pretty straightforward. It is unlikely that you got a student loan that is not deductible if you used it for most types of college or vocational education in the United States. If you did something truly weird with the loan, seek additional help. You can deduct interest for you or your spouse, or your dependent. The dependent part is a little weird because they don't have to be a dependent on the tax return you're filing now. Instead, they had to be your dependent in the year you took the loan out and you have to be obligated to pay the loan. Paying your child's loan that is in their name doesn't count.

The deduction is not part of itemized deductions, so you get it even when you take the standard deduction. You get a maximum of $2,500 PER RETURN, not per person. You should get a Form 1098-E or a letter with similar information from your loan holder. There is an income limitation on the deduction, and, as usual, you can't be MFS. You also can't be claimed as a dependent on someone else's return and take the deduction.

One additional piece of advice: Don't ignore your student loans. If they become delinquent, the government has significant avenues for collection. These include taking your federal tax refund and your spouse's federal tax refund. If your refund is taken for your spouse's delinquent student loans, you may be able to file as injured spouse to get some refund back. Or you can file as injured spouse when you initially file to keep some refund from being taken.

Here are the details:

1. Loans from relatives or your employer don't count.
2. The student has to be enrolled at least half-time in a program leading to a degree, certificate or other recognized education credential at the time the money is borrowed.
3. The loan proceeds have to be received within a reasonable period within the time the education is received. This is assumed to be met if they are paid for specific periods of education and you actual attend school during the specific period.
4. The loan proceeds need to be for tuition, room and board, books, supplies and equipment, and transportation. If you use them for general living expenses, these cannot exceed what the educational institution would have charged you for room and board.
5. You get a maximum of $2,500 per return.
6. You must be legally obligated to repay the loan. This means the loan must be made in your name, or with you as a co-signor.
7. You can't deduct the interest in more than one place on your tax return.

8. If you file MFJ, the deduction phases out as your AGI increases above $130,000, and is gone at an AGI of $160,000. If you are Single, HH or QW, the deduction phases out as your AGI increases above $65,000, and is gone at an AGI of $80,000.

9. If you are married, and both of you are paying back student loans, you need to consult an expert to determine the effects of filing status on Income Based Repayment plans.

Military: Not a lot of differences for you here, though if you have pre-service student loans at higher than 6% interest, you should look into getting a reduced interest rate through the Soldiers and Sailors Civil Relief Act.

59. I'm Changing Jobs

There are a few big issues to consider, but first, I want to point out that this assumes you already have the new job, or have it lined up. There is another section for losing your job, which you might want to review if you lost your job and then found a new one. This section here is the one to read if you made a transition that did not involve a significant unemployment period. This section is going to cover two big things: your 401k (or other employee retirement plan) and your move (if applicable).

401k's or other employee retirement plans:

For your 401k, you will need to do something with it, though you are allowed to leave it with your former employer sometimes. I'm not a financial advisor, but my non-professional suggestion is to roll it over to an Individual Retirement Account with a financial services company. Seek professional assistance from a licensed financial advisor, or if you are good at handling your investments, do it yourself. DON'T HAVE THEM SEND THE MONEY TO YOU! Do a trustee-to-trustee transfer, where you tell the destination financial institution to go get the money from your old employer. You don't have to do it this way, but trust me, this is the safe and easy way to do it. You can also move it to your new employer's plan if they offer one. Work through your new employer's plan administrator to make it happen.

If you absolutely have to take money out of your 401K, take the absolute minimum that you need to SURVIVE. Make sure they withhold the maximum (generally 20%) and realize that this probably won't be enough. You will probably pay a 10% penalty, plus your regular tax rate (probably AT LEAST another 15%).

Moving Expenses:

Moving expenses should be simple, but the IRS insists on making them complicated. I'll try to simplify the rules you need to qualify, then go over the usual expenses, and then talk some about reimbursement and other complicated crap.

Here are the rules to see if your move qualifies:

You have to be moving to get or maintain a job. You don't actually have to have a job in the place you move to, but if not, you need to get one within a year. If you start a new job in a new place, you need to move yourself and your family within a year. If you move within a year but your family doesn't, you can deduct your moving expenses, but not theirs. If you have a good reason for not moving within a year, such as you wait to move your family for 18 months so your kids can finish school, that's okay, and you can deduct the expenses. The idea of all these rules is that you really have to be moving for job reasons, and not other reasons.

You need to be moving a decent distance. Just moving from house to house to lower your commute is not enough. Simple test, take your old commute from home to work, add 50 miles to it. If your new job is at least this distance from your old house, you're good. It's not really a tough test to meet. If you are military moving on Permanent Change of Station orders, you don't need to meet this test.

There's one more test that's complicated, but rarely comes into play. The gist of it is that you have to be moving near your new place of work. This is generally a no brainer. You basically can't move from Georgia to Texas when your job is in California. Duh. Ask a professional for help if this doesn't apply to you in an obvious way.

You have to do full-time work in your new location for at least 39 of the first 52 weeks after the move. Full-time is that which is typical for your job type. If you are self-employed these are more restrictive—seek professional assistance. If your job is seasonal, you can consider yourself to have worked the full year if you work the normal season in the first 52 weeks, and the "off-season" is less than six months. This most commonly applies to teachers who are good if they work full time for the normal school schedule for the first 52 weeks. Seasonal tax pros who work 4 out of 12 months can't use that exception. If you lose your new job due to employer's convenience and not for willful misconduct, you don't have to meet the test. Obviously, it's possible to need to file a tax return before you have met these tests. There are a number of ways to handle this, but my recommendation, if you're pretty sure you'll meet the test, is to take the deduction assuming you'll meet the test (this is allowed) and if you end up not meeting the test, amend the tax return to remove the deduction. You can also not take the deduction, and then amend to add it on when you do meet the test.

That's pretty much it for qualifying to deduct expenses.

Here's what you can deduct:

You can deduct only reasonable expenses for moving you, your family and your household goods. You must move by the most direct route and not take side trips or excess vacations. If you have some of your household at a different location, you can deduct the moving expenses for them, but not any more than it would have cost to move them by the direct route from your old home to new home. Make sure to save all receipts.

If you drive you can deduct 19 cents a mile, or actual costs for oil and gas ONLY. In addition to that, you can deduct parking and tolls.

You can deduct lodging, but not meals for you and your family members. You get lodging for the day you have to leave your old house, up to the day you get ANY lodging (including hotel) in the area of your new job. You can't deduct meals. You can deduct plane, rail or train fare for you and your family. You don't have to travel together, but you only get one trip per person. (You can't go back and forth moving kids and keep deducting your travel, but you can deduct each kid's plane ticket.)

You can deduct expenses for moving your household goods, if you pay them. This includes truck rental and supplies, or professional moving services.

You can deduct thirty days of storage either before or after the move (or combination of before and after, but not more than 30 days).

You can deduct the cost of connecting and disconnecting utilities (but not deposits or regular monthly charges).

Here's how to handle reimbursements:

First of all, if your company uses a professional relocation services company to move you, you probably got more reimbursement than you could have deducted, and they also tend to cover any additional taxes you might pay for extras they throw in. Refer to the information packet provided by the relocation company to see how it should be handled tax-wise. The good companies will actually provide a sample tax form with numbers filled in for your move.

Outside of that, you need to know how your employer reimbursed you. You probably need to contact them to see what happened, as they can handle reimbursement in a number of ways. Obviously, if they did not reimburse you, report all your allowed expenses and you're good to go. If you have a W-2 with a Code P in Box 12, or your employer reimbursed you and you have no code P in Box 12, read on...

Determine from your employer if all reimbursements are in Box 12 with Code P, Box 1 with your wages, or a combination. Reimbursements in Box 12 get reported, unless they exactly match your expenses. Reimbursements in Box 1 do not get reported (they are included as income and already taxed). Here are specific situations:

- If all reimbursements are in Box 12 with Code P, and they exactly match your expenses, don't report anything.

- If all reimbursements are in Box 12 with Code P, and the allowable expenses are different, report all expenses and reimbursements (the number from Box 12 with Code P).

- If all reimbursements are in Box 1 with your wages, report your allowed expenses, but no reimbursement.

- If there is a combination of reimbursements between Box 1 and Box 12 with Code P, report all allowed expenses and only the reimbursement from Box 12 with Code P.

These are reported on Form 3903

Military: Moves related to discharge from the military are exempt from the distance test.

Not discussed: Self-employed moves, International moves.

60. What the Hell is Alternative Minimum Tax and Why the Hell am I Paying It?

I'm not going to go into a ton of detail here, mainly because the Alternative Minimum Tax is a completely different tax system from the income tax we are used to. What it is, is a neat trick that the government came up with a number of years ago to make sure that even the super rich, with tons of deductions, paid their fair share. It now affects millions of people, and can be quite disturbing if you are subject to it. Early in my career as a Tax Super Genius, I would be working on tax returns and find that the refund stopped changing, even though there was plenty of room for deductions, and I kept adding them in. I soon learned this was the Alternative Minimum Tax (AMT).

The AMT basically gives you very few deductions, but has a very large standard deduction. It has only two tax rates, 26% and 28%. You generally get sucked into this if you have a large income, and/or lots of deductions.

To make things more confusing, the tax forms don't have a separate return where you calculate AMT and then compare it to your regular tax. What they do have is a short form that essentially undoes everything not allowed in AMT, and then adds in the stuff that's allowed. It then compares your AMT tax to regular tax, and if the AMT is higher, adds the difference to your regular tax. This makes it very difficult to really understand what's happening to your return because of AMT, and makes it hard to strategize to minimize taxes.

If, when you are reviewing your tax return, there is a number on Form 1040 Line 45, you have been hit with AMT. You should consider talking to a professional to see if there's anything you can do, and to develop strategies for future years to minimize it.

Charitable deductions are one of the few rock solid ways to minimize AMT. Check out the I Give to Charity section.

Military: Not much different here for you.

61. I Run a Home-Based Business Like Amway, Party Lights, Mary Kay, etc.

This section is for all the would-be home-based business millionaires selling AdvoCare, Amway, Pampered Chef, Mary Kay, etc. The time to think about taxes is before you open the business, but if you already have, the time is now! This section will tell you virtually everything you need to know about how taxes should, and do, work for a Multi-Level Marketing (MLM) type business. This is the kind of business where someone in the business recruits you to sell the products, and, eventually, recruit others into the business. This section works for Amway, Mary Kay, Avon, Pampered Chef, Herbalife, Isagenix, Scentsy and dozens of others you've never heard of.

Most clients I see trying these businesses out have not given a thought to taxes and are getting very little help from the businesses they are making money for. In fact, the first piece of advice I'll give is to ignore virtually everything the company, other associates or friends tell you about how to handle taxes for these businesses. To go further, I'll tell you to ignore every piece of tax information the company provides, except the 1099MISC they issue you (if you gross >$600) and the invoices for the products you buy and sell. You can, and should, keep better and more useful records all by yourself. More on that point later.

First, a couple of terms, some basic advice, and some warnings:

1. You should be, at this point, a sole proprietor. This means that you own and run the business by yourself, with no employees. You will file the business taxes as a part of your personal taxes, usually on a Schedule C. I strongly encourage you not to have any partners, even your spouse. Your spouse can help, but should generally not be an employee, and not have any true decision making power, except the power that is normal in a healthy spousal relationship (advice and support, but no "official" role). The reasons for this are myriad, and anyone who's delved into a partnership can attest to the issues that arise. For now, just trust me. Later you may want to form a more complicated business entity, but that will require professional assistance and guidance.

2. You are going to spend more time doing taxes, and it's going to cost more. Even if you use software (which I highly discourage if you are running a business) you will pay more for the programs.

3. You might not actually be a business. Most of the people starting these businesses will never have a dime of profit, and after a few years, the IRS will put the kabosh on taking a negative income from your business off of your regular taxable income. This is called Hobby Income. It means you do it more for fun than for profit. You still have to claim the income (on Line 21, Other Income), but you deduct the expenses on your Itemized Deductions (subject to 2% of income limit, maximum deductions equal to income and a bunch of other restrictions that ensure that you pay taxes on the income instead of getting write-offs). My advice

is to go full-bore, gung-ho toward making a profit for 3 years. File the Schedule C's and take the losses on your taxes (improving your refund). If, after three years, you haven't made a profit, and gross revenues aren't approaching 5 digits ($10,000), take real stock of where you're at. If revenues are growing and profitability seems close, keep things going. If revenues are flat, profits are a distant dream, and/or your enthusiasm is waning, bite the bullet and either shut the business down, or tone it back and start filing it as a Hobby.

4. The IRS doesn't like your business model. They tend to believe most MLM businesses are actually hobbies. They will scrutinize the line between business and personal expenses. They think pretty much every seminar you attend is a personal expenses. Be very careful to document everything that you deduct and be prepared to explain how it will actually benefit your business and is not a personal expense.

Moving along. Here's the advice you need to make things work...

Record Keeping: This is where the rubber meets the road. Good record keeping will save you when it comes to tax time. Your records don't need to be extensive, but they do need to be accurate and useable. I hate double entry bookkeeping and would never recommend it as a tool for a home-based business. I also have found that the various bookkeeping software programs are virtually useless when it comes to taxes. They may help when it comes to managing the business, but they suck for doing taxes. The best and easiest record keeping method I've found involves a small notebook, a big notebook and an envelope or box. The small notebook is for mileage, discussed below. The big notebook is for every other expense. You need simple columns set up: date, description, cost and payment received (if you pay something, it goes in the cost column, if you're paid it goes in the payment received column). You can add categories, but don't really need to. If you're unsure something is deductible, write it down and let your tax professional tell you if it's deductible. The box/envelope is for receipts—just throw them in. Really? No sorting, categorizing or organizing? No. Simply put, your odds of ever needing them for an audit are slim to none. Save the box, notebooks and tax returns for 7 years, and then throw it all away. If you ever do get audited, there's plenty of time to sort through the box and organize it to match the notebooks—but why do it if it's not necessary? If I'm doing your taxes I'm going to use the notebooks, and remind you that you should have a receipt for everything. You don't have to prove things to me (though I may question unbelievable things). It's important to not to over-think things. For example, if you make a sale involving sales tax, which you know a portion will go to the government, you still write down 100% of what you were paid (including the tax). Later, when you remit the sales tax to the government, it is entered as a payment (deduction). Get it—you get money, it's entered as income; you pay money, it's entered as a deduction.

The trick to your kind of business is that sometimes you don't make the sale, it happens through a website and is fulfilled by the company, with the payment going straight to the company, the product going straight to the consumer, and you getting a commission. Generally the company will only report the commission as income to you, which means you don't need to track any expenses like shipping, sales tax or the wholesale price—just the commission, which you can track when the payment comes to you. Just make sure your company handles it this way, and you'll be good. If the product is paid for by you, comes to you, and then you pass it on to the client for a markup, the entire price paid goes into your records as income, and all the costs to you (shipping, wholesale price, sales tax) go into your records as an expense.

Expenses: You can deduct any ordinary and necessary expenses for your business. I generally describe the requirements like this: If it will make you more money, is required by someone in authority, or makes your business more efficient or your life as a business person easier, it's probably deductible. Here's a non-exhaustive list:

1. Pretty much anything the company charges you for. If they deduct it off your commission check, deduct it off your taxes (you report the gross commission, not the commission after deductions).

2. Marketing Expenses: Business cards, website fees, posters, signs, sponsorships, commercials, advertising, pretty much anything you do to get someone to call YOU when they want your product.

3. Insurance: I'm not talking about homeowner's insurance here. I'm talking about "Oops! I screwed up and someone is suing me" insurance. Sometimes this is called Errors and Omissions Insurance, sometimes it's a liability bond, or a rider on your homeowner's insurance. Also, if you pay a rider to your car insurance for business use, the difference between that and regular insurance is deductible. There is also a self-employed health insurance deduction that allows you to deduct your health insurance costs if you have no other insurance source (if you can get insurance through your spouse's work this is a no-go).

4. Entertainment Expenses: Those party expenses count: the food, the favors, the entertainment. It all counts if you expect there's a chance you'll make money. Eventually you'll be with a client, or potential client, and pick up the tab for lunch or dinner. Generally, if you expect the expense to result in a sale that makes you money, either immediately or in the future (whether it ultimately does or not doesn't matter, as long as you expect it to), it's deductible. I recommend writing the name of the client on the receipt, as well as a quick description: "referral source," "potential client" or something like that.

5. Travel Expenses: These are a toughie. People love conflating personal and business travel. If you travel to Maine to visit family and see the lobster festival, and try to sell to some family and friends, the trip is primarily personal. You can

deduct expenses DIRECTLY RELATED to the sales efforts, but little else. I recommend keeping business and personal travel separate. You can visit a friend for dinner on a three day business trip, but don't do business for an hour on a three day personal trip. Also avoid what I call BS travel. Flying to Vegas to assess potential markets is transparent vacationing disguised as business travel, especially if you spend 23 out of every 24 hours in the casino! Be reasonable! Go on trips that are going to increase your money-making potential. Stay away from any others. For legitimate travel, you get airfare, rental car, tips, taxis, laundry, internet and phone, as well as 50% of meals and any other reasonable and necessary expenses. Travel assumes overnight trips away from your home area. The IRS is very skeptical of the sales seminars your company puts on. They consider that they are more motivational than instructional, and thus not deductible.

6. Cell phones, laptops and tablets: Do yourself a favor, get a business only laptop, cell phone, tablet and/or computer. It is simply too difficult to calculate expenses on a part-personal and part-business electronic device. Don't share your business number with friends and family (other than wife and kids). If you keep everything separate, the deductions are easy and legitimate. If you don't, you have to establish a business use percentage, and worry about listed property rules— which suck! This behavior also helps with the Hobby vs. Business discussion we've already had.

7. Vehicle Expenses: Keep a mileage log. Let me say it again, unless you have a vehicle that is 100%, no kidding, total business and no personal use, keep a mileage log. Don't worry about gas, repairs, oil changes, insurance or any other car expenses (except as discussed above under insurance). There are other ways to track vehicle expenses, but mileage is the best. Do track annual car taxes and finance charges. The easiest mileage log is a notebook where you write the date, the trip purpose and the miles driven. You will also need to know the total miles the vehicle is driven for the year, so write the odometer reading down every January 1st! Mileage will be one of your biggest expenses, so keep track of it religiously! 10,000 miles of properly tracked vehicle mileage can result in $1,500 or more of tax savings!

8. Home Office: Set aside a space in your home that is 100% business use. It should never be used for anything else, and regularly used for business. This is where you keep your business records, your business computer or laptop, make your sales calls from and meet clients. The tax term is regular and exclusive business use. If you do this, you deduct a percentage of the household expenses (rent, interest, taxes, utilities, insurance, repairs, etc.) based on the square footage of the office ratioed to the home square footage. Expenses directly related to the office, such as a dedicated phone line, do not have to be ratioed. You can also take a small depreciation deduction for the home losing value (let your tax professional handle this—it's a pain!). The IRS "simplified" this, allowing you to take $5 for every square foot of Home Office, up to $1,500, but it's BS to call it

simplifying, because any tax professional worth their salt is going to run the numbers both ways and take the number that makes the most sense.

9. Depreciation: Some items that you buy for your business, that have a useful life longer than a year will have to be depreciated over time rather than deducted all at once (examples include computers, digital cameras, machinery, big tools or office furniture). There are many options for deducting it up front, but be wary of this. There are tripwires that can cost you if you dispose of something before it has passed its useful life. Talk about these items with your tax advisor.

10. The stuff you buy to sell: This can get tricky. If everything you sell is paid for and shipped through the company, it's easy, as discussed above about commissions. If you order the stuff, pay for it and either deliver it or ship it to the customer, you have to track the wholesale price, shipping, sales tax and the amount you received. Even worse, if you order items to keep on hand for later sale directly to customers, you need to track all the purchases you made (at your cost is my recommendation) and track what is sold and what is on hand. This is the devil called inventory. You need to know what you have on hand at the beginning and end of the year, what you bought, and what you sold. The easiest way to do this is with an inventory notebook—now you have three notebooks. If you buy something to later sell, write it down with date, description and price paid. Have columns for date sold, and price sold for, and another column to make a note if it's disposed of without selling it (given away, used by yourself, or expired/lost/stolen). Track each item as it's sold or disposed of. At the end of the year, total everything left (that's Ending Inventory), everything bought during the year (that's Cost of Goods Sold), and everything sold (that's Gross Receipts). Ending Inventory this year becomes Beginning Inventory next year. If you sell some this way and some through the company on commission, you'll have to add commissions to your Gross Receipts, but I think you get the point. If I ran a business like this I would desperately try to avoid inventory; however, that might cost you some sales. Do what works best for you.

11. Taxes: These are mainly sales taxes. You need to work with your state or county to make sure you collect and remit sales taxes. Don't blow this off. Things get bad if you do. The sales tax you collect and remit is deductible if included in the price you charge, and the income you report. You also may need to pay business taxes and licensing fees to state/county/city. These are deductible, but you need to work these out on your own—this is an income tax guide, and these other taxes vary too much by locale to cover here. Again, don't screw these up. The local governments can be worse than the IRS if you mess up.

There's more that's deductible, but I think you get the idea.

Keep the record keeping up to date. It's a nightmare to back fill. Work your butt off to generate business and make money. Research best practices and talk to the people making money doing this. The idea is to MAKE money, and then be pissed off that you are paying taxes on it. Getting a big tax deduction from your unprofitable business is only good at tax time. Paying taxes is a sign of success!

Military: If you live in military housing your office in home deduction might be minimal. Consider using the $5 per square foot safe harbor.

62. I'm an Independent Contractor or I Got a Form 1099-MISC

What's an independent contractor? For the purpose of this section, I'm considering an independent contractor as anyone who's paid for **work** on a Form 1099-MISC vice on a W-2, or who works for themselves and is paid cash (or check or credit card) by their customers. I say work because I'm not talking about an Engineer getting paid a few bucks for coaching softball. I'm talking about someone who is in the business of doing the work they get paid for. This section is best used by someone who earns the majority of their income from the work they do that's paid in cash or via a 1099-MISC. If you're a painter who gets most of your money on a W-2, and gets a minor portion of their income on a 1099-MISC, this section can be helpful, but it's really not the prime focus. This section is also intentionally generic, so it can apply to a variety of businesses. Some specific businesses have their own sections, so check the <u>Table of Contents</u>.

There are a lot of reasons you might get a 1099-MISC that aren't because you're an independent contractor. An independent contractor will have a number in Box 7 of the 1099-MISC. However, even that doesn't mean you're in the business of whatever they paid you for on a 1099-MISC. If you are unsure, seek professional help.

What does this section not do?

Foremost, it assumes you are either a Sole Proprietor, or a Single Member LLC. In other words, the business is reported on your personal tax return, vice the business filing its own tax return. There are advantages and disadvantages to forming other business entities, but those are best discussed face-to-face with a professional you trust.

Second, it is mostly for contractors who provide services, vice those who make or buy items to sell. There is some good information for them, but I won't be covering inventory or cost of goods sold.

Third, it's not a guide on how to do your taxes. It's a bunch of best practices I've found to make running your business easier, your taxes simpler, and your life better. It's not the only way to do things, but it's what I've found works best. I assume you either have a tax pro who does the tax return, or you're pretty smart and capable of using tax software yourself (though I recommend having a professional check it the first couple years - the money you spend on this can pay you back in spades, both in not paying excess taxes, and getting great advice for the future).

Fourth, it's for SMALL businesses. If you're approaching 7 figures of gross income, thinking about hiring employees, or bringing on a partner, get a professional CPA involved.

How does a 1099-MISC / cash business work for taxes?

You'll be filing a Schedule C and reporting ALL income, and then taking any legitimate deductions to come up with 'net' income. This is what you pay taxes on. You have to pay it all as you go, or at the end of the year when you file your tax return. Also, there's nobody to pay for Social Security taxes except, well, you. Most people are barely cognizant of the 7.65% that's taken right off the top for Medicare and Social Security taxes out of their paycheck. What even the most aware don't realize is that their employer matches this deduction! As a 1099 recipient (self-employed is the IRS term) you have to pay both the employee and employer portion! This means a 15.3% additional tax! Imagine you're in the 15% tax bracket—that means you actually pay 30.3% taxes! And this doesn't even cover state taxes!

The good news is that, unlike a W-2 employee, you only pay these taxes on your 'net' income. This means you get to take all ordinary and necessary expenses off the top, before you pay a dime in taxes. Even employees with business expenses still pay their half of Social Security and Medicare taxes before any deductions. So what is 'ordinary and necessary'? I like to boil it down into two main categories: 1. things you pretty much have to pay, such as licensing, commissions and fees; 2. Things you pay because you expect them to increase your income, or make running your business easier or more efficient. If the expense meets either of these requirements, they're pretty much a lock as being deductible.

Knowing the above, it's important that I give one of my biggest pieces of advice— you pretty much should NEVER do something just because you expect it to help on your taxes. Spend money only if you have to, or because it's the best idea for your business! This has two benefits: 1. You don't waste money on stupid stuff; 2. Chances are the deduction is legitimate.

So what can I deduct?

Here's a non-exhaustive list: Supplies, rent, vehicle mileage, travel, bank fees, taxes, licensing, insurance, home office, office supplies, equipment, marketing, advertising, subcontractors, employees, postage, education, legal and professional expense, bank interest and much, much more. I'm going to give details on a few here:

Marketing Expenses: Business cards, website fees, posters, signs, sponsorships, commercials, advertising, pretty much anything you do to get someone to call YOU when they need your type of services.

Training, Education and Licensing: Whatever you pay to maintain your ability to do your business is deductible, as well as things you do to increase your skills or what you are allowed to do in your field. Classes, seminars, books and certificates mostly all qualify. Commercial Drivers License is another example.

Insurance: I'm not talking about homeowners insurance here. I'm talking about "Oops! I screwed up and someone is suing me" insurance. Sometimes this is called Errors and Omissions Insurance, sometimes it's a liability bond, or a rider on your homeowner's insurance. Also, if you pay a rider to your car insurance for business use, the difference between that and regular insurance is deductible. There is also a self-employed health insurance deduction that allows you to deduct your health insurance costs if you have no other insurance source (if you can get insurance through your spouse's work this is a no-go).

Entertainment Expenses: Eventually you'll be with a client, or potential client, and pick up the tab for lunch, dinner, or drinks. Generally, if you expect the expense to result in a sale that makes you money, either immediately or in the future (whether it ultimately does or not doesn't matter, as long as you expect it to), it's deductible. I recommend writing the name of the client on the receipt, as well as a quick description, such as "referral source" or "potential client."

Travel Expenses: These are a toughie. People love conflating personal and business travel. If you travel to Maine to visit family and see the lobster festival, and go to dinner with a client that is moving to your area, the trip is primarily personal. You can deduct expenses DIRECTLY RELATED to the meeting with the client, but little else. I recommend keeping business and personal travel separate. You can visit a friend for dinner on a three-day business trip, but don't do business for an hour on a three-day personal trip. Also avoid what I call BS travel. Flying to Vegas to assess potential markets is transparent vacationing disguised as business travel, especially if you spend 23 out of every 24 hours in the casino! Be reasonable! Go on trips that are going to increase your money-making potential. Stay away from any others. For legitimate travel, you get airfare, rental car, tips, taxis, laundry, internet and phone, as well as 50% of meals and any other reasonable and necessary expenses. Travel assumes overnight trips away from your home area.

Cell phones, laptops and tablets: Do yourself a favor, get a business only laptop, cell phone, tablet and/or computer. It is simply too difficult to calculate expenses on a part-personal and part-business electronic device. Don't share your business number with friends and family (other than wife and kids). If you keep everything separate, the deductions are easy and legitimate. If you don't, you have to establish a business use percentage, and worry about listed property rules—which suck!

Vehicle Expenses: Keep a mileage log. Let me say it again, unless you have a vehicle that is 100%, no kidding, total business and no personal use, keep a mileage log. Don't worry about gas, repairs, oil changes, insurance or any other car expenses (except as discussed above under insurance). There are other ways to track vehicle expenses, but mileage is the best. Do track annual car taxes and finance charges. The easiest mileage log is a notebook where you write the date, the trip purpose and the miles driven. You will also need to know the total miles the vehicle is driven for the year, so write the odometer reading down every January 1st! Mileage will be one of your biggest expenses, so keep track of it religiously! 10,000 miles of properly tracked vehicle mileage can result in $1,500 or more of tax savings!

Home Office: Set aside a space in your home that is 100% business use. It should never be used for anything else, and regularly be used for business. This is where you keep your business records, your business computer or laptop, make your sales calls from and meet clients. The tax term is regular and exclusive business use. If you do this, you deduct a percentage of the household expenses (rent, interest, taxes, utilities, insurance, repairs, etc.) based on the square footage of the office ratioed to the home square footage. Expenses directly related to the office, such as a dedicated phone line, do not have to be ratioed. You can also take a small depreciation deduction for the home losing value (let your tax professional handle this—it's a pain!) The IRS "simplified" this, allowing you to take $5 for every square foot of Home Office, up to $1,500. However, it's BS to call it simplifying, because any tax professional worth their salt is going to run the numbers both ways and take the number that makes the most sense.

Depreciation: Some items that you buy for your business that have a useful life longer than a year will have to be depreciated over time rather than deducted all at once (examples include computers, digital cameras, machinery, big tools or office furniture). There are many options for deducting it up front, but be wary of this: there are tripwires that can cost you if you dispose of something before it has passed its useful life. Talk about these items with your tax advisor.

Employees or Subcontractors: If you pay someone to do work for you in your business you can deduct it. Usually you will hire them as a subcontractor, and may even pay them in cash (use a check!) If you pay them more than $600 in a year, you will need to issue them a 1099-MISC – see your tax pro about this as soon as you pay a subcontractor. If you want to hire regular employees, you will have to withhold taxes from their check. Get help with this! Make sure you talk with your tax pro about the difference between an employee and a contractor. If you call an employee a contractor, you could be in trouble. But if you just have a few guys that you call when you have excess work and they can decline to do the work, and you only pay them if they do the work, they are probably a contractor.

What about Record Keeping?

This is where the rubber meets the road. Good record keeping will save you when it comes to tax time. Your records don't need to be extensive, but they do need to be accurate and useable. I hate double entry bookkeeping and would never recommend it as a tool for a basic contractor. I also have found that the various bookkeeping software programs are virtually useless when it comes to taxes. They may help when it comes to managing the business, but they suck for doing taxes.

The best and easiest record keeping method I've found involves a small notebook, a big notebook and an envelope or box. The small notebook is for mileage, discussed above. The big notebook is for every other expense. You need simple columns set up: date, description, cost and payment received (if you pay something, it goes in the cost column, if you're paid it goes in the payment received column). You can add categories, but don't really need to, if you're unsure something's deductible, write it down and let your tax professional tell you if it's deductible. The box/envelope is for receipts—just throw them in. Really? No sorting, categorizing or organizing? No. Simply put, your odds of ever needing them for an audit are slim to none. Save the box, notebooks and tax returns for 7 years, and then throw it all away. If you ever do get audited, there's plenty of time to sort through the box and organize it to match the notebooks—but why do it if it's not necessary? If I'm doing your taxes I'm going to use the notebooks, and remind you that you should have a receipt for everything. You don't have to prove things to me. It's important to understand not to over-think things. For example, if you make a sale involving sales tax, which you know a portion will go to the government, you still write down 100% of what you were paid (including the tax). Later, when you remit the sales tax to the government, it is entered as a payment (deduction). Get it—you get money, it's entered as income; you pay money, it's entered as a deduction.

Do I need a Separate Bank Account?

This one might be a little controversial, but I believe it's the be-all end-all of successful businesses. Combined with record keeping discussions above, and budgeting discussions below, this will make everything easier. Open a separate bank account for your business. It doesn't have to be in a different name, just separate from your personal business. If you use credit, get a second credit card that is exclusively for business (again, it doesn't have to actually be a business credit card, just one that you use only for business). Put all contractor business income in this account, and pay all business expenses out of it, or with the business credit card. Pay off the business credit card out of this account (don't carry a balance). The only expenses not paid out of the account are car expenses (especially gas) and home office expenses that will be divided based on square footage as discussed under home office above (utilities would not be paid out of the account, but office supplies and business-only cell phone would). The beauty of this method is that it simplifies budgeting, as we'll discuss below, and it allows reconciling of expenses to make sure your notebook covers everything. A good tax expert should be able to compare your account statements with your notebooks, and know if you missed something (assuming you don't intermingle personal and business expenses).

How do I Budget if my Income goes up and down?

Now that you have an account that is separate for business, you can start thinking about budgeting. Your income may fluctuate wildly, so you can use the business account to pay a "salary" to your personal account. I recommend letting some money build up in the business account until you have a feel for your income level. It will probably start small, but build up over time. Once you have a good feel, you can pay yourself this "salary". The "salary" should be no more than 50% of your annual gross income or 60% of your net income (divide it by twelve obviously, to get the monthly amount). You need to play around with it. Start small and raise it if income exceeds expectations, but NEVER pay yourself more than 60% of net income. Having a "salary" allows you to budget like you had a normal job. Keeping a buffer amount in the account allows you to have a "salary" even during lean months. By paying yourself a "salary" and saving the rest, if you have a really big month, you end up saving more, which in turn allows you to have the money to pay the tax bill that the big month will generate. When you file your taxes, you should have plenty of money to pay the tax bill, and still have money left to maintain a buffer. If you're lucky, you will have the ability to pay yourself a bonus to your personal account for a big purchase or vacation! The reason "salary" is in quotes is because it's not really a salary. It's just you living on the profits from your business. None of the baggage that comes with real salaries applies to this (like W-2's and tax withholding). The "salary" will not come into play on your tax return.

Do I need to make Estimated Payments?

My advice is that you should use the budgeting advice above to pay your taxes. You'll still need to make estimated tax payments if you're making good money, but you should pay the minimum required to avoid an underpayment penalty. Your tax pro will calculate them for you, but to explain simply: you need to pay at least as much as your prior year's total tax liability in withholding or estimated taxes to avoid a penalty (oversimplified explanation, but really all you need to know). This is an easy calculation for your tax pro, who can set up quarterly payments and provide vouchers for paying them. (The timing is a little weird. You pay 4/15, 6/15, 9/15 and 1/15.) You can also pay varying payments to try to avoid a tax bill, but it gets complicated, and the government won't pay you interest. You can also make these payments online now, and it's really quite easy.

Military: If you live in military housing your office in home deduction might be minimal. Consider using the $5 per square foot safe harbor.

63. I Drive for UBER (or other taxi like business)

This Tax Guide is written with very specific information for UBER drivers of all types. It can be used by LYFT and other casual taxi drivers, but may not have enough information for true professional non web based taxi drivers. Most clients I see trying these businesses out have not given a thought to taxes, but UBER does a fairly good job of helping out. The yearend statement you receive has a wealth of useful information. That said, there are a lot of deductions that aren't included that are a slam dunk, as well as some others that might be more shaky. As with all new business models, a lot of how these things apply specifically to UBER have not been fought out with the IRS, so some things may evolve over time. I'm going to start with a general discussion of things that every UBER driver should understand about taxes, and then get into the specifics of your documentation, and then get really specific on deductions.

First, some things you should know and understand:

1. Your business model is a bit unique, and you're doing some things that are fairly common in the tax world, but on a much higher scale than normal. You're using your own car for business, but the business side may be a very small percentage (or very large) of the use of your car. Your car is now a business asset (in part) and thus there are potential implications when you buy, sell or trade it. Keep things simple by only using one vehicle at a time, and taking the standard mileage rate (discussed later).

2. You should be, at this point, a sole proprietor. This means that you own and run the business by yourself, with no employees. You will file the business taxes as a part of your personal taxes, usually on a Schedule C. I strongly encourage you not to have any partners, even your spouse. Your spouse can help, but should generally not be an employee, and not have any true decision making power, except the power that is normal in a healthy spousal relationship (advice and support, but no "official" role). The reasons for this are myriad, and anyone who's delved into a partnership can attest to the issues that arise. For now, just trust me. Later you may want to form a more complicated business entity, but that will require professional assistance and guidance. If your spouse or partner also drives for UBER, they will have a separate and independent business, with it's own Schedule C, and, hopefully, their own car. Co-mingling cars at this point will greatly complicate your taxes and probably seriously confuse your, or your preparer's, tax software.

3. You are going to spend more time doing taxes, and it's going to cost more. Even if you use software (which I highly discourage if you are running a business) you will pay more for the programs. Based on the returns I've done so far, the more you drive, the more likely it is that you will also generate taxable income after expenses. This income will be taxed at a much higher rate. 15.3% minimum for self employment taxes (the self-employed person's Social Security and Medicare).

The good news is, you only pay taxes on the profit. We'll talk more about budgeting for taxes later.

4. You might not actually be a business. There's some tension between Hobby and Business income. If you take losses year after year, the IRS may put the kabosh on taking a negative income from your business off of your regular taxable income. This is called Hobby Income. It means you do it more for fun than for profit. UBER recruiting has not helped with this, as they sell it more like a Hobby than a Business. As a Hobby, you still have to claim the income (on Line 21 - Other Income), but you deduct the losses on your Itemized Deductions (subject to 2% of income limit, maximum deductions equal to income and a bunch of other restrictions that ensure that you pay taxes on the income instead of getting write offs.) Most UBER drivers will quickly find themselves turning a profit, making this a moot point. My advice is to go full bore, gung-ho towards making a profit for 3 years. File the Schedule C's and take the losses on your taxes (improving your refund). If, after three years, you haven't made a profit, and gross revenues aren't approaching 5 digits ($10,000), take real stock of where you're at. If revenues are growing and profitability seems close, keep things going. If revenues are flat, profits are a distant dream, and/or your enthusiasm is waning, bite the bullet and either shut the business down, or tone it back and start filing as a hobby.

Moving along. Here's the advice you need to make things work...

Income: This is the easy part. UBER will issue you a 1099-K and (maybe) a 1099-MISC. The 1099-K reports the income from all the rides you gave and the 1099-MISC reports all other income. You just need the totals from these, though some software lets you enter the whole form and pulls the relevant data. Box 1a of the 1099-K and Box 7 of the 1099-MISC is your Gross Receipts for your Schedule C. I've seen UBER drivers that took tips, and others that did not. If you get tips, add them to these amounts. Any other income you make as a driver should also be added, but I think UBER frowns on this.

Record Keeping: This is usually the biggest deal for a small business, but for UBER it should be very simple. Keep a mileage log!!!!! We will discuss mileage below but, know this, the one piece of information from UBER you should ignore is the mileage number - this is where you will save the most in taxes. (There are some great phone Apps available on the web for this. MileIQ is my favorite.) Other than that, have a notebook and an envelope for receipts. When you make a purchase for the business, write down date, description and cost, if you get income not tracked by UBER, add it here as well. Throw the receipt in the envelope. You can add categories, but don't really need to, if you're unsure something's deductible, write it down and let your tax guy tell you if it's deductible. That's it. Really? No sorting, categorizing or organizing? No. Simply put, your odds of ever needing them for an audit are slim to none. Save the box, notebook, mileage log and tax returns for 7 years, and then throw it all away. If you ever get audited, there's plenty of time to sort through the box and organize it to match the notebooks - but why do it if it's not necessary. If I'm doing your taxes I'm going to use the notebooks, and remind you that you should have a receipt for everything. You don't have to prove things to me. It's important to understand not to over think things. You get money, it's entered as income, you pay money, it's entered as a deduction. Keep in mind that UBER will report every penny you make, and then give you a report of deductions they took off. This is the easy part. For a lot of people, especially casual drivers, these will be all the deductions they have - except for the mileage log that you MUST have. You can use UBER's mileage, but you'll be leaving your best deduction on the table (or in the car!)

Expenses: You can deduct any ordinary and necessary expenses for your business. I generally describe the requirements like this: If it will make you more money, is required by someone in authority, or makes your business more efficient or your life as a business person easier, it's probably deductible. The list below is actually a fairly exhaustive list of normal business deductions, tailored to UBER. Some won't apply at all, but I'm leaving them there to stimulate your own thoughts. First some things most UBER driver's could or should be deducting (details in the numbered lists): Mileage, any tolls, parking or access fees not included in the UBER statement, driving gloves, insurance riders, office supplies for the business, steering wheel covers, car equipment specifically for driving passengers that is not normal car equipment or maintenance, mileage tracking apps or equipment, business cards, commercial driver's license, car seat additions that help for long driving, and a percentage of cell phone bills if you use your cell phone for the UBER app. Also any safety clothing or equipment that would not be considered normal for a car that was not used for driving paying passengers. Examples might be first aid kit, flares, fire extinguisher, or a reflective vest. Some might argue that these are normal for a regular driver, but how many people do you know that have these in their car? I would deduct them. Second, things you should not be deducting: Car maintenance including car washing, oil changes, gas, repairs or any other vehicle expenses unless they are specific alterations or additions to allow you to drive commercially (the mileage deduction covers all these things). Meals and entertainment would be unlikely. Uniforms or clothing would not be deductible, though possibly dry cleaning of a specific set of "driving clothes" - this would be shaky.

Here's the exhaustive list:

1. Pretty much anything the company charges you for. If they deduct it off your commission check, deduct it off your taxes (you report the gross commission, not the commission after deductions). These are all the deduction numbers listed on your annual UBER tax summary (except the income, of course). They generally fit into nice categories on your Schedule C, mostly as commissions.
2. Marketing Expenses: I'm thinking most of this will be handled by UBER, but if you spend money for business cards, signage, websites, etc, these will be deductible. I'm guessing you might have some for finding new drivers for UBER

and getting the referral fee, though I'm not sure you should be recruiting your own competition.

3. Insurance: I'm not talking about homeowners insurance here. I'm talking about 'oops I screwed up and someone is suing me insurance.' There's a lot of argument right now as to whether your personal car insurance is good enough for the business, and I'm the wrong guy to answer the question (tax guy - not insurance guy. See how that works? Don't take tax advice from a non tax guy, and don't take investment or insurance advice from your tax guy (except as how it relates to taxes). That said, if you have just regular, personal car insurance - no deduction. If you pay extra for commercial insurance, or a rider for commercial use, or a special 'UBER' rider that some companies are providing, that cost is deductible.

4. Entertainment and Meal Expenses: You really shouldn't have any of these. Your meals aren't deductible, even when waiting for a customer. I also can't really envision you taking someone to lunch. Since UBER provides the customers, this is a no-go. Some drivers have had mints or such in the car - I call those supplies (and they are deductible). I guess theoretically you might take a potential driver to lunch to talk to them about driving for UBER in hopes of getting the referral fee. In that case, save the receipt and write the person's name, and the topic of discussion on the receipt. That would be deductible entertainment expense - don't abuse this.

5. Travel Expenses: Unless UBER starts running those educational seminars that the IRS hates, you won't have much of this. I guess theoretically, you might drive to a big metropolis for a special event so you can make boatloads of money, so I guess we'll talk about it. If you travel specifically to drive and make money for UBER, you can deduct airfare (though how would you get your car there), car rental (I guess you could rent a car and drive it, but I'll bet that violates a lot of terms of use), lodging, mileage, meals, tips, tolls and other necessary travel expenses. For meals you can take a standard Federal daily rate for the area you are in (google 'per diem rates' and you'll find a list). If the travel is not 100% for business - like you visit family and do a few rides, or drive to Vegas or New York City for a long weekend and some shows, and do some driving while you're there - it gets complicated. You can take a portion of the travel based on the percentage of time spent "on the clock" for UBER.

6. Cell phones, laptops and tablets: You can take a portion of the phone and data costs for the phone you use for UBER. Ratio based on time or data usage. Don't go crazy figuring the exact ratio. If you do a lot of driving, or it's your main source of income, you may want to get a business only phone, and/or laptop. You can take a portion of your personal stuff, but it might not be worth it unless the ratio is high. We'll talk about business use of home later. The purchase of laptops or phones that you use for business generally requires them to be depreciated (taking a portion every year for several years.) Your tax professional or software should handle this, but make sure you put the information in right.

7. Vehicle Expenses: Keep a mileage log. Let me say it again, unless you have a vehicle that is 100%, no s**t, total business and no personal use, keep a mileage log. Don't worry about gas, repairs, oil changes, insurance or any other car expenses (except as discussed above under insurance). There are other ways to

track vehicle expenses, but mileage is the best. Do track annual car taxes and finance charges. The easiest mileage log is a notebook where you right the date, the trip purpose and the miles driven. You will also need to know the total miles the vehicle is driven for the year, so write the odometer reading down every January 1st! Mileage will be one of your biggest expenses, so keep track of it religiously! 10,000 miles of properly tracked vehicle mileage can result in $1500 of tax savings! UBER only tracks miles with passengers. If you're "on the clock" driving around waiting for a call, driving to or from a pickup, or driving to do other things to support your business - write it down! You pretty much get no other deductions for the vehicle, but the mileage deduction is very generous.

8. Home Office: If your business is getting big, set aside a space in your home that is 100% business use. Never used for anything else, and regularly used for business. This is where you keep your business records, your business computer or laptop, and do other business related things. The tax term is regular and exclusive business use. If you do this, you deduct a percentage of the household expenses - rent, interest, taxes, utilities, insurance, repairs, etc, based on the square footage of the office ratioed to the home square footage. Expenses directly related to the office, such as a dedicated phone line; do not have to be ratioed. You can also take a small depreciation deduction for the home losing value (let your tax guy handle this - it's a b**ch!) The IRS "simplified" this, allowing you to take $5 for every square foot of Home Office, up to $1500, but it's BS to call it simplifying, because any tax guy worth their salt is going to run the numbers both ways and take the number that makes the most sense.

9. Depreciation: Some items that you buy for your business, that have a useful life longer than a year will have to be depreciated over time rather than deducted all at once (examples include computers, digital cameras, machinery, big tools or office furniture). There are many options for deducting it up front, but be wary of this, there are tripwires that can cost you if you dispose of something before it has passed its useful life. Talk about these items with your tax advisor.

10. Licenses: If you get a commercial driver's license, that is deductible. If you have to pay for special licenses, tags, access fees or other things to let you pick up passengers in an area or work in an area, those are deductible. UBER pays some of these for you and accounts for them on your statement, so don't double deduct!

11. Taxes: Unlikely, but sales or other taxes may come into play in some super psycho jurisdictions. UBER should handle this, but don't assume they do. You also may need to pay business taxes and licensing fees to State/County/City. These are deductible, but you need to work these out on your own - this is an income tax guide, and these other taxes vary too much by locale to cover here. Again, don't screw these up. The local governments can be worse than the IRS if you mess up. There's more that's deductible, but I think you get the idea.

Do I need a Separate Bank Account? This one might be a little controversial, but I believe it's the be all end all of successful businesses. Once your business really gets going, and is more than just a little side income, it's this, combined with record keeping discussions above, and budgeting discussions below, this will make everything easier. Open a separate bank account for your business. It doesn't have to be in a different name, just separate from your personal business. If you use credit, get a second credit card that is exclusively for business (again, it doesn't have to actually be a business credit card, just one that you use only for business). Put all business income in this account, and pay all business expenses out of it, or with the business credit card. Pay off the business credit card out of this account. The only expenses not paid out of the account are car expenses (especially gas) and home office expenses that will be divided based on square footage as discussed under home office above (utilities would not be paid out of the account, but office supplies and business only cell phone would). The beauty of this method is that it simplifies budgeting as we'll discuss below, and it allows reconciling of expenses to make sure your notebook covers everything. A good tax expert should be able to compare your account statements with your notebooks and know if you missed something (assuming you don't intermingle personal and business expenses).

How do I Budget if my Income goes up and down? Now that you have an account that is separate for business, you can start thinking about budgeting. Your income may fluctuate wildly, so you can use the business account to pay a "salary" to your personal account. I recommend letting some money build up in the business account until you have a feel for your income level. It will probably start small, but build up over time. Once you have a good feel, you can pay yourself this salary. The salary should be no more than 50% of your annual gross income or 60% of your net income (divide it by twelve obviously, to get the monthly amount). You need to play around with it. Start small and raise it if income exceeds expectations, but NEVER pay yourself more than 60% of net income. Having a salary allows you to budget like you had a normal job. Keeping a buffer amount in the account allows you to have a "salary" even during lean months. By paying yourself a salary and saving the rest, if you have a really big month, you end up saving more, which in turn allows you to have the money to pay the tax bill that the big month will generate. When you file your taxes, you should have plenty of money to pay the tax bill, and still have money left to maintain a buffer, and, if you're lucky, have the ability to pay yourself a bonus to your personal account for a big purchase or vacation!

Do I need to make Estimated Payments? My advice is that you should use the budgeting advice above to pay your taxes. You'll still need to make estimated tax payments if you're making good money, but you should pay the minimum required to avoid an underpayment penalty. Your tax advisor will calculate them for you, but to explain simply: you need to pay at least as much as your prior year's total tax liability in withholding or estimated taxes to avoid a penalty (oversimplified explanation, but really all you need to know). This is an easy calculation for your tax guy and he will set up quarterly payments and provide vouchers for paying them. (The timing is a little weird. You pay on 4/15, 6/15, 9/15 and 1/15.) You can also pay varying payments to try to avoid a tax bill, but it gets complicated, and the government won't pay you interest.

That's all! Keep the record keeping up to date. It's a nightmare to back fill. Work your ass off to generate business and make money. Research best practices and talk to the people making money doing this. The idea is to MAKE money, and then be pissed off that you are paying taxes on it. Getting a big tax deduction from your unprofitable business is only good at tax time. Paying taxes is a sign of success!

64. I am (or will be) a Real Estate Agent

So you've got your real estate agents license and that first commission is finally on the way. No way around it now, you have potentially taxable income. The question is, how much? And, how do you pay as little as possible? This section assumes that you will be paid on a 1099-MISC, as a self-employed Real Estate Agent. If you're getting a W-2, some of this will be useful, but not all. I'm also assuming that you work for a real estate company, and aren't completely independent. Much of this advice isn't gospel, it's just what I've seen and think works best. In some ways, it's a list of "best practices." As always, you should use this post as a starting point, and seek professional assistance when it comes to your personal situation. I am also going to assume you have not formed a complex business entity such as an S Corporation or Multi Member Limited Liability Corporation. There are benefits and disadvantages to these, but you need to talk to a professional to understand them.

I'm going to start with some basics, and then get into details. The first big surprise you will have is that nobody's taking taxes out of your paycheck. You have to pay it all as you go, or at the end of the year when you file your tax return. The second thing is that there's nobody to pay for Social Security taxes except, well, you. Most people are barely cognizant of the 7.65% that's taken right off the top for Medicare and Social Security taxes out of their paycheck. What even the most aware don't realize is that their employer matches this deduction! As a 1099 recipient (self-employed is the IRS term) you have to pay both the employee and employer portion! This means a 15.3% additional tax! Imagine you're in the 15% tax bracket—that means you actually pay 30.3% taxes! And this doesn't even cover state taxes!

The good news is that, unlike a W-2 employee, you only pay these taxes on your 'net' income. This means you get to take all ordinary and necessary expenses off the top, before you pay a dime in taxes. Even employees with business expenses still pay their half of Social Security and Medicare taxes before any deductions. So what is 'ordinary and necessary'? I like to boil it down into two categories: 1. Things you pretty much have to pay such as licensing, commissions and fees. 2. Things you pay because you expect them to increase your income or make your business easier or more efficient. If they meet either of these requirements, they're pretty much a lock as being deductible.

Knowing the above, it's important to tell you one of my biggest pieces of advice—you pretty much should NEVER do something just because you expect it to help on your taxes. Spend money only if you have to, or because it's the best idea for your business! This has two benefits: 1. You don't waste money on stupid stuff. 2. Chances are the deduction is legitimate.

So now comes the part you've been waiting for: What the heck can I deduct? Here's a non-exhaustive list, with some details, to get you started:

Marketing Expenses: Business cards, website fees, MLS dues, lead-generating expenses, posters, signs, sponsorships, commercials, advertising, pretty much anything you do to get someone to call YOU when they want to buy or sell a house. As a non-tax aside, you need to evaluate these carefully, and talk to experienced agents to find the best of these. Your commissions are big, but come infrequently. You need to understand how much you spend for each commission so you can properly evaluate what works best.

Gifts and Referral Rewards: Gifts to clients are generally limited to $25 per person, per year. (That's the deductible amount, you can give more.) Be careful of referral fees. You should have received more training on this than me to get your license, but I will simply remind you that there are varying rules from state to state, as well as RESPA requirements that restrict what amounts, how and to whom you may pay a referral fee—check with your senior brokers before paying these. If the referral fees are legal, there are ways to deduct them, but talk to your tax professional about them.

Training, Education and Licensing: Whatever you pay to maintain your ability to be an agent is deductible, as well as things you do to increase your skills or what you are allowed to do in your field. Classes, seminars, books and certificates mostly all qualify.

Insurance: I'm not talking about homeowners insurance here. I'm talking about "Oops! I screwed up and my client is suing me" insurance; or someone who's not my client is suing me. Sometimes this is called Errors and Omissions Insurance. If your state or agency doesn't require it, get it anyway! Also, if you pay a rider to your car insurance for business use, the difference between that and regular insurance is deductible. There is also a self-employed health insurance deduction that allows you to deduct your health insurance costs if you have no other insurance source (if you can get insurance through your spouse's work this is a no-go).

Entertainment Expenses: Eventually you'll be with a client, or potential client, and pick up the tab for lunch, dinner, or drinks. Generally, if you expect the expense to result in a sale that makes you money, either immediately or in the future (whether it ultimately does or not doesn't matter, as long as you expect it to), it's deductible. I recommend writing the name of the client on the receipt, as well as a quick description, such as "house hunting," "referral source," or "potential client."

Travel Expenses: These are a toughie. People love conflating personal and business travel. If you travel to Maine to visit family and see the lobster festival, and go to dinner with a client that is moving to your area, the trip is primarily personal. You can deduct expenses DIRECTLY RELATED to the meeting with the client, but little else. I recommend keeping business and personal travel separate. You can visit a friend for dinner on a three-day business trip, but don't do business for an hour on a three-day personal trip. Also avoid what I call BS travel. Flying to Vegas to assess potential real estate markets is transparent vacationing disguised as business travel, especially if you spend 23 out of every 24 hours in the casino! Be reasonable! Go on trips that are going to increase your money-making potential. Stay away from any others. For legitimate travel, you get airfare, rental car, tips, taxis, laundry, internet and phone, as well as 50% of meals and any other reasonable and necessary expenses. Travel assumes overnight trips away from your home area.

Cell phones, laptops and tablets: Do yourself a favor, get a business-only laptop, cell phone, tablet and/or computer. It is simply too difficult to calculate expenses on a part-personal and part-business electronic device. Don't share your business number with friends and family (other than wife and kids). If you keep everything separate, the deductions are easy and legitimate. If you don't, you have to establish a business use percentage, and worry about listed property rules—which suck!

Vehicle Expenses: Keep a mileage log. Let me say it again, unless you have a vehicle that is 100%, no s**t, total business and no personal use, keep a mileage log. Don't worry about gas, repairs, oil changes, insurance or any other car expenses (except as discussed above under insurance). There are other ways to track vehicle expenses, but mileage is the best. Do track annual car taxes and finance charges. The easiest mileage log is a notebook where you write the date, the trip purpose and the miles driven. You will also need to know the total miles the vehicle is driven for the year, so write the odometer reading down every January 1st! Mileage will be one of your biggest expenses, so keep track of it religiously! 10,000 miles of properly tracked vehicle mileage can result in $1,500 or more of tax savings!

Home Office: Set aside a space in your home that is 100% business use. It should never be used for anything else, and regularly be used for business. This is where you keep your business records, your business computer or laptop, make your sales calls from and meet clients. The tax term is regular and exclusive business use. If you do this, you deduct a percentage of the household expenses (rent, interest, taxes, utilities, insurance, repairs, etc.) based on the square footage of the office ratioed to the home square footage. Expenses directly related to the office, such as a dedicated phone line, do not have to be ratioed. You can also take a small depreciation deduction for the home losing value (let your tax professional handle this—it's a pain!) The IRS "simplified" this, allowing you to take $5 for every square foot of Home Office, up to $1,500, but it's BS to call it simplifying. Any tax professional worth their salt is going to run the numbers both ways and take the number that makes the most sense.

Employer Reported Expenses: In many cases your employer is going to charge you for a number of different things, such as marketing and insurance. They will generally track the expenses and then deduct them from your commission check when you make a sale or broker a purchase. Virtually everything they charge you for will be deductible, but they will report the full amount of your commission on the 1099-MISC at the end of the year, and then give you a report of what they charged you. This simplifies things for record keeping, except that you need to make sure not to deduct something from the employer report twice by tracking it in your own records.

Depreciation: Some items that you buy for your business that have a useful life longer than a year will have to be depreciated over time rather than deducted all at once (examples include computers, digital cameras or office furniture). There are many options for deducting it up front, but be wary of this. There are tripwires that can cost you if you dispose of something before it has passed its useful life. Talk about these items with your tax advisor.

Record Keeping: This is where the rubber meets the road. Good record keeping will save you when it comes to tax time. Your records don't need to be extensive, but they do need to be accurate and useable. I hate double entry bookkeeping and would never recommend it as a tool for a Real Estate Agent. I also have found that the various bookkeeping software programs are virtually useless when it comes to taxes. They may help when it comes to managing the business, but they suck for doing taxes. The best and easiest record keeping method I've found for Real Estate Agents involves a small notebook, a big notebook and an envelope or box. The small notebook is for mileage, discussed above. The big notebook is for every other expense (except employer reported expenses.) You need simple columns set up: date, expense and cost. You can add categories, but don't really need to. If you're unsure something's deductible, write it down and let your tax professional tell you if it's deductible. The box/envelope is for receipts—just throw them in. Really? No sorting, categorizing or organizing? No. Simply put, your odds of ever needing them for an audit are slim to none. Save the box, notebooks and tax returns for 7 years, and then throw it all away. If you ever do get audited, there's plenty of time to sort through the box and organize it to match the notebooks—why do it if it's not necessary? If I'm doing your taxes I'm going to use the notebooks, and remind you that you should have a receipt for everything. You don't have to prove things to me.

Separate Bank Account: This one might be a little controversial, but I believe it's the be-all end-all of successful businesses. Combined with record keeping discussions above, and budgeting discussions below, this will make everything easier. Open a separate bank account for your Real Estate Agent business. It doesn't have to be in a different name, just separate from your personal account. If you use credit, get a second credit card that is exclusively for business (again, it doesn't have to actually be a business credit card, just one that you use only for business). Put all Real Estate income in this account, and pay all Real Estate expenses out of it, or with the business credit card. Pay off the business credit card out of this account (don't carry a balance). The only expenses not paid out of the account are car expenses (especially gas) and home office expenses. Home office expenses will be divided based on square footage as discussed under home office above (utilities would not be paid out of the account, but office supplies and business only cell phone would). The beauty of this method is that it simplifies budgeting as we'll discuss below, and it allows reconciling of expenses to make sure your notebook covers everything. A good tax expert should be able to compare your account statements with your notebooks and know if you missed something (assuming you don't intermingle personal and business expenses).

Budgeting and Saving: Now that you have an account that is separate for business, you can start thinking about budgeting. Your income may fluctuate wildly, so you can use the business account to pay a "salary" to your personal account. I recommend letting some money build up in the business account until you have a feel for your income level. It will probably start small, but build up over time. Once you have a good feel, you can pay yourself this "salary". The "salary" should be no more than 50% of your annual gross income or 60% of your net income (divide it by twelve obviously, to get the monthly amount). You need to play around with it. Start small and raise it if income exceeds expectations, but NEVER pay yourself more than 60% of net income. Having a "salary" allows you to budget like you had a normal job. Keeping a buffer amount in the account allows you to have a "salary" even during lean months. By paying yourself a "salary" and saving the rest, if you have a really big month, you end up saving more, which in turn allows you to have the money to pay the tax bill that the big month will generate. When you file your taxes, you should have plenty of money to pay the tax bill, and still have money left to maintain a buffer. If you're lucky, you will have the ability to pay yourself a bonus to your personal account for a big purchase or vacation! The reason "salary" is in quotes is because it's not really a salary. It's just you living on the profits from your business. None of the baggage that comes with real salaries applies to this (like W-2's and tax withholding). The "salary" will not come into play on your tax return.

Estimated Payments: My advice is that you should use the budgeting advice above to pay your taxes. You'll still need to make estimated tax payments if you're making good money, but you should pay the minimum required to avoid an underpayment penalty. Your tax advisor will calculate them for you, but to explain simply: you need to pay at least as much as your prior year's total tax liability in withholding or estimated taxes to avoid a penalty (oversimplified explanation, but really all you need to know). This is an easy calculation for your tax professional, who will set up quarterly payments and provide vouchers for paying them. (The timing is a little weird. You pay 4/15, 6/15, 9/15 and 1/15.) You can also pay varying payments to try to avoid a tax bill, but it gets complicated, and the government won't pay you interest. You can also now make these payments online, which makes things easier.

Military: If you live in military housing your office in home deduction might be minimal. Consider using the $5 per square foot safe harbor.

65. I'm Renting out my Former Home

This section is designed for the average homeowner who is converting their personal residence into rental property, either because they are unable to sell it, intend to reside in it later, or simply hope to use it as an investment. It does not cover all the specifics of how to file a Rental Property tax return; rather, it covers record keeping and tax issues that an owner of Residential Rental Real Estate should be aware of. This section does not discuss Alternative Minimum Tax implications of Rental Property. I feel strongly that you should have a tax pro help you, at least for the first year, and have any self-prepared tax returns checked once in a while.

When is it Rental Property?

It's rental property the day it is available for rent. This is when you can start deducting expenses. Generally, when you put the sign out front, put the ad in the paper, or tell your co-workers to find you a tenant, you have made it available for rent.

What is Rent?

Rent is the full amount of rent received. If you have a property manager who deducts a commission, the rent is the full rent paid (including the commission) and the commission is a deduction. Similarly, if your tenant performs a repair and deducts the cost from the rent, the rent is the full amount of the rent and the deducted amount is a repair expense. If someone pays advance rent, include it in the year received. If a security deposit is paid, it becomes rent when you keep it to cover an expense (and the expense becomes a deduction). If the deposit is agreed as non-refundable (such as a pet cleaning deposit) it is rent when received. If the tenant is supposed to pay rent and doesn't, do not include the amount not paid as rent. This means there is no "bad debt" deduction for rental—if you don't get it, it's not rent.

Deductible Expenses:

You can deduct all reasonable and necessary expenses for the rental of your home. Some items must be depreciated over their useful life (defined by the IRS). Be careful and make sure to do this right—there's more information coming later in the section. These must be expenses you pay for—your labor is not an expense. A fairly comprehensive list of expenses:

Mortgage interest (pro-rate by day for the first year of rental)
Taxes (pro-rate by day for the first year of rental)
Insurance (pro-rate by day for the first year of rental)
Mortgage insurance premiums (pro-rate by day for the first year of rental)
Homeowner's association dues

Pest control
Utilities you pay (including those paid when unoccupied but available for rent)
Advertising expenses
Repairs
Landscaping
Painting
Legal expenses for collecting rent, preparing leases, evicting tenants
Improvements
Tax prep fees for rental-related forms
Management fees
Cleaning expenses
Travel and mileage to manage the rental property (the primary purpose of the trip must be to manage the rental property—don't try to deduct a vacation during which you "check on" the rental.)

Save receipts for all of these and report the amounts to your tax preparer.

Depreciation:

Depreciation is how you deduct the cost of major items with a life longer than 1 year. You will deduct a portion of the cost a little at a time over a specified number of years. Don't let someone tell you not to depreciate so you can avoid recapture—you have to recapture any depreciation allowed (whether deducted or not).

You will depreciate the building, appliances and any improvements to the property, as well as certain landscaping items (fences, trees, etc.). It's important to understand that if you have a major expense that increases the value, or prolongs the life of your property, it will be depreciated vice deducted. Repairs that do not increase the value or extend the life may be deducted. Examples of improvements are air conditioner replacement, roof replacement, and additions. Examples of repairs are painting, replacing garbage disposal, repairing hole in roof, repairing air conditioner unit.

When converting your home to rental you need to know the Basis. This is generally the price you paid for the home, plus any improvements you made to it (see IRS Pub 551, or a tax professional for other things that might affect it). If the Fair Market Value (FMV) the day you convert it to rental property is less than this value, then this is your basis. The FMV is what your house would sell for to a willing buyer. You also need to know what the land is worth. You subtract this from the basis before depreciating the basis. You can determine the land value from your property tax card or by comparing to other similar properties sold in the area. You will depreciate the house by taking an even portion of the basis every month for the next 27.5 years (this means the first year's deduction will be smaller, and the deduction for the rest of the years will be about the same). Your tax pro will need the basis, land price, FMV, date purchased and date available for rent for your house.

Improvements are depreciated for 27.5 years just like the house. Appliances are depreciated for 5 years and landscaping improvements are depreciated for 15 years. See IRS Pub 527 for how to depreciate 5- and 15-year property. Your tax preparer will need to know the date you bought these items and the price you paid for them (including installation if you paid for it).

Do I need a Property Manager?

I like property managers. They will keep about 10% of your rent, but if they can save you 1 month of vacancy, they've paid for 10 months of commissions. If you try to rent without one, and can generally keep the place occupied, you probably are okay without one. If you try to rent it and it goes more than a month empty, get referrals and hire a property manager. Similarly, if you have a property manager and your house goes vacant more than a month, find a new property manager.

Active Participation:

It generally behooves you to be an active participant in the renting of your property. You can be an active participant even if you have a property manager. If you make the decisions about what rent to charge, what repairs to make, and whether to allow pets, you are actively participating. Even if the manager says: "I think we should raise the rent to $1,200." and you have to give the OK, you are actively participating. By being an active participant, you can generally deduct up to $25,000 of rental loss from the rest of your income (subject to income and filing status limitations). If you are totally passive in the rental, you cannot deduct any losses. If you are passive, or you have losses in excess of the limit, you will have to carry them over until you have a gain or dispose of the property.

At Risk Issues:

You may be asked if you are "At Risk" for the full amount of your rental. This means that you are not protected from losses on the property should everything go south on you. Generally speaking, unless you have some sort of a loan that you would not have to pay back (such as from a family member) you are At Risk for the full amount.

Tax Implications When Selling:

When selling a house that has been used as rental property, it is generally treated as a sale of a business asset. Thus, it is a fully taxable transaction. It will be reported on Form 4797 (Sale of Business Assets). The form will ask for the date purchased, date sold, the sale price (minus expenses of sale) and the Basis. Other than basis, these entries are fairly self-explanatory. The basis is that which you are using to depreciate the home. It is the price paid (or FMV when converted to rental if this was lower than the basis) + the cost of any improvements – any depreciation taken or allowed. There are other things that might affect the basis, but they are unusual and won't normally be seen. The gain or loss is the difference between the basis and the sales price.

It is possible to use the exclusion for the Sale of Main Home if you meet the requirements. This will normally only occur if you lived in the home for at least two years before you rented it out and sold it within three years of renting it. If this is the case, you may be able to exclude up to $250,000 of the gain ($500,000 if MFJ). You may use this exclusion for all gain, except that attributable to depreciation. See the I'm Selling my Rental Property section.

Personal Use or Part-Year Rentals:

If you rent your property for only part of the year, or you rent only a portion of your property (such as a room or a duplex) you need to pro-rate your expenses. Your tax pro will need to know the status of the property for each day of the year (rented, occupied by you, occupied by family, vacant, vacant but available for rent). They will also need to know the square footage of the property that is rental use, personal use and communal use, as well as which expenses cover the whole property (mortgage, taxes, etc.) and which are exclusive to the rental portion (repairs to that portion, utilities billed separately, etc.). There are more intricacies of this—contact your tax pro for more details.

State Issues:

If you rent out a property in a state that is not your state of residency, make sure you make this clear to your tax pro and make sure you understand how each state handles it. South Carolina, for example, requires you to add an out-of-state rental loss back and subtract an out-of-state rental gain from income.

Military: For selling your home as discussed above for the main home exclusion, the 2 of 5 year rule is extended by up to 10 years. See the Military discussion in the I'm Selling my Rental Property section.

66. What about the Affordable Care Act (Obamacare)

I wanted to do a section on the Affordable Care Act; however, I'm a tax expert and this is a tax book, so I will be primarily focused on the tax implications of the law. I have read the entire law several times, and I'd like to help people understand more than just the tax implications of the law. Use this section as a starting point, but PLEASE don't rely on it as your sole source of information.

Healthcare Marketplaces:

The easiest way to access the marketplaces is via www.healthcare.gov. The big "Apply Now" button is hard to miss. Just below that is a "Want to Learn More" statement with a "Start Here" button. I highly recommend clicking it and reading the information. In addition, at the bottom of that page, you can put in your zip code to find local help centers.

If you don't have insurance, and can't get it through your job, this is the place to start. It will work you through the subsidy (called the Premium Tax Credit) available. You can get a subsidy if you are ineligible for insurance from another source (generally your employer or another government program), and your income is below 400% of the poverty level for your family size. You may also be eligible for Medicaid if you are below 133% of the poverty level. You can also use the marketplace if you have insurance available, but you won't get a subsidy— I'm not sure if you can get a better deal here than your current insurance, but you can try.

The biggest points I will make on it are:

1. Keep the Marketplace notified about changes to your income or family status.
2. You don't have to get a Silver Plan. You get the same subsidy no matter which plan you choose.
3. To clarify the second point, the subsidy is designed to cap your out-of-pocket costs for a Silver Plan at 9.5% of your income. If you get a lower tier plan, you will have lower out-of-pocket costs for premiums, but higher costs for care. If you get a higher level plan, you will have higher costs for premiums, but lower costs for care.
4. The first point is the big one, though. The subsidy goes right to the marketplace, is estimated based on 2014 income, and gets reconciled on your 2016 tax return (for 2017 calendar year it is based on your 2015 income, and is reconciled on your 2017 tax return). Any changes that increase your subsidy between 2014 and 2016 get you a bigger refund, but, if your income goes up from 2014 to 2016, you may have to pay back the difference in subsidy! This is the BIG pitfall that MUST be avoided.

The Premium Assistance Tax Credit (subsidy):

You can get a subsidy if you are ineligible for insurance from another source (generally your employer or another government program), and your income is below 400% of the poverty level for your family size. The subsidy is generally paid directly to the insurance company, and is designed to keep your costs below 9.5% of your income. In the bullets I use 2016 for the year you are getting the subsidy but for many of you we will be talking about your 2017 calendar year. In that case, the tax return used to determine your subsidy would be 2015. The pattern continues for future years. Here are the details:

1. The term subsidy really refers to the refundable Premium Assistance Tax Credit (PATC).
2. The PATC is calculated on a monthly basis using 1/12 of the annual income for 2016.
3. The PATC may be applied directly to premiums for insurance obtained through the exchanges. The 2016 tax return will reconcile the amounts paid with the actual credit eligible and the difference applied to 2016 tax.
4. If you receive too much credit, you may have to repay the excess as an additional tax on your 2016 return. My research indicates that this amount could be in the **tens of thousands of dollars**! The good news is that if your income is below 400% of the poverty level, the repayment is capped at between $300 and $2,500, depending on filing status and income. Still, if you go above 400% of poverty level, you could be in **REAL TROUBLE!**
5. To avoid the above, it is vital that you keep the exchange informed of changes in income, marital status and family size on a month-to-month basis if they occur.
6. I ran 2 scenarios using numbers from various exchanges. My worst-case scenario involved a 62-year-old with a family of four where a significant (somewhat unrealistic) increase in income from 2014 to 2016 could result in a repayment in excess of $30,000. I also ran a 55-year-old single person, with 2014 income of $35,000 and 2016 income of $46,100. This fairly plausible scenario would result in a repayment of just under $7,000. These numbers will vary based on changes in rates and various states, but they are for warning purposes only.
7. The Healthcare Exchanges will offer plans categorized as Bronze, Silver, Gold and Platinum based on the percentage of costs covered. In any case, out-of-pocket expenses will be capped annually at a fairly reasonable amount. Some of the exchanges don't specifically or obviously use these categorizations, but they do specify cost, subsidy, deductibles, and caps.
8. The subsidy is calculated based on the second cheapest Silver Plan price for the state exchange the taxpayer uses. The credit is designed to cap out-of-pocket expenses for insurance premiums for this plan at between 2 and 9.5% of income for persons below 400% of the poverty level (2% for persons at or below 133% ranging up to 9.5% for people at 400%).
9. The PATC is calculated per above regardless of the plan actually accepted. This means that accepting a lower tier plan will result in lower out-of-pocket expenses for premiums while a higher plan will cost more out-of-pocket for premiums.

10. MOST IMPORTANT: I said this above, but I cannot emphasize enough how important it is for someone receiving the PATC to keep the Healthcare Exchange informed if their income changes significantly or their family status changes.

Individual Shared Responsibility Payment (penalty for not having insurance):

If you fail to maintain minimum essential coverage as defined by the Act, you can be charged a penalty. Your insurance provider should be able to tell you if your plan qualifies, and you will receive a form documenting your coverage around the time you get your W-2 for the tax year. Here are the details:

1. Penalty amounts:
 -In 2015, the penalty for not having qualifying health insurance will be the larger of:
   2% of income -or-
   $325 dollar per adult and $162.50 per child in the household, up to $975 max
 -In 2016, the penalty for not having qualifying health insurance will be the larger of:
   2.5% of income -or-
   $695 dollar per adult and $347.50 per child in the household, up to $2,085 max
2. The penalty is calculated on a monthly basis for each month of non-coverage; however, there is no penalty for any one period of no more than 3 months of non-coverage for each year. (If the 3 months is exceeded, you pay the penalty for all 12 months, it's not a 3-months-free exception.)
3. There is no penalty if your income is below the filing threshold
4. There are other exceptions for hardship (to be defined later), incarcerated individuals, religious objectors (very restrictive rules), illegal aliens, Native Americans and persons with very limited income (out-of-pocket expenses for premiums would exceed 8% of income). There are other exceptions, but these are the big ones.
5. There is an IRS form (1095 A, B, or C) that will detail insurance coverage and periods that will be required to be sent by insurance providers to taxpayers by January 31st of the tax filing season. This form will list the persons covered by name and SSN, and provide the dates coverage was in force. This form could cause you to have to wait for it to file, even after you have your W-2.
6. There is a provision for the IRS, with the assistance of the Secretary of Health and Human Services, to inform taxpayers without coverage as of June 30th of each year that they are not covered and to provide information on services available through Health Care Exchanges.
7. The IRS will not be allowed to enforce the Health Care Penalty through liens or levies.

If you are Filing Married Filing Separately:

If you are receiving an Affordable Care Act subsidy, MFS is NOT an option for you. The only exception is domestic abuse (which is discussed later under Note

1). If you file MFS, you are ineligible for the Premium Assistance Tax Credit, and will have to pay your half of the subsidy back when you file taxes (the person you are married to pays the other half, unless you received all the subsidy on your own in which case you pay it all back).

You need to pay attention to this as the end of the year approaches. If you are not divorced or LEGALLY separated as of December 31, 2016, you are married for tax purposes, and your only choice for filing status is MFJ, MFS or (under a difficult to meet standard—see Note 2 below) HH. If you can't file MFJ in this case, and don't meet the requirements for HH, you will have to pay back the subsidy (subject to limits based on income—but you'll pay some or all of it back).

Keep this in mind when considering changing your marital status, whether through divorce, marriage or separation toward the end of this year. Also take this into account when deciding how to file with your soon to be ex-spouse.

Note 1: If you are forced to file MFS due to domestic abuse, you have to meet the following requirements, and indicate that you meet them on the tax return to avoid the repayment: You must be forced into filing MFS due to domestic abuse (unable to file MFJ) and you must be living apart from your spouse at the time you file the tax return.

Note 2: If you are not legally divorced or separated and want to file MFS, make sure to see the section on Filing Status. The following is just the bare bones and there are lots of tricky parts. If you are married at the end of 2016, but live apart from your spouse for the last 6 months of the year and paid more than 50% of the cost of maintaining a home for you and your dependent child, you might be able to file HH by being considered unmarried for tax purposes.

Military: Tricare and Tricare Prime for you, your spouse and children counts as minimum coverage for the ACA, as does your active military medical services.

67. I Get Health Insurance Through the Healthcare Marketplace

This section is not going to go over every detail of getting insurance through the marketplace, since this is, after all, a tax book. I'm also not going to run numbers in detail, since even I find it extremely difficult to rationalize them, with or without using forms. I don't like depending on software, but I have found that reconciling an Affordable Care Act (hereafter abbreviated ACA) subsidy requires software first, and then checking to make sure it's right. I pity anyone trying to get this right using pen and paper.

One thing as an aside, I found last year that a lot of people didn't realize they had insurance through the marketplace. Insurance companies hired a lot of people to sell policies through the ACA, many paid on commission, and I guess some of the agents found it easier to sell insurance if they neglected to mention that the incredible low price was due to a subsidy. The IRS was all over this and we saw dozens of letters requiring filing of the proper forms before the IRS would release the refund. If you get a letter saying you were missing a Form 8962, that means you had marketplace insurance, and should have gotten a 1095A.

If you get insurance through the ACA marketplace, you WILL be getting a form 1095A from the insurance company. This form has the information needed to reconcile your subsidy (the Advance Premium Tax Credit). This reconciliation occurs using form 8962. In practice, you pretty much just have to copy the information from your 1095A into your software (or provide the 1095A to your tax pro) and the software will work it out (if you are doing it by hand, God help you.) In theory, if you provided accurate information about your expected 2016 income when applying for the health coverage (and it matched what you expected exactly) this will result in no change to your tax return.

If you guessed to high on your income, you will get the FULL amount of the difference between what your subsidy was, and what it should have been. This amount will be added directly to your refund (or will lower your balance due.) If you guessed too low on your income, you have to pay the difference back - maybe. There are limits to how much they can make you pay back as long as your income was below 4 times the poverty level for your family size. If your income is more than 4 times the poverty level - you pay the FULL difference back. To avoid these paybacks, keep the marketplace informed of changes in income or family size.

You should have online access to an account. If you don't, get it, and don't lose the login information.

Everyone reading this section should read the previous section on the Affordable Care Act. There are a number of warnings about filing status and other tricks. In fact, you should read it NOW, and not wait until tax time.

I highly recommend having a tax professional at least look over your numbers to make sure you got it right. It took me a few weeks to really get comfortable with how these numbers should transfer onto the various forms. There also a few tricks if you get married or divorced during the year.

Military: I can't imagine a military member getting insurance through the exchange.

68. I Don't Have Health Insurance

This is not going to be a comprehensive discussion of every detail, but it will help you determine if you might have to pay a penalty, and how to avoid paying it through exemptions. If you, or anyone in your household, didn't have qualifying insurance for all 12 months of the year, this chapter is for you.

If you had health insurance that qualifies as minimum coverage per the Affordable Care Act (ACA), but not for the whole year, you should know what months you had health insurance. If you had health insurance, and aren't sure it qualified, you should contact your employer and/or provider and ensure it did. They should be able to tell you if it qualified, and how and when you will be getting your "proof". The proof is a 1095 form (A, B or C depending on how you get your coverage.) Make sure you know how to get it (mail, email, delivered to your desk, pick up at Human Resources, carrier pigeon). You will need this for your taxes. The 1095 form shows what months you had coverage. It also tells you how much coverage they offered you that you didn't take would have cost - and this is useful later.

I hate to send people to a government website, but, this little tool actually works pretty well. If you didn't have health insurance for all 12 months for everyone in your household, this is actually a good place to start. I recommend using it with your spouse (if applicable) and having a good idea what your household income for the year was or will be. The tool will ask you a bunch of questions, and will help you determine what exemptions apply, and how to apply for them. Many of them you can apply for right there, or print the form to apply by mail. If you qualify for the ones online or by mail, you will get a code you can put into your tax return or give to your tax pro that will eliminate or reduce the penalty. Others you will calculate directly on your tax return - we'll cover those in a second. Make sure to click the information link for details on any you might qualify for. For example, the utility shut-off notice exemption applies if you received a notice anytime in the last THREE years. Here's the website and a list of some of the exemptions you might be able to use directly from the website or by mail:

www.healthcare.gov/exemptions-tool
You were homeless
You faced eviction or foreclosure
You got a utility shut-off notice
You are a victim of domestic violence
You suffered a significant disaster
You filed for bankruptcy
You are caring for an ill or disabled family member and expenses went up
A close family member died
Someone else is supposed to provide health insurance (ex spouse) and you can't get Medicaid
There are a lot more, but they aren't nearly as common, so use the tool!

Here are a few that you do on your tax return, listed in order of probability/ease:

1. You had less than 2 months without insurance: Most software has you check boxes for the months you have insurance. If the gap is 2 months or less, it shouldn't calculate a penalty.

2. You don't have to file taxes: If your income is low enough that you aren't required to file, you don't have to pay the penalty. Your software or tax pro should handle this for you.

3. If you live in the following states: AL, AK, , FL, GA, ID, KS, LA, ME, MI, MO, MS, MT, NC, NE, OK, SC, SD, TN, TX, UT, VA, WI, WY, then your state did not expand Medicaid coverage like they were expected to for the ACA. This means that if your household income is below 138% of the poverty line for your family size, you don't have to pay the penalty. The poverty line used is not the one for the current tax year, so here are the numbers for 2016: Family size of 1: $16,242. 2: $21,983. 3: $27,724. 4: $33,465. 5: $39,205. 6: $44,946. 7: $50,687. 8: $56,428. Add $4,160 per person above that. For Alaska, the numbers are different so check the form instructions. Your software may do this automatically, but you should check to make sure, and also make sure your tax pro does it.

4. If your job offered health insurance, and it costs more than 8.13% of your household income, you might not have to pay the penalty. If they only offer a plan for YOU (as opposed to your family), and it exceeds 8.13% of your household income, only YOU are exempted. You will have to provide the cost information to your software or tax pro, and you should be prepared to prove it. You might have a 1095 form with this information.

5. If your employer doesn't offer insurance, you can check to see if the marketplace insurance exceeds 8.13% of your household income. There is a tool on the healthcare website you use to figure out the cost: www.healthcare.gov/tax-tool.

I highly recommend talking to a tax professional if you can't find a way around the penalty. Good luck!

Military: Not a lot of differences for you.

69. State by State Tax Guide for Military

This section is just an overview. Also, many states update their information at the last minute, so some of this information will be out of date at the time of publishing. Use this info as a starting point with hints, and double check with your state. I will start with some general information, and then continue with state by state details.

Military Spouses Residency Relief Act (MSRRA)

Most states have begun to treat this in a similar manner to each other. In general, the spouse of a service member has two choices for state of residency: the state they are stationed in, or the military member's state of residency. In order to claim the military members state, they must have established a domicile in that state at some time before moving to the current state. For those qualified to make the election to claim the military members state, it is important to weigh the benefits properly, for example, a spouse who works in SC married to a military resident of MI might assume that since MI does not tax the military member that they should choose this state. This would be wrong because MI will tax the non-military income of the spouse. SC is far more generous to the spouse of a service member stationed in SC. Expert assistance may be required making this determination. It can also be difficult to get the current state to stop withholding from the spouses wages. Each state Dept of Revenue has different procedures for handling this.

Residency

A military member normally retains residency in the state they resided in when they joined the military unless action is taken to change this. The W-2 can generally be relied upon as to the state of residence of the military member. The states in which a service member are stationed will not tax the members military income unless they are residents. They will tax any income earned from other employment or business activities conducted in the state by the member and their spouses (subject to the MSRRA discussed above.) The discussions below talk about the taxation of military income for residents of the respective state.

Filing Requirements:

Not having to file discussed below assumes there is no withholding from the given state. A member may file even if not required and should do so if they have withholding from the given state so they can get the money back. If a member would not be required to file except for the existence of withholding, they should adjust their state withholding through MyPay so no taxes are withheld from that state. They may also consider stopping withholding even if they are required to file, for states that do not tax their income (MI for example.) Many people do not file required tax returns when there is no refund or balance due. This could result in a letter from the state requesting a return but rarely any penalties – but there can be!

Death Benefits:

Many states exclude death benefits and military pay for service members killed in a combat zone or while on active duty. The specifics are not discussed here. Survivors of service members killed on active duty can obtain assistance for this from CACO personnel.

States with **Bold** names either require a tax return or other document to be filed by military residents, or a tax return should be prepared to determine if any refundable benefits are available from that state.

Alabama:
Alabama treats military residents the same as all other residents. Alabama does not tax military retirement.

Alaska:
Alaska does not have an income tax. Alaska Permanent Funds Dividends are taxable on the Federal Return.

Arizona:
Arizona does not tax active duty military pay, and does not require filing if the only AZ source income is active duty pay.

Arkansas:
Beginning in 2014, Arkansas no longer taxes active duty military pay. A tax return is still required.

California:
California does not tax military pay of CA residents stationed outside of the state of CA. They do tax military income of their residents when stationed in CA. They also treat military spouses generously, similar to SC. Form 540NR is used to account for this. You write "MPA" to the left of column A for non-resident military income and enter the military income in column B but exclude it from column E.

Colorado:
Beginning in 2015, Colorado no longer taxes active military income. Before 2015, Colorado taxed military residents the same as other residents unless the member was stationed outside the US for >305 days in the year.

Connecticut:
Connecticut allows resident military personnel stationed outside of CT to be treated as non-residents for tax purposes. This can be confusing but the point is that they are still a resident, just not treated that way for tax purposes. In order to be treated as a non-resident they must meet all three of the following requirements:

1) Not maintain a permanent place of abode in CT for the entire year (a parents house is not a permanent place of abode.) 2) Maintain a permanent place of abode outside of CT for the entire year. 3) Spend no more than 30 days in CT for any reason during the year. If they meet these requirements they can file as a non-resident and exclude any military wages from gross income and need not file unless they have other CT source income.

Delaware:
DE taxes military residents the same as all other residents.

Washington DC:
DC taxes resident military personnel the same as all other residents.

Florida:
Florida does not have an income tax.

Georgia:
GA taxes military residents the same as all other residents however Reserves or National Guard called to active duty for more than 90 days may be able to take a credit against their individual income tax based on their income from the National Guard or Reserves.

Hawaii:
Hawaii taxes military residents the same as all other residents except that they do not tax the first $6076 of reserve pay or HI national guard pay.

Idaho:
ID residents stationed in ID pay taxes on all military income; however, if the member was on active duty >120 days and stationed outside of Idaho they can exclude any military income earned while stationed outside of ID. If they are stationed outside of Idaho the entire year they do not need to file an ID tax return, however Idaho has a Grocery Credit that a military member is eligible for that is refundable so it is possible to get a refund from Idaho even though there was no tax withheld. This makes Idaho one of the States that a military member should file even when not required to.

Illinois:
IL does not tax military pay; however, the member must file a tax return if they file a Federal return. Military members with children who get Federal Earned Income Credit may get up to 10% of the Federal amount even if they have no taxes due to IL.

Indiana:
Indiana taxes military income but allows a deduction of the first $5000 of military income for the taxpayer and/or the spouse ($10000 for military couple.) If a

military member changes state of residency to another state they must submit the DD Form 2058 with the tax return for the year they changed state of residency.

Iowa:
IA does not tax military income and military income is not used in determining filing requirements (if the only significant sources of income are military income, a tax return is not required.) Starting in 2014, Iowa no longer taxes military retirement.

Kansas:
Kansas taxes military income but allows a deduction for recruitment, sign-up and retention bonuses paid that are included in Federal taxable income (if the bonus was tax free to federal do not deduct it from KS. Kansas starts with Federal AGI so it is already excluded.) The subtraction is made on Adjustments line A21.

Kentucky:
Beginning with 2010, KY does not tax military income and does not require a tax return if the only KY source income is military pay.

Louisiana:
Louisiana requires a tax return from military personnel the same as any other resident; however, LA gives an exclusion of up to $30000 of military pay if the person has been on active duty outside of Louisiana for at least 120 days during the tax year. The subtraction is taken as a Schedule E subtraction, Code 10E, by entering military pay up to $30000 on the schedule.

Maine:
Maine allows resident military personnel stationed outside of ME to be treated as non-residents for tax purposes. This can be confusing but the point is that they are still a resident, just not treated that way for tax purposes. In order to be treated as a non-resident they must meet all three of the following requirements: 1) Not maintain a permanent place of abode in ME for the entire year (a parents house is not a permanent place of abode.) 2) Maintain a permanent place of abode outside of ME for the entire year. 3) Spend no more than 30 days in ME for any reason during the year. If they meet these requirements they can file as a non-resident and exclude any military wages from gross income and need not file unless they have other ME source income. Maine calls this the General Safe Harbor Rule.

Maryland:
Maryland taxes military residents just like other residents; however, they allow a subtraction for up to $15000 of military pay earned outside of the U.S. (Military Overseas Income.) The deduction phases out dollar for dollar as ALL military income goes above $15000 and there is no exclusion if the total military income exceeds $30000. The subtraction is taken on Form 502SU and the Military Overseas Income Worksheet is used to calculate the deduction. Military members are also subject to local income taxes.

Massachusetts:
There are no special tax benefits for military, however, the Massachusetts Dept of Veterans Affairs will give a onetime payment of $500 to any resident after they served at least 6 months active duty in the military. They also have a $1000 benefit for personnel who serve in Iraq or Afghanistan. Check their website for details.

Michigan:
Michigan requires military members to file a tax return; however, they subtract active duty pay from income (Schedule 1, Line 11). Military members with children who receive Earned Income Credit on their Federal return may collect 6% of the federal amount, even if they pay no taxes to MI. (This was 20% for 2011 and prior years.)

Minnesota:
Minnesota subtracts Active Duty Military pay from income of MN residents. If Gross Income on Federal return other than military is less than $10000, no MN return is required.
Minnesota pays $120 per month a military resident spends in a combat zone. This is paid separately from the tax return and is claimed on Minnesota form M99. Check their website for the form.

Mississippi:
Mississippi taxes military residents the same as other residents except that they do not tax National Guard and Reserve pay up to $15000.

Missouri:
MO allows resident military personnel stationed outside of MO to be treated as non-residents for tax purposes. This can be confusing but the point is that they are still a resident, just not treated that way for tax purposes. In order to be treated as a non-resident they must meet all three of the following requirements: 1) Not maintain a permanent place of abode in MO for the entire year (a parent's house is not a permanent place of abode.) 2) Maintain a permanent place of abode outside of MO for the entire year. 3) Spend no more than 30 days in MO for any reason during the year. If they meet these requirements they can file as a non-resident and exclude any military wages from gross income and need not file unless they have other MO source income. If your spouse works but claims MO as your state of residency through the MSRRA their income is taxable to MO and must file a tax return if they earn more than $1200. As of 2014, Missouri exempts 75% of military retirement income from tax and starting in 2016 all military retirement income will be tax exempt.

Montana:
Montana requires military residents to file a tax return but exempts active military pay from taxation on Schedule 2, Line 8. Verification of active duty status must be attached to the return.

Nebraska:
Nebraska taxes military residents just like other residents. Nebraska has implemented an incredibly complicated option to exclude certain amounts of military retirement income for some years. It's too stupid to attempt to explain, but if you are retiring or retired from the military in Nebraska you should research this on their website.

Nevada:
Nevada does not have an income tax.

New Hampshire:
NH does not have an income tax but they do tax interest and dividends. Generally these would need to exceed $2400 for an individual and $4800 for a couple.

New Jersey:
NJ allows resident military personnel stationed outside of NJ to be treated as non-residents for tax purposes. This can be confusing but the point is that they are still a resident, just not treated that way for tax purposes. In order to be treated as a non-resident they must meet all three of the following requirements: 1) Not maintain a permanent place of abode in NJ for the entire year (a parent's house is not a permanent place of abode.) 2) Maintain a permanent place of abode outside of NJ for the entire year. 3) Spend no more than 30 days in NJ for any reason during the year. If they meet these requirements they can file as a non-resident and exclude any military wages from gross income and need not file unless they have other NJ source income. (NJ does not consider barracks maintaining a permanent place of abode outside NJ)

New Mexico:
New Mexico does not tax active duty military pay however; NM residents are required to file a NM return if they were required to file a Federal return.

New York:
NY allows resident military personnel stationed outside of NY to be treated as non-residents for tax purposes. This can be confusing but the point is that they are still a resident, just not treated that way for tax purposes. In order to be treated as a non-resident they must meet all three of the following requirements: 1) Not maintain a permanent place of abode in NY for the entire year (a parents house is not a permanent place of abode.) 2) Maintain a permanent place of abode outside of NY for the entire year. 3) Spend no more than 30 days in NY for any reason during the year. If they meet these requirements they can file as a non-resident and exclude any military wages from gross income and need not file unless they have other NY source income. NY specifically excludes barracks as an abode outside of NY for the purpose of this rule. Also, if a NY return is required to be filed to get back state taxes withheld and this exemption results in zero income (as it usually does) the return may have to be mailed in vice electronically filed.

North Carolina:
NC taxes military residents the same as other residents.

North Dakota:
ND taxes military residents the same as other residents, however, National Guard and reserve members called to active duty can exclude their active duty pay form ND income.

Ohio:
Ohio does not tax military pay of OH residents stationed outside of the state of OH. They do tax military income of their residents when stationed in OH. Ohio does not tax military retirement pay.

Oklahoma:
Oklahoma allows military members to exclude active duty pay. This exclusion is accomplished using Schedule 511-C. Military members are required to file an OK tax return if they were required to file a federal return.

Oregon:
Oregon allows a subtraction of all military pay earned while stationed outside of OR and up to $6000 earned while stationed in Oregon (Subtraction Code 319). OR also allows military residents to be treated as non residence if they spent less than 31 days in OR, did not have an abode in OR and had a permanent abode outside OR the entire year.

Pennsylvania:
Pennsylvania does not tax Active Duty Military Income of residents stationed outside of PA and does not require a tax return; however, they do require the service member to mail or fax a copy of their orders stationing them outside of PA and their W-2. If filing a tax return a copy of the orders must be included when mailing the return, or sent separately to the address below.
PA DEPT OF REVENUE
NO PAYMENT OR NO REFUND
2 REVENUE PLACE
HARRISBURG PA 17129-0002
May also be faxed to : (717) 772-4193

Rhode Island:
Rhode Island taxes military residents the same as other residents.

South Carolina:
SC taxes military residents just like regular residents except that it does not tax reservist drill pay. SC is very generous to the spouses of military (residents of another state) in that they allow you to exclude the active duty income of the non-resident military member from the calculation of what percentage of deductions to allocate to the spouse. This generally results in 100% of the deductions against

only the spouses SC income. It is very difficult to get tax software to handle this correctly. Line 1 of the SCNR should have no active duty military income in the Federal column. SC is phasing in a reduction in taxes for military retirees between now and 2020. Make sure you get credit for it.

South Dakota:
SD does not have an income tax.

Tennessee:
TN does not have an income tax but they do tax interest and dividends. Generally these would need to exceed $1250 for an individual and $2500 for a couple.

Texas:
Texas does not have an income tax.

Utah:
Utah taxes resident service members the same as other residents.

Vermont:
Vermont does not tax military pay of VT residents stationed outside of the state of VT. They do tax military income of their residents when stationed in VT. Military pay is subtracted on line 32. A tax return is not required if the only income is military pay while stationed outside VT.

Virginia:
Virginia taxes military residents just like other residents except that they give a subtraction of basic military pay of up to $15000. The subtraction phases out dollar for dollar as income goes from $15000 to $30000 and is completely gone at $30000 of income. (If a military member made less than $15000, it would all be subtracted. If they made $20000, they get to subtract $10000.) The subtraction code is 38.

Washington:
Washington does not have an income tax.

West Virginia:
West Virginia taxes military residents unless they spent less than 30 days in WV. In this case they file as a non-resident. WV does not tax military income of reserves or national guard called to active duty by Executive Order of the President.

Wisconsin:
Wisconsin taxes military residents the same as other residents except that they do not tax military pay of reserves or national guard called to active duty. Rent paid by the military member in a state other than WI is allowed to be used for the School Property Tax Credit (not military housing.) If a military member is stationed outside the United States, they may take a credit of up to $300 for pay

received while stationed outside the U.S. Wisconsin does not tax military retirement.

Wyoming:
WY does not have an income tax.

70. The IRS Called and is Threatening Me!

No they didn't.

Really. Getting a call from the IRS is incredibly rare and will only occur as a follow-up from several letters, or an arrangement YOU made to have them call you.

99% chance this is a SCAM!

Even if they seem to have your personal information like SSN, address or other private stuff. It's a scam.

These guys are PROFESSIONALS! They do this all day, every day and are very good at sounding real. Some have even ordered transcripts to be sent to the victim and refer to that as a way to seem more legitimate.

Do NOT give any information out over the phone!
Do NOT send them any money!
Do NOT give them access to your bank!
Do NOT give them a chance to engage you with questions. The longer you talk to them, the more chance they have to sound legitimate.

How can you be sure it's a scam?

One: Google the phone number, chances are you aren't the first person they've called and the phone number will show up as a scam.
Two: They claim to be the Treasury Department, an agent of some kind, and there is a warrant for your arrest.
Three: Contact the IRS either by phone or through irs.gov. The IRS website has lots of information about these scams right on their front page.
Four: Call your tax guy.
Five: They want you to pay with gift cards.
Six: They insult you, threaten you, swear at you or behave in any way that would be considered unprofessional.

How do you stop them from calling?

Make it ABSOLUTELY clear that you know it's a scam and that they are wasting their time. Yelling and bad language are a plus here. Be brief, loud, emphatic and angry, then hang up. They won't call back because there are easier targets out there.

Here's an amusing aside: One of my best days in the office was when a long time client walked in with a scammer on her cell phone - she was terrified. I asked for the phone and went full retired Navy Master Chief on the guy. He hung up and never called back. Good times.

Military: Not a lot of differences here for you.

71. I Got a Letter From the IRS

Open it...

Seriously, this isn't a joke. You would be stunned how many of my clients bring me letters from the IRS...unopened. Sometimes months after they get it.

OPEN IT!

But don't panic. Even though the first page will almost certainly tell you that you owe money (it might not, but be prepared). Just because it says you owe money doesn't mean you do. You should never pay on a letter from the IRS unless you are absolutely certain you owe the money...and often you don't. You would be stunned (again) how often my clients pay money to the IRS they don't owe without consulting me. It's much easier to not pay money you don't owe than it is to get it back.

And the IRS has gotten a little more evil lately. A lot of times these letters are generated because you forgot a small W-2 or other tax form that doesn't amount to much. In the past, the IRS wouldn't even bother if the amount was small. But recently the IRS has started doing this weird trick where they combine a basic "you missed a form" letter with an audit type letter. Usually (in my recent experience) this is with Education Credits. You get a letter saying you forgot a W-2, and we're denying your education credit until you send documentation for it. A $100 missing W-2 letter now is a $2,000 missing W-2 and denied Education Credit letter. To make matters worse, they don't do a good job of explaining that they don't have any reason to suspect the Education Credit is invalid, they just want more proof - kind of like a spot check. I think this is intentional, and the IRS is getting a good chunk of money from people who just pay, or who ignore the letter.

Which brings me to a very important point...

NEVER ignore an IRS letter or allow the response date to pass without communicating with the IRS. PERIOD! The IRS hates 2 things - being lied to and being ignored - don't do either!

Well, this was going to be a nice long chapter on letters, but now the scammers have stepped it up a notch. They are actually sending some VERY convincing letters that look a LOT like IRS letters. So I can't in good conscience suggest that anything other than seeing a professional is a good idea. Take the letter and your tax return to a competent professional and, for not too much money, confirm that it's legit, see if it's accurate, and get some advice on how to respond - or pay them to handle it. I am including a sample response letter in Appendix C, but don't use it without consulting a professional first. Sorry.

72. I got this Form

Below is a listing of forms you may come across while managing your finances and preparing your taxes:

W-2: I'm pretty sure you know what this is, but I'll cover some basics. Boxes 1 through 6 are your income and withholding for federal taxes, Social Security and Medicare. Only Boxes 1 and 2 affect your federal tax return, unless you have multiple jobs that put you above the maximum income for Social Security withholding, (that's pretty rare).

Boxes 7 and 8 are about tips, I have a <u>section</u> on that.

Box 10 is what your company gives you to put your kids in daycare. If you spend it on daycare, you're good; if you don't, its taxable income. You report it on Form 2441, which is the form you get your daycare credit on. Speaking of which, you have to subtract Box 10 from your daycare expenses before you calculate your credit for daycare expenses.

You shouldn't see anything in Box 11. If you do, seek a tax professional.

Box 12 is information that might be used in your tax return. This is where 401k-type plans, healthcare benefits, HSA contributions and other information is reported to you.

Box 13 has special check marks for unique situations. If statutory employee or third-party sick pay is checked, you need help (or you already know what to do). If retirement plan box is checked, that affects your IRA contribution limits as discusses in the <u>IRA</u> section.

Box 14 can hold a lot of information, and you should understand what's in there. Some companies put a lot of weird stuff in there.

Boxes 15 and beyond are state information for filing state taxes (though the tax withheld is a federal <u>Itemized Deduction</u>).

W-2G: This is income from gambling or lottery. Make sure to report it on your tax return.

W-4: This is the form you use to tell your employer to adjust your withholding. Some employers do it online via a payroll site. The instructions work great for a single or married person with one income and no kids. After that, it's pretty much crap.

W-9: This form is used by your employer to get information from you to verify your SSN so they can properly report your income to the IRS. You have to fill it out if you want the job.

1095-A: This form reports the health insurance you got through an Affordable Cara Act (Obamacare) marketplace. It includes information on covered persons and the subsidy received. It serves as both proof of insurance, and is used to determine any reconcile the amount of subsidy received and whether you owe money back, or get more. You will need to file form 8962 to reconcile the credit amount and might need to file additional forms if you weren't covered the entire year.

1095-B: This form is provided to you (and the IRS) by your health insurance provider to report on health insurance that they provide to you. You will need it to prove that you had minimum essential health insurance coverage to avoid the Shared Responsibility Payment (penalty for not having insurance).

1095-C: This form is provided to you (and the IRS) by your employer to report on health insurance that they provide to you. You will need it to prove that you had minimum essential health insurance coverage to avoid the Shared Responsibility Payment (penalty for not having insurance).

1098: This form provides your mortgage interest, points and mortgage insurance premiums paid on a residence that might be deductible on Schedule A or Schedule E (for rental property). You can also usually find your real estate taxes and sometimes homeowners insurance on this form, or on the same page as the form. Make sure you get a 1098 from every lender who has serviced your loan over the course of the year.

1098-C: You'll need to get this form from a charity you donate a car to if you want to deduct more than $500.

1098-E: This form reports the student loan interest you paid during the year. Often this comes in the form of a letter that looks nothing like a 1098-E, but will say "substitute 1098-E" on it. See I Paid on Student Loans for more information.

1098-MA: This form reports information on government mortgage assistance programs that helped you with mortgage payments. Seek help if you get this form.

1098-T: This form has most of the information you need to claim education credits or deductions. It should show the amount of tuition you paid, and the scholarships you received. You should not rely solely on this form, but should get an account transcript from your school's finance department. See I am Going to College for more information.

1099-A: This form indicates that someone has taken possession of your property, usually to satisfy a debt. Generally you will see this for foreclosure on real property or repossession of a vehicle. For tax purposes, this represents a deemed sale of the property and it must be reported on Schedule D or Form 4797 (for business property). You cannot take a loss on the repossession of personal property. Determine gain by subtracting your basis (how much you paid for it, generally) from either the FMV (Box 4) or balance outstanding (Box 2). Generally, you will use FMV if Box 5 is checked; use the outstanding balance if Box 5 is not checked (though you should seek advice from a local tax professional because state lending laws can impact this determination). Box 1 is the sale date, and the date acquired is when the taxpayer acquired the property.

If this was a foreclosure of your personal residence, any gain might be excluded following the same rules as for Sale of Main Home. Details are linked in the Foreclosure section.

1099-B: This form reports proceeds from investments that you sold during the year. They can vary in form and are often combined with 1099-DIV and 1099-INT. They will report the total price that you received for all assets you sold during the year (with that particular investment company). Further in the package they will provide information for each asset: the date purchased, (if they have it), date sold, sales proceeds and basis (if they have it—basis is generally what you paid for an asset, but can change due to a variety of factors). If the information is provided and accurate, simply report it on your tax return. If information is missing or inaccurate, work with your broker and a tax professional to find it. ALWAYS report sales on your tax return, even if you broke even or lost money!

1099-C: This form is used to report debt that you owed to a company that has been written off for one reason or another and will not be collected. It is generally income to you, but there are lots of exceptions. You'll want to check out these sections as applicable: I Had Debt Written Off by the Company I Owe Money To and I Lost my House (Foreclosure, Short Sale or Bankruptcy).

1099-G: The 1099-G is used for a lot of things, but you generally only need to be concerned with two: unemployment compensation, and state income tax refunds. I find it irritating that the two are mixed such that state refund information is right in the middle of unemployment information.

Box 1 reports any unemployment compensation you received. There's a line for this on your 1040.
Box 4 reports any federal income tax withheld on your unemployment compensation. This is included on your tax return with your withholding from W-2's and other forms.
Boxes 10 and 11 report state information for your unemployment compensation, including state tax withheld.

Box 2 is your state refund from the year indicated in Box 3. If you itemized deductions in the prior year, this is probably taxable income to you. (If you owed and paid taxes on your state return the prior year, that would be a deduction.) It is only taxable to the extent that it improved your tax situation, so if you were only $100 above your standard deduction and received a refund of $200, only $100 would be taxable.

If any other boxes have entries, seek professional help.

1099-K: This form reports payments you (probably your business) receive from credit card processors. It should be reported on your Schedule C (or other business return you file), but make sure it doesn't duplicate income recorded in your own records. (If you keep good records this form should have no new information for you.)

1099-Q: This form contains information on the amount of money withdrawn from Qualified Tuition Plans or Education Savings Accounts. These are plans that allow you to save money in tax-deferred accounts for education. If you had education expenses, this form will assist you in determining the benefits you get for education (see the I am Going to College section). If you don't have education expenses, the amount in Box 2 is taxable income to you.

1099-R: This form is used to report retirement plan distributions (state, federal, private, military and more), annuity distributions, IRA distributions, some insurance plan payments and many other distributions from tax advantaged accounts. Some situations are simple, and some are amazingly complicated. If your 1099-R has a number in Boxes 1 and 2, and the code 7 in Box 7, you have a simple situation (the amount in Box 2 is taxable income and is reported on your return and taxed). Anything else and you might have some work to do. See the I am Retired section for some help.

1099-S: You receive this form when you sell real estate. It has the gross proceeds from the sale. You generally only need to make sure the gross proceeds on this form match your records of the sale—the information on the 1099-S is reported to the IRS. Assuming they match, use your documents to report the sale. If they don't match, contact the person who provided the 1099-S to find out why.

1099-SA: This form reports distributions from Health Savings Accounts of various types. See I Have an HSA and HDHP through Work for more details.

1099-INT: This form reports interest you received from bank accounts, Certificates of Deposit and bonds. It comes in many forms and may be combined with 1099-DIV and 1099-B. See I Have Investments Outside of Work for more information.

1099-OID: This form reports interest you received from bonds, which accrue due to buying the bond at a discount from its face value. It comes in many forms and may be combined with 1099-DIV, 1099-INT and 1099-B. See I Have Investments Outside of Work for more information.

1099-DIV: This form reports dividends you received from ownership of stocks and mutual funds. It comes in many forms and may be combined with 1099-INT and 1099-B. See I Have Investments Outside of Work for more information.

1099-MISC: This is the catchall form for when someone pays you money and there's no other form for it. I'm going to tell you what Boxes 1, 2, 3, 4 and 7 generally mean; if you have anything in another box (other than the state info boxes), you should seek additional help.

Box 1 represents rent received. Most people with numbers in this box have rental property and either have a property manager, or receive government rent payments for low income housing. This is reported on your Schedule E for the rental.

Box 2 would be royalties from art, writing or even possibly oil wells on your land. It is also reported on Schedule E.

Box 3 is money paid to you that doesn't fit anywhere else. It is generally reported on Line 21 of Form 1040.

Box 4 is federal income tax withheld from the payments that were made to you. You include it with all the other federal tax withheld on your tax forms.

Box 7 is "usually" income you receive as a contractor or as a self-employed business person, and would go on your Schedule C. There are situations where this would be reported on Line 21 of Form 1040, but you should seek guidance to be sure before you report it there.

1099-PATR: This form reports distributions from a cooperative. If you aren't sure how to handle this information, you should seek additional help.

1099-RRB (RRB-1099): This form reports Railroad Retirement Benefits, which is an alternative to Social Security. If you aren't sure how to handle this information, you should seek additional help.

1099-SSA (SSA-1099): This form reports Social Security payments. If you receive this form, your payments are potentially taxable (even if they are for disability). See I am Receiving Social Security for more information. If there is a number in Box 4 or information on prior year's payments in the big box (description of amount in Box 3), you might want to seek professional assistance.

2439: You might get one of these if you invest in certain types of investments, mainly Real Estate Investment Trusts. They represent capital gains that they had but did not distribute. You have to claim them on your tax return. They generally go right on your Schedule D (the form instructions tell you where) or the worksheet in the Schedule D instructions.

3921: This reports exercise of incentive stock options (ISO). You need to determine if the stock was sold in the year exercised. If the stock was sold in the same calendar year it was exercised, determine if the income was included on the W-2 (cashless exercises almost always are.) You can do this by inquiring from your employer or comparing Boxes 1 and 5 on the W-2 to see if the difference can be accounted for as the gain from the option (ISO gains are not taxed for Medicare or SS). If it is on the W-2, you need only report the proceeds on Schedule D and enter the basis as the same as the proceeds. If it is not on the W-2, you add it on Line 7 of Form 1040. Also enter it on Schedule D as above.

If the stock option was not sold in the calendar year purchased, you only report the difference between the option price and FMV on Line 14 of the 6251 (alternative minimum tax.) This value can be calculated by subtracting the amount in Form 3921 Box 3 from Box 4, and multiplying the difference by Box 5. Save this information, you will need this when you sell the stock. When the stock is sold you will need to determine if it meets holding periods (see IRS Pub 525 under stock options) and report it as capital gain and/or ordinary income in accordance with the instructions. If you paid AMT on the exercise, you may not have to pay as much tax when you sell it.

3922: This represents transfer of stock from the employer to the employee under an incentive stock purchase plan where the value of the stock transferred is higher than the price paid. No action is required until the stock is sold, at which point it is reported on Schedule D and/or Form 1040 Line 7 IAW IRS Pub 525. If the stock was not sold during the tax year, I recommend recording the data from the form in a note with your tax records so it is available when the stock is sold.

5498: This form reports information on your IRA contributions and the value of your account. Most people will have already used their year-end statement to report this information on their tax return, since this form comes out late in the tax season. SAVE ALL of these forms in your tax records where you can get them easily. A lot of companies send these forms in a format that looks very little like the IRS form, so pay attention to your brokerage statements to find them.

5498-SA: This form reports information about your Health Savings Account. See I have an HSA and HDHP through Work for more information.

Schedule K-1: You get this form when you are a participant or beneficiary of a partnership, estate or trust. You might get this if you invested in a limited partnership (even if you thought it was regular old stock). Basically, the partnership, trust or estate files its own tax return, and then breaks the results down by ownership interest (if you own 10% of a partnership, you get 10% of their income and deductions). These forms can be very complicated, but the information generally carries directly to your tax return. They come with instructions that tell you where to put things, but you might want some extra help.

Military: Not a lot different for you here.

Appendix A
Support Worksheet

This is actually pretty tough. The IRS has a worksheet, that they would prefer you to use, and it's actually pretty well thought out. The problem is that it doesn't explain how or why it works, and doesn't give you enough detail to really understand what you are doing, and why you are doing it. So I'm going to attempt something a bit unique. I'm going to go through each section, and explain its purpose. Then I'm going to use letters for each value you need, and then describe how to get that number. I will then tell you what to do with each letter in order to determine if you passed the support test that applies to your situation. You will probably need to write the letters and the appropriate answer on a separate sheet. I am going to post printable worksheets, as well as an excel spreadsheet on my website, so feel free to use them. Here's the address: www.supertaxgenius.com/book-owner-exclusives.html. As the title implies - it's just for you as a thank you for buying the book, so please keep it between you and me. Do a separate worksheet for each potential dependent.

Who should not use this worksheet and instead seek professional help (though having the numbers for this can be useful to the professional): If it is for a child in college, and the college is being paid for in large part by student loans, scholarships or trusts, you should get professional help. People with weird living situations - such as you and the potential dependent living with a third person who pays the bills, or in a third person's house. The information below is somewhat over simplified for these situations, and may not be accurate for your personal details.

Obscenely Oversimplified Test: Use the tests below if the person lives with you in your home, is not in college, and there aren't any weird situations involved.

Test 1: Take the total annual expenses for the household (rent paid or what it would cost to rent), plus utilities and other expenses and divide by the number of people living there and add any other expenses, no matter who paid them, that support the potential dependent (clothing, entertainment, cars, medical, education and travel.) If the potential dependent's income, plus savings withdrawals, minus money put into savings, is more than half of that amount, you fail the test and cannot claim the person.

Test 2: Take the total annual expenses for the household (rent paid or what it would cost to rent), plus utilities and other expenses and divide by the number of people living there and add any other expenses, no matter who paid them, that support the potential dependent (clothing, entertainment, cars, medical, education and travel.) If the amount you paid is more than half of that amount, you pass the test and can claim the dependent if all other tests are met.

If you can't use the simplified test, let's see if we can make the complicated one work.

Funds Belonging to the Person You Supported: This section uses a roundabout method to figure out how much money your potential dependent used to support them self. The test pretty much assumes that any money they had, and didn't save or give away was used for support. So the worksheet takes the amount in savings or investment accounts at beginning of the year, income received or borrowed during the year, and then subtracts the amount in savings and investment accounts at the end of the year. This essentially ensures that you account for what is saved (or withdrawn from savings) without needing to account for each dollar. This allows you to ignore investment earnings and bank interest, and just focus on income from work, businesses and borrowing. Investment earnings are handled automatically by comparing year start and year end investment accounts. Now let's start getting some numbers:

A. Savings and Checking Account balances at the **beginning** of the year. Include all accounts in the child's name, custodial accounts and joint accounts with the child's name on them (unless you can VERY convincingly prove that the child's name is on the joint account for some purpose that makes the funds yours and not theirs.)

B. Investment Account balances at **beginning** of the year. You should include all funds, but you can ignore accounts that no money is added to or removed from, such as Savings Bond Accounts that are just sitting there, or 401k accounts (even if currently contributing to them). These would include mutual funds, brokerage accounts and other investments.

C. Trust Account balances at the **beginning** of the year.

D. Any other account balances at the **beginning** of the year. I threw this in even though A through C should cover everything, but sometimes things have weird names, or you might not realize what falls into the above categories. Examples would be CD's, Money Market accounts or stock certificates.

E. Add together the total of A, B, C, and D.

F. Savings and Checking Account balances at the **end** of the year. Make sure you are consistent with the treatment of the accounts from the beginning of the year.

G. Investment Account balances at **end** of the year. Make sure you are consistent with the treatment of the accounts from the beginning of the year.

H. Trust Account balances at the **end** of the year. Make sure you are consistent with the treatment of the accounts from the beginning of the year.

I. Any other account balances at the **end** of the year. Make sure you are consistent with the treatment of the accounts from the beginning of the year.

J. Add together the total of F, G, H, and I.

K. Income from jobs. Use Box 1 from the W-2 to be the most accurate.

L. Income from self employment. Include net earnings from their schedule C if used and/or total amounts of money paid for odd jobs.

M. Amount of money borrowed, even if it's from you. If they are obligated to pay it back, include it. Include student loans, even if you cosigned for them (unless you are prepared to PROVE that you will be the one repaying - and it better be ROCK SOLID proof). Include car loans and credit cards and other borrowed money that is in their name. If you take out a loan for something like a car for them, but they are making the payments, you should include it here.

N. Amount received for pensions, annuities, and social security in their name. Use the numbers from 1099R's, 1099SA's. If the income is non-taxable, use the amount actually received.

O. If the potential dependent served in the military and has GI Bill from that service, include any amount of money received from the GI Bill, or paid to the college. If the GI Bill was earned by you and transferred to them, I don't think it should be included here, but I can't say for sure.

P. Amount received in grants and Education Savings Account distributions (if child has reached the age where they gain control of the account for your state). Do not include Qualified Tuition Plan (State prepaid tuition or college savings plans) unless the potential dependent put the money into the accounts. Do not include scholarships.

Q. Gifts received during the year not from you or your spouse. This is complex, and assumes the money was given with no strings attached. If it was given for specific purposes - get help from a pro (unless it was a small amount compared to the other numbers and doesn't really put the results in question.) Do not include Child Support payments here.

R. Add together amounts from K through Q.

S. Amount of money not used for support - this is pretty much gifts and charitable giving. I have a tough time figuring out anything else that would apply.

T. Funds available for support is $E + R - I - S$.

Expenses for Entire Household (where the person you supported lived): This section figures out how much the place the potential dependent lived costs, and how much is attributable to the potential dependent. If the person goes away to school, but comes back to your house, this is about your house. If they live in a nursing home or their own house, this is expenses for THEIR house or the nursing home.

U. If you rent, the amount of rent paid for the year. If you own, the "fair rental value" of the residence. You can get the rental value at zillow.com, or, if you want government numbers (which aren't as property specific) you can got to huduser.gov/portal/datasets/fmr.html and find averages for your area.

V. Total utilities for the year that aren't included in rent. Don't miss netflix, cable, internet...get everything that's entertainment or consumable. Don't include taxes, insurance, mortgage interest, warranties or pest control.

W. Amount paid for the year for repairs (not general maintenance) for the property.

X. Amount paid for other home expenses that aren't general maintenance or upkeep.

Y. Total U through X.

Z. Number of people who live in the house or apartment.

AA. Divide Y by Z (Holy crap that feels like algebra from school!)

Expenses for the Potential Dependent: Here we are going to figure out the specific amounts spent to support the potential dependent's life. We will add in their share from above. Include amounts spent, regardless of who spent them. Some of this will have to be estimated, but if this is going to come up every year, you might want to start tracking things and saving documentation.

BB. How much was spent on clothing for the person.
CC. How much was spent on education. Include private school, college, or technical school. Include room and board, books, tuition, fees and anything else. Sports fees and equipment go either here or entertainment, but don't duplicate.
DD. How much was spent for medical and dental that wasn't paid for by insurance. Include insurance costs.
EE. How much was spent on travel, recreation, entertainment, and other fun.
FF. If you bought big items, like cars, furniture, or electronics, for the person, even if financed (in your name) include them here.
GG. Include any other expenses you paid during the year for them.
HH. If the person bought something on credit in the past, it would have been included in funds for their support, but, I would argue that if you end up making the payments for them, even if not obligated, those payments should count...include them here. (This is not rock solid.)
II. Total BB through HH. This is the expenses for the potential dependent.

Test 1:
JJ. Divide II in half.
KK. If AA represents expenses for a place owned by the potential dependent, enter that value here, otherwise this line is zero.
LL. Add T to KK.

If LL is more than JJ, then you pass this test and the dependent qualifies (with regard to support).

Test 2:
MM. Divide II in half.
NN. Enter the amount of Foster Care Payments received by you or your potential dependent here.
OO. Enter amounts paid or provided by the state for Welfare, Housing, AFDC, Food Stamps, WIC, or any other government or third party payments here (do not include Child Support payments you receive.
PP. If AA represents expenses for a place owned by the potential dependent, enter that value here, otherwise this line is zero.
QQ. Total lines NN through PP.
RR. Subtract QQ from II.

If RR is more than MM, then you pass this test and the dependent qualifies (with regard to support).

Appendix B: Insolvency Worksheet Instructions

This Appendix is going to go line by line through the insolvency Worksheet from the IRS. You can get a copy of the worksheet in Publication 4681, located here: https://www.irs.gov/pub/irs-pdf/p4681.pdf. You should have gotten here from the chapters on cancelled debt, either: I Had Debt Written Off by the Company I Owe Money To or I Lost my House (Foreclosure, Short Sale or Bankruptcy).

The first, most important thing you need to know is the date of debt cancellation. This date can be found right on the 1099C you received. If you don't think this is the right date, you can try to get the 1099C issuer to correct it (good luck) or gather documentation to support the date you think is right. Either way, start with this date and determine your insolvency on the day BEFORE this date (I'm going to refer to this as the DATE for the rest of the chapter). This means the cancelled debt from the 1099C counts as a liability and should be included on the worksheet. If the 1099C has a Fair Market Value for an item the debt secured, this is included as an asset.

The worksheet should include ONLY assets owned or co owned by the person for whom the debt was cancelled, unless you lived in a community property state, in which case I HIGHLY recommend getting professional help, but, if you don't, research how property is divided in your state. In general, for a community property state, each person is responsible for half of the liabilities and owns half the assets, but that varies by state. Assuming you don't live in a community property state, include the full value of the assets that are fully in your name, and the appropriate percentage of jointly owned assets (generally 50% for married couples, but may vary for other assets for which you own only a part). For liabilities, include the full amount of money you are fully responsible for, and the appropriate percentage for assets you are only partially responsible for (again, generally 50% for married couples). If the cancelled debt was in both of your names, use your combined assets and liabilities. All of the instructions below assume you are NOT in a community property state.

You MUST be responsible for the debt in order to include it as a liability. If you are paying your child's car loan or student loan, but are not REQUIRED to do so, such as by being a co-signor on the loan, you cannot include it as a liability.

I have a fillable form available on the internet at www.supertaxgenius.com/book-owner-exclusives.html. As the title implies - it's just for you as a thank you for buying the book, so please keep it between you and me.

So with all that said, this is how you fill out the worksheet:

Liabilities: This is actually the easy half, because people you owe money to generally are pretty helpful reminding you.

Line 1: Credit card debt. If possible, pull up the actual statement that covers the month the debt was cancelled. Take the amount owed at the beginning of that statement, and add any additional charges made up until the DATE, and subtract any payments made. Do this for every credit card you had outstanding. You might want to pull your credit report to make sure you don't forget anything. If there are authorized users on the account, but they are not liable for payment, you can include the full amount. If there is a joint owner of the account, you only include half.

Line 2: Mortgage Debt. Include your personal residence, any vacation homes, investment or business property for which you are personally liable. If the business debt is limited such that the business must pay, but you are not personally liable, do not include it. Pull up the amortization schedule or bank statements for the month in question and determine the amount owed. If you are the only one liable, include the full amount, otherwise divide by how liability is divided, or, more likely, ownership percentage (50% for joint ownership).

Line 3: Auto Loans. For any car loans outstanding at the DATE, determine the amount you owed at the time. This may be harder than it looks if you don't have online access to the loan account. You may need to contact the creditor to get this information. Don't just add up the total of remaining payments at the time, this is not accurate.

Line 4: Medical Bills. Be careful with this. Only include the amount owed after insurance payments, but DO make sure to dig deep for debts you may owe. Even one hospital visit can result in dozens of bills from various medical practitioners.

Line 5: Student Loans. Include all loans you are liable for, including ones in deferment.

Line 6: Accrued or past due Mortgage Interest. These are probably included in Line 2, but make sure to check on it.

Line 7: Accrued or past due Real Estate Taxes. Most counties charge you by month for real estate taxes, and you pay them at the end of the year. So this means you just divide the tax bill for the year by 12, and multiply by the number of months that passed before the DATE. Add in any past due bills still owed on the DATE.

Line 8: Accrued or past due Utilities. Unless you have past due bills, it's probably not worth bothering trying to figure out what you owed on the DATE, but you can calculate by day to get a number.

Line 9: Accrued or past due Child Care Costs. Most places make you pay by month, but it is possible that they let you go for a couple of months or so. Just contact the agency or pull up bills for the month the DATE occurs.

Line 10: Federal or State Income Taxes Due. This should only be for prior years. You can get an account transcript from the IRS if you don't have these numbers. Your state probably has a similar method for determining this amount.

Line 11: Judgments. Any amounts that a court has determined you must pay. Make sure not to duplicate amounts from other lines just because they went to court.

Line 12: Business Debts. Make sure you are personally liable for these. Debts owed as a Sole Proprietor or partner might qualify, but verify by reviewing the loan documents.

Line 13: Margin Debt. Your brokerage account statements should specify the amount that you owe for money borrowed to buy stocks or bonds, or for short selling.

Line 14: Other Liabilities. This is where you account for any other money you owe. Examples might be signature loans, other taxes outstanding, furniture loans, 401k loans, life insurance or annuity loans, title loans, payday loans or any other money you borrowed that you are LEGALLY OBLIGATED to pay back. The IRS will be doubtful of money you borrow from family or friends unless you have some rock solid proof.

Line 15: Total all your liabilities from lines 1 through 14.

Assets: This can be a bit hard, and can require a little work, but I'm going to tell you something that might make it easier: If your liabilities are so big that they exceed the cancelled debt plus a huge over estimation of your assets by tens of thousands of dollars, you can be a bit more cavalier in this section. If it's anywhere close however, you will want to be very careful here and document where you got your values.

Line 16: Cash and Account Balances. Go to bank statements for the DATE and look up the balance on the exact date. Don't forget savings, checking, and money market accounts. Cash should be whatever was available to you that DATE (if any). Print the account statement in question.

Line 17: The value of real property (houses, land, investment property). Ideally you want an appraisal, but very few people have the forethought to make this happen in advance of debt cancellation. The next best thing is a good real estate agent's assessment of the value (on the DATE) based on comparable sales in the area. Lacking that, you can use tax assessments, online values or any other reasonable method. Just realize that the IRS can dispute these values. I would definitely get a real estate agent involved. If the property was part of the cancelled debt, the 1099C probably has a Fair Market Value that you should use unless you can prove that it's unreasonable. Try to get a written report showing how you valued the property.

Line 18: Cars and other Vehicles. The best source for these values is kbb.com and edmunds.com. I would check both and use the lower value unless they are way off from each other, in which case I would make sure I could defend whichever value I used (or split the difference). If you recently purchased the vehicle from a non-dealer, that value is probably good. If more than a year has passed since the cancelled debt, you might need to tweak the model year of the car to make the car seem older. For example, if it's 2016, and the cancelled debt is for 2013, you would put a 2005 car into edmunds or kbb as a 2002 car. This can be hard if the models have changed significantly. Print the web results and note any adjustments you made. Also save the bill of sale from the purchase.

Line 19: Computers. This can be hard, but, if you have the details on your system, gadgetvalue.com does a pretty good job, though I think a bit high on values. Ebay and other secondary sales sites can help as well. If it's really old, it may be near worthless. Print any web pages you use to value it.

Line 20: Household Goods and Furnishings. This is hard. How much is everything in your house (other than computers, jewelry, tools, clothing and books) worth? The "right" way to go about this is to walk through your house (I would use a camera) and start adding up the values - writing it down would help. Go through every drawer, shelf, closet. Sound insane? It kinda is. Some insurance websites say 10 to 20% of your home's value, but that seems really high based on my life experience (and the website's goal of selling you more insurance would make them want to inflate this value.) To be honest, I would do every other part of the worksheet and see if this number even matters. If you are barely insolvent without adding this in, you're not insolvent, so don't bother. If you are HUGELY insolvent without this number, then you can relax and be somewhat casual about this number. If it's close, spend some time trying to figure out what the expensive things are worth, and get more casual as quantity and value of items go down. This is the one you might get some pushback on.

Line 21: Tools. I'll bet if you're a tool guy (or gal) you have a pretty good idea what your stuff is worth. If you just have the minimum of tools that the average person has, you can probably just lump this in with household above. If you have a lot, or expensive stuff, make a list and check values on ebay, craigslist or other used tool sites.

Line 22: Jewelry. Identify and value expensive pieces, though you can probably use the price you paid for diamonds. Don't forget the engagement ring. Small, inexpensive jewelry can be considered lumped in with household.

Line 23: Clothing. Another tough one. IRS publications say Goodwill type donations are worth a fraction of what you paid for them, so I would agree with them here. Designer clothes and shoes can add up, but you should be able to quickly go through your closet to figure out a good number. If you need help with approximate values, check out thrift shops in your area. You can also use charitable donation value calculators from tax software or other sites.

Line 24: Books. I would go $2 a hardback and 25 cents a paperback for most books unless they are textbooks or collectibles.

Line 25: Stocks and Bonds. This should be easy to obtain from your account statements or websites. Items from lines 31, 33, and 35 might be on the same account statements, so make sure you don't duplicate them.

Line 26: Investments in Coins, Stamps, Paintings or Other Collectibles. As a former collector, this one bugs me a bit. You shouldn't have too much trouble getting values for a lot of this from various books, trade magazines and online sources, but anyone who's ever tried to sell a collectible knows how hard it is to get what the catalog says it's worth from anyone. Consider trying to get a written appraisal from a dealer if you have a significant amount of stuff and haven't valued it lately.

Line 27: Firearms, Sports, Photographic or Other Hobby Equipment. Same caveats from Line 26 apply here.

Line 28: Interest in Retirement Accounts. This line we're talking about accounts outside of work. Some people may have accounts that cross the line between work and personal, but the main thing is to not duplicate between this line and the next. The most common accounts we're talking about here are Traditional and Roth Individual Retirement Accounts (IRA's). Also Myra's SEP's and SIMPLE's (though some of these might be technically considered part of the next line - again - just don't duplicate). I know you're not supposed to be able to get the money without penalty, but that's irrelevant here (according to the IRS). Include the full value of the accounts on the DATE. Do not try to account for potential taxes due or other penalties. Include the FULL value.

Line 29: Interest in a Pension Plan. Here we are talking about both traditional pensions (called Defined Benefit Plans) and 401k type pensions (called Defined Contribution Plans - including the Thrift Savings Plan, 457 plans, 403b plans, etc). There has been a lot of litigation on this, and some court cases have clarified the rules quite a lot, but there is still some argument. I'm going to include the commonly accepted method, and suggest that you use it unless you are willing to get a HIGHLY SKILLED professional on your side. Include the full amount of any money that you, or your employer contributed, as well as all earnings that are fully vested (meaning it's not forfeited if you are fired or quit). Include these amounts even if you can't withdraw it until you retire. If you are already receiving a pension or Social Security (do not include disability pensions) include the amount of money in the account, or, if there is no underlying account, how much money would need to be invested to generate the pension amount (See Example C). Loans taken against these accounts should have been included as liabilities. Here are some examples to help guide you:

Example A: You have a 401k plan that you contribute 6% of your income to and your employer matches what you contribute. The matching isn't vested until you've worked there for 5 years. You would include the value of the account attributable to your contributions, but not your employers, until after you meet the 5 year requirement, at which point you include all of it.

Example B: You are in the military, which has the traditional pension that pays out if you serve 20 years, and the Thrift Savings Plan (TSP - similar to a 401k), to which you contribute 5% of your salary with no matching. The TSP account value is all included, but none of the military pension is included until you actually start receiving it. Once you start receiving the military pension (do not include disability payments), you must include an amount that, if invested, would generate that amount of income (See Example C for a discussion of this calculation.)

Example C: You are receiving non-disability Social Security payments each month (or military retirement, or a traditional pension like governments and old big businesses used to pay, that is not based on you or your employer putting money in an account). You have to figure out how much money would have needed to be invested to generate this income. The IRS has an entire publication dedicated to this (Pub 1457) but it is nearly incomprehensible to the average person. It involves your age, survivors ages if applicable, the survivor benefit structure and interest rates based on government bond rates - and tables - lots of tables. You will definitely need a professional to help with this. The good news (actually bad) is that this probably means you aren't insolvent since this will probably be a big number. Even a modest $1000 a month amount probably results in hundreds of thousands of dollars in assets to be included, so, if your insolvency calculation was close, this just ruined it.

Line 30: Interest in Education Accounts. This is another area where there is some room for doubt. I think the IRS will take the position that any 529 plans or other education accounts which have not passed permanently to another's control (such as the child reaching a certain age per state laws) should be fully included on this line since most of them can be revoked. I would include the FULL amounts that you control or could withdraw. If this is a deal breaker, and the dollars involved are big, you could consider getting a professional to help you argue this point.

Line 31: Cash Value of Life Insurance. Generally we're talking Whole Life policies here, but the insurance companies give them a ton of weird names like "universal", "variable" and others. Bottom line, if it's not traditional term insurance where the only way you get money is by dying, there is a cash value that should be included. Your insurance company should be sending you statements with this information, but if they're not, give them a call.

Line 32: Security Deposits with Landlords, Utilities or Others. If you make a deposit that you will get back if you don't destroy things or fail to pay, include it.

Line 33: Interest in Partnerships. This line and the next line can get conflated so again, don't duplicate. Also, you may have partnership money recorded above as stocks, since some partnerships basically sell as stocks. I know you get it - don't duplicate. It's not a big deal if they're on the wrong line as long as you can translate the numbers into where they came from. That's why you print out your source data. If you own some of a partnership, you and/or the partnership should be able to figure out the value. If it's publicly traded, this is easy, if it's not, talk to the partnership's accountant.

Line 34: Value of Investment in a Business. Same basic deal as the above line.

Line 35: Other Investments. Annuity contracts, guaranteed investment contracts, mutual funds, commodity accounts, hedge funds and options are the examples the IRS provides. This list can be extensive. If you invest in something, it has a value. Include that value here.

Line 36: Other Assets. Anything else you own of value. Put that value here.

Line 37: Total of all your assets from lines 16 through 36.

Total Insolvency:
Line 38: Subtract Line 37 from Line 15. If this is zero or less, you are not insolvent. If it's more than zero, this is the number you use on Form 982.

I've seen a few different insolvency worksheets floating around out there from various tax companies, but the names should be easily decipherable using the information above.

Appendix C: Sample IRS Response Letter

I use the same basic style of letter for all of my IRS responses. It's not based on anything required, or suggested by anyone in authority, it has just worked for me and I've had decent success. It's designed to be respectful, to the point and easy to follow and respond to. It's not complicated and should not be difficult to compose. Don't over think it! Be honest! Be Nice!

Here's the format:

Today's Date

To: Internal Revenue Service
From: Your Name, followed by your Social Security Number

Subj: IRS Letter (put the type and any control numbers here - you can find them in the upper right corner of the letter) dated (date on the letter)

1. I received your letter referenced above.
2. Start by telling them any pertinent background, like you didn't get the form referenced
3. Or you forgot to include something
4. Each number should have one, specific piece of information.
5. Acknowledge information they provide that is correct.
6. Then identify where you think they are wrong, but don't be rude
7. Once you've identified accurate and inaccurate information above.
8. Give them your bottom line belief as to what you feel the result should be.
9. If you don't owe them anything, and they don't owe you....
10. Say, "Based on the above, I don't believe I owe any additional taxes."
11. If you owe a smaller amount, tell them the amount
12. Ideally tell them you are sending the money, if not, tell them how much you are sending, and how you plan to pay the rest.
13. Tell them what forms and documentation you are enclosing.
14. Thank them for their attention, and/or, if you made a mistake, apologize for the trouble.
15. Tell them to feel free to contact you, and include a method of contact with the information needed to reach you.

Very respectfully,

Your Signature

Your Printed Name

65619228R00139

Made in the USA
Charleston, SC
29 December 2016